The Unfinished Agenda for State Tax Reform

edited by
Steven D. Gold

National Conference of State Legislatures
William T. Pound, Executive Director

1050 17th Street, Suite 2100
Denver, Colorado 80265

444 North Capitol Street, N.W., Suite 500
Washington, D.C. 20001

November 1988

Table of Contents

List of Tables and Figures v

Foreword vii

Acknowledgments ix

   I Introduction 1

General Issues

  II A Review of Recent State Tax
      Reform Activity 11
      Steven D. Gold, NCSL

 III The Meaning of Balance for State-Local
      Tax Systems 31
      Helen F. Ladd, Duke University

  IV Principles of a High-Quality State
      Revenue System 47
      *Committee of legislators and legislative staff
      sponsored by Lincoln Institute of Land
      Policy and NCSL*

      Appendix: A Checklist of Characteristics
      of a Good State Revenue System 57
      Steven D. Gold and Corina L. Eckl

   V State Tax Expenditure Budgets—
      And Beyond 65
      Richard D. Pomp, University of Connecticut

  VI State Legislators and Tax Administrators:
      Can We Talk? 83
      *Harley T. Duncan, Federation
      of Tax Administrators*

 VII Suggestions for Improving the
      Administration of State Taxes 101
      Robert C. Witzel, RJR-Nabisco

Nonbusiness Taxes

VIII   Models of State Income Tax Reform 107
       Harvey Galper and Stephen H. Pollock,
          Peat Marwick Main

  IX   The Florida Sales Tax on Services:
          What Really Went Wrong? 129
       James Francis, Florida Department
          of Revenue

       Appendix: Chronology: Florida Sales Tax
          on Services 151

   X   State Tax Relief for Low-Income People . . 153
       Robert Greenstein and Frederick
          Hutchinson, Center on Budget
          and Policy Priorities

Business Taxes

  XI   State Business Taxes: The Policy and
          Research Agendas 177
       Michael Vlaisavljevich, Price Waterhouse

 XII   Are States Overtaxing or Undertaxing
          Corporations? 197
       Robert S. McIntyre, Citizens for Tax Justice

XIII   Constructive State and Local Tax Policy . 219
       David R. Burton, U.S. Chamber
          of Commerce

 XIV   Virtues of a State Value-Added Tax 227
       Gerald H. Miller, National Association
          of State Budget Officers

  XV   Should States Adopt a Value-Added Tax? . 235
       Robert J. Cline, Hope College

About the Authors 255

Index 257

List of Tables and Figures

Chapter II

Table 1:   State and Local Tax Revenue per $100
of Personal Income, 1970 to 1987 13

Table 2:   Summary of Major Personal Income, Sales,
and Corporation Income Tax Changes
in 1987 and 1988 18

Table 3:   Marginal Tax Rates for State Personal Income Taxes,
Joint Returns, Once Currently Enacted Reforms
Are Fully Phased In 22

Chapter III

Table 1:   Balance Among State and Local Government
Tax Sources, 1984 34

Chapter VIII

Table 1:   Major Changes in the Federal Income Tax
and the Tax Laws of Five Selected States 118

Table 2:   Distribution of Income and Tax
by Income Class 122

Table 3:   Suits Indexes of Progressivity 124

Table 4:   Elasticity of Tax Liability with Respect
to Changes in Real Income 125

Table 5:   Change in Number and Percentage of Families
with Positive Federal and State Income Tax ... 126

Table 6:   Number of Families with State Taxes Greater
Than Federal Taxes Before the Earned
Income Credit 127

Chapter X

Table 1:   State Income Tax Thresholds for Two-Parent
Families of Four in 1986 and 1988 158

Table 2:   State Income Tax for Two-Parent Families of Four
with Wage Income of $10,000 in 1986 and 1988 . 160

Chapter XI

Table 1:   Sales Taxation of Equipment Purchases
           by Manufacturers and Contractors   186

Table 2:   Annual Tax per $100 of Capital Investment
           for Rural Locations, 1985   192

Chapter XII

Table 1:   State Statutory Corporate Tax Rates, Current
           Law, 1986, 1980, and 1970   199

Table 2:   Composition of State Tax Revenues in 1986   202

Figure 1: State Corporate Tax Rates, 1970 to 1986   206

Figure 2: Federal Corporate Tax Rates, 1970 to 1988   207

Table 3:   Revenue Effects of Corporate Changes
           in the 1986 Tax Reform Act   208

Chapter XIII

Table 1:   Federal Personal Income Tax Revenue
           by Income Class, 1981 to 1984   223

Table 2:   Distribution of Federal Personal Income Tax
           Burden by Income Class, 1981 to 1984   223

Chapter XV

Table 1:   Michigan Single Business Tax Base:
           Components of Value Added, 1983   242

Table 2:   Distribution of Quarterly Single Business Tax
           Payments by Industry, 1979 to 1986   245

Table 3:   Michigan Single Business Tax Revenues,
           Fiscal Years 1978 to 1987   246

Foreword

This book represents a continuation of the National Conference of State Legislatures' efforts to provide state officials with the best information available about how to cope with the complex fiscal problems facing state and local governments. Just as tax reforms in earlier periods helped strengthen state revenue systems and enabled states to assume greater responsibilities in our federal system, tax reform now is also vitally important.

Most of the chapters in this book are based on presentations made at a conference sponsored by NCSL in Washington, D.C., in October 1987. The great interest in this subject was evidenced by the attendance at that conference, which was the largest in NCSL's history for a conference on a single theme. The views expressed are those of the authors and do not represent the official position of NCSL.

We are extremely grateful to the Ford Foundation, whose financial support of NCSL's Fiscal Federalism Project made possible the conference and this volume.

NCSL will continue to work on state tax policy, state-local relations, and related issues.

William T. Pound
Executive Director
National Conference of State Legislatures
October 1988

Acknowledgments

This book reflects the efforts of many people. Aside from the authors, Sharon Schwoch has done her usual excellent job of editing the manuscript and managing production. Discussions with many people helped me identify the key issues to be covered. Hal Hovey deserves special recognition for his insightful suggestions, and Bob Ebel was also a great help. Kae Warnock was outstanding in processing the manuscripts and communications with the authors. Bruce Holdeman illustrated the cover.

Especially appreciated is the support of David Arnold of the Ford Foundation in encouraging our work in this area.

Steven D. Gold
October 1988

Introduction

Every few decades state governments go through a period of intense tax reform activity. During the 1930s, states responded to the Great Depression by enacting many new income and sales taxes. In the 1960s and in 1971, they strengthened their tax systems by enacting new taxes, broadening tax bases, and increasing tax rates as they strained under the pressure of educating the Baby Boom generation and financing new programs that developed as they modernized their operations.

Now we are in the midst of another major round of reform. The issues are more complex than in early periods because most states already have income and sales taxes in place. In the 1930s and 1960s, enacting a new broad-based tax was usually at the heart of the reform effort, but in the 1980s, improving the operation of those and other taxes is generally the essence of reform.

Overview of This Book

This is NCSL's second major publication surveying the issue of tax reform. The first, *Reforming State Tax Systems,*[1] covered each major state tax as well as several systemic issues, such as tax simplification and interstate tax competition. Its publication in late 1986 occurred shortly after the passage of federal income tax reform, which led states to embark on the greatest round of tax reform activity ever in a single year.

This book builds upon the foundation established in *Reforming State Tax Systems*, focusing on two areas—the major issues raised by the reforms enacted by the states in 1987 and the major neglected issues confronting the states in the years ahead. It is divided into three parts. The first deals with general issues, reviewing recent reform activity and considering issues of how tax systems ought to be structured and administered. The second part focuses on nonbusiness taxes—the personal income tax, the general sales tax, and tax relief for the poor. The final section concentrates on business taxes, both existing and potential ones.

There are two reasons for devoting so much attention to business taxation. First, interstate tax competition and economic development are preeminent issues at the state level, and the taxation of businesses is close to the heart of both. Moreover, business taxation has not been on center stage in the past two years because states devoted most of their attention to the personal income tax. But state tax policy is operating in a new environment, which calls for reconsideration of the principles of business taxation.

Part I

The first chapter reviews recent state tax reform activity, with special emphasis on the personal income tax reforms enacted in 1987. Major themes of recent tax reforms include reducing tax rates when they are above average, increasing standard deductions and personal exemptions or credits, reducing the tax burden on the poor, and simplifying the tax structure by making it conform more closely to the federal tax code.

The next two chapters deal with the basic strategy of putting a tax system together. Helen F. Ladd discusses the meaning of balance in state-local tax systems, criticizing the position advocated by the U.S. Advisory Commission on Intergovernmental Relations (ACIR) that states should strive for *balance among revenue sources* (i.e., the personal income tax, general sales tax, and property tax should each account for between 20 and 30 percent of state-local tax revenue). Instead, she endorses the goal of *balance among policy goals*—revenue growth and stability, fairness, avoiding behavioral distortions, and competitiveness—and elaborates on its implications for design of a tax system.

The following chapter contains a statement of 10 principles of a high-quality revenue system developed by a group of 13 legislators and legislative staff who have played leading roles in efforts to reform tax policy in their respective states. The purpose of the statement is to stimulate discussion within each state about how its tax system might be improved. An appendix to this chapter provides a checklist derived from the statement to facilitate analysis of areas possibly deserving attention from reformers.

Richard D. Pomp's chapter discusses the utility of tax expenditure budgets. These are documents prepared in at least 15 states that measure the revenue forgone as a result of granting tax preferences. Pomp argues that "the concept of a tax expenditure is a powerful analytical tool that has revamped traditional ways of viewing a tax system" but that these documents would be more useful if they intensively focused on particular tax provisions rather than attempting to be relatively comprehensive. He also advocates that states reveal the identities of the major corporate beneficiaries of tax expenditures.

The final two chapters in this section deal with tax administration from the perspectives of a state tax department and a major corporation. Harley T. Duncan, former secretary of the Kansas Department of Revenue, discusses how the operation of the tax system could be improved if legislators would place a higher priority of administrative considerations in the formulation of tax policy. Robert C. Witzel, RJR-Nabisco's senior director for state and local tax, makes numerous suggestions for improving tax administration.

Part II

The personal income and general sales tax are the mainstays of state tax systems, each accounting for more than 30 percent of total state tax revenue. The chapters by Harvey Galper-Stephen Pollock and James Francis focus on the most important developments affecting these taxes in 1987. Galper and Pollock show how state tax reforms tended to increase the progressivity and reduce the elasticity of the personal income tax. In other words, the distribution of the income tax burden was shifted from low-income to high-income taxpayers, while the responsiveness of income tax revenue to the growth of the economy was diminished. They also explain why state policymakers should have access to micro-simulation models to understand how their income tax operates and the effects of potential reforms.

Francis analyzes Florida's experience in attempting to expand its sales tax to cover a large number of services. This action not only raised considerable revenue but also promised to increase the elasticity of the tax system. The tax on services, of which Francis was one of the principal architects, was repealed after being in effect for six months. He argues that it operated successfully, raising more revenue than originally anticipated and withstanding legal challenges.

Greenstein and Hutchinson discuss the various ways in which

states relieve tax burdens on the poor. Federal tax reform removed poor families from the federal income tax rolls, and most states also provided some tax relief for the poor in 1987. The authors note, however, that most states still impose an income tax burden on the poor and that the property and sales taxes were more significant for low-income households even before their income tax liability was reduced.

Part III

Michael Vlaisavljevich leads off the concluding section of the book by providing an overview of state business tax issues. He describes the tensions surrounding business tax policy, the ways in which federal policy affects the state tax environment, and the leading issues to be confronted in the next five years. One of his major conclusions is that states ought to develop estimates of how their own state-local taxes on business compare with those in other states with which they are competitive.

The next two articles provide opposing views about whether states should raise or lower corporate taxes. Robert S. McIntyre, whose research was instrumental in building momentum for increasing federal corporation income taxes in 1986, argues that states should increase their reliance on the corporation income tax. Between 1970 and 1986, states increased the nominal tax rate of this tax significantly, but the effective rate decreased because the tax base became considerably narrower. McIntyre also attacks the notion that low business taxes are needed for a state to have a good business climate.

David R. Burton, on the other hand, argues that constructive state and local tax policy requires low taxes on businesses and individuals. He maintains that redistributionist tax policies seriously impair a state's prospects for economic growth, job creation, and a higher standard of living. Burton urges states to avoid following the precedent of the federal government in increasing taxes on business and investment income.

The final two articles advocate that states consider adoption of a value-added tax (VAT), drawing heavily on the experience of Michigan, which in 1975 replaced most of its existing business taxes with the Single Business Tax (a form of VAT). Gerald H. Miller argues that such a change would make the tax system fairer, simpler, more stable, and more conducive to capital investment. It also would extend coverage of the tax system to the rapidly growing service sector, which tends to be undertaxed.

Robert J. Cline reinforces Miller's arguments and provides more detailed discussions of the Michigan experience and some of the technical aspects of value-added taxation. He also suggests that a VAT might be substituted for a state general sales tax rather than business taxes, particularly since the incidence of a VAT and a retail sales tax are somewhat similar and the latter is no longer deductible for federal income tax purposes.

The Outlook for Tax Reform in the Years Ahead

The author has been on record for several years predicting that a significant wave of state tax reform was in the offing.[2] While that was not a widespread sentiment at the time, the events of 1987 alone are sufficient to conclude that the prediction was accurate.

It appears likely that 1987's tax reforms ultimately will be seen as just the first chapter of a more extended period of state tax reform. Success begets success. Just as the federal tax reform of 1986 led to many state reforms in 1987, so those reforms may stimulate similar or related actions in a large number of additional states over the next several years.

What is the unfinished agenda for state tax reform? It varies considerably from one state to another, but four major areas apply in many states. These areas involve the personal income tax, the general sales tax, business taxes, and local taxation.

Personal income tax. While the changes in the personal exemption and standard deduction that many states adopted in 1987 are significant, they are much less far-reaching than the realignment of rates in the seven states that may be characterized as having enacted thorough income tax reforms. Some additional states probably will go further in the coming years, moving in the direction of reducing the number and level of tax rates and curtailing at least some tax expenditures. Several of the states that have thus far done relatively little if anything in the way of reform (such as Arizona, Mississippi, Missouri, and North Carolina) also are likely to move in the reform direction over the next few years. States that have a relatively low reliance on the personal income tax may increase their tax rates, as many other states did approximately 20 years ago.

One of the main reasons why reform may be widespread is that state income tax structures have been relatively neglected for many years. Another is that reform may be seen as progressive, since many of the accomplishments at the federal and state level are being favorably commented upon. Reforms in many areas, not just in fiscal policy, often sweep across the states in broad waves, and this is likely to happen in the tax area. Other contributing factors will be the need to diversify revenue systems in energy states and the enhancement of legislative staff capacity for developing and analyzing tax proposals.

General sales tax. The sales tax also is likely to experience considerable reform. Interest in extending the sales tax to services undoubtedly suffered a serious setback as a result of Florida's repeal of its initiative, but many states eventually are likely to broaden the coverage of the sales tax to include many consumer services that are currently exempt. Nearly half of the 45 states that impose a sales tax do not tax services at all except for utilities, admissions, and transient accommodations, and many of the other states have only limited taxation of services.[3]

Business taxes. Tax reform is also likely and, in fact, already has emerged in several areas of business taxation strongly affected by technological change and/or deregulation, particularly telecommunications, banking and finance, insurance, and transportation.

If there really is the widespread reform of personal income, sales, and business taxes envisioned here, it could have either of two effects. Most likely, reform momentum would spill over into other taxes, such as the property tax, because lessons learned and the capacity developed in reforming one tax might be applied in other places. A good example of such serial tax reform occurred in 1987 in New York, which reformed its personal income tax in April and then reformed its corporation income tax in June. Kansas provides another example. It reformed its property tax after years of effort in 1986 and then overhauled its income tax in 1988. On the other hand, the effort of reforming one or several taxes might exhaust the participants in the process, and interest in tax reform might wane.

Local taxation. Important developments are likely to occur in local tax policy, where the taxes that local governments can tap are circumscribed by state law. In an era of "fend-for-yourself federalism" (to cite John Shannon's phrase), states are likely to remove many of the shackles that constrain local revenue choices. These changes may occur as part of a general reform of state-local policies, including revisions of state aid policy and a reconsideration of sorting out responsibilities between levels of government.[4]

This view of tax reform prospects may be too optimistic. Significant tax reform is not normally easy to accomplish. As Joseph Minarik has written about the federal experience, "The passage of tax reform required the most incredible confluence of circumstances—almost like an alignment of the planets."[5] There are several significant barriers to successful reform efforts: 1) There are normally more winners than losers, but the losers tend to put up a much stronger fight than the winners because they are more aware of the effects of reform, because the average loser may lose more than the average winner gains, and because the losers from an elimination of tax preferences are often better organized politically than the potential winners from reform. 2) The economic advantages of reform, such as improving efficiency in the allocation of resources, are hard to explain and hence are only dimly perceived at best. 3) There is some truth to the adage "an old tax is a good tax" in that taxpayers learn to live with flawed taxes and to adjust to their deficiencies, so opposition to existing tax provisions may not be as strong as might be expected. As explained in the following chapter, the conditions in 1987 were particularly favorable for income tax reform because of the impact of federal tax reform. To some extent, 1987 was a special case.

One important factor that will influence the chances for tax reform is the fiscal condition of the states, which probably will deteriorate badly if the economy slips into a serious recession. In such a situation, states would need to bolster their revenue to avoid budget deficits or large cuts in expenditures, so they would be more receptive to drastic actions such as broadening the tax base.

To summarize, the state tax environment has been transformed fundamentally as a result of at least three developments:

- The reverberations of federal tax reform will continue to be felt. In a setting of relatively low federal tax rates, many states will find it desirable to reform their tax structures to assure their economic competitiveness.
- Now that the genie of tax reform has gotten out of its bottle and states have one round of tax reform under their belts, reform is likely to become habit forming, with opposition to reconsidering long-established policies crumbling.
- Economic, regulatory, and technological change will force states to rationalize their tax systems, moving in the direction of a level playing field, broader tax bases, and lower tax rates.

If a serious economic recession is added to these factors, it will stimulate tax reform further. In an atmosphere of serious fiscal stress, options once considered taboo suddenly may become acceptable. This could lead, for example, to adoption of income and sales taxes in many of the states that do not currently impose them.

The other major influence likely to affect the course of state tax reform is federal tax policy. Most informed observers believe some form of significant federal tax increase can be expected within a year or two, but its shape is uncertain. If the federal government enacted a value-added tax, it might discourage states from relying as much as they traditionally have on consumption taxes. On the other hand, if income tax rates were increased, that would tend to dampen interstate tax competition and might have other effects that are difficult to anticipate.[6]

What Is Tax Reform?

Tax reform is in the eye of the beholder. One person's reform may be another's abomination. Tax reform can be defined as any change that improves the operation of the tax system. It might encompass, for example, changes in the tax system to:

- Raise more revenue (so that "needed services" can be provided);
- Raise less revenue (to lessen the "oppressive hand of government");
- Make the tax system more or less progressive;
- Make tax burdens more uniform for households that are similarly situated;
- Increase the degree to which tax burdens are related to the benefits received from government;
- Make a particular tax or the entire tax system simpler to understand and cope with;
- Improve tax administration;
- Reduce the distortions in resource allocation caused by the tax system;
- Promote economic development and job creation;
- Increase the stability of tax revenue;
- Increase the responsiveness of tax revenue to economic growth; and
- Increase accountability so that governments cannot increase tax rates by a large amount without overt action.

This list of 12 goals of tax reform is not exhaustive, but it does cover most of the major goals of tax reform. If tax reform can mean so many different things, is it an empty concept? Not at all. Whatever the goals of a reform effort, it is usually possible to make improvements in the existing system. The chapters of this book suggest many ways of moving closer to achieving these goals.

Besides discussing policies to accomplish tax reform, some of the authors describe tools for improving the reform process. Policymakers need better information than they normally have if they are to understand how their tax system operates. Galper and Pollock describe models of state personal income taxes and Vlaisavljevich discusses models of state business taxes. An investment of time and money in such models is indispensable for making wise tax policy. Their use is likely to spread considerably in the coming decade.

Notes

1.   Steven D. Gold, ed., *Reforming State Tax Systems* (Denver: National Conference of State Legislatures, 1986). More specialized NCSL books on tax reform include Steven D. Gold, *State Tax Relief for the Poor* (Denver: National Conference of State Legislatures, 1987) and Mitchell A. Zahn and Steven D. Gold, *State Tax Policy and Senior Citizens: A Legislators' Guide* (Denver: National Conference of State Legislatures, 1985).

2.   For an early prediction that a wave of tax reform was imminent, see Steven D. Gold, "A Pivotal Year for State Finance," *State Legislatures* (January 1985), pp. 20-25. The prediction also was made at an NCSL tax conference held in Denver, Colorado, October 11-12, 1985.

3.   John L. Mikesell, "General Sales Tax," in Gold, *Reforming State Tax Systems,* pp. 220.

4.   NCSL's Task Force on State-Local Relations has approved a set of recommendations for changes along the lines discussed in this paragraph.

5.   Joseph Minarik, "How Tax Reform Came About," *Tax Notes* 37 (December 28, 1987), p. 1372. For a more detailed description of the perilous course of federal tax reform, see Jeffrey Birnbaum and Alan Murray, *Showdown at Gucci Gulch* (New York: Random House, 1987).

6.   Higher federal income tax rates would make deductions more valuable, which would tend to favor reliance on state and local income and property taxes rather than on sales taxes. On the other hand, an increase in the federal income tax could discourage states from increasing the income tax because of "crowding out" by the federal government.

II

A Review
of Recent State
Tax Reform
Activity

by
Steven D. Gold

$\mathbf{F}$ederal tax reform touched off an unprecedented burst of state tax reform activity, with more important reforms enacted in 1987 than in any other year within recent memory. This chapter reviews state tax activity in the wake of federal tax reform and places it in its historical context.

Background

Table 1 traces fluctuations in state and local tax revenue per $100 of personal income from fiscal year 1970 to fiscal year 1987.

Several important conclusions emerge from this historical record:

- State tax revenue as a proportion of personal income rose sharply in the early 1970s, reaching a peak in fiscal 1978. It declined in response to the celebrated Tax Revolt, recovered when states raised taxes in reaction to the severe recessions of the early 1980s, and then dipped again as states removed many of the tax increases enacted in response to the fiscal emergencies of 1982 and 1983. In 1987, the proportion of personal income claimed by state taxes was slightly lower than before the Tax Revolt but higher than in 1970.
- To an important extent, the reason why state taxes were a higher proportion of personal income in 1987 than in 1970 is that states relieved local governments of much of their responsibility for raising tax revenue. Local taxes declined more than 20 percent as a proportion of personal income between 1972 and 1987. With state taxes rising faster than personal income and local taxes rising slower than personal income, combined state-local tax revenue per $100 of personal income in 1987 was virtually the same as it had been in 1970.
- General sales and personal income taxes are the mainstays of state tax systems, accounting for 63 percent of total tax revenue. Their relative importance has increased steadily since 1970.
- Corporation income tax revenue is lower as a proportion of personal income than it was between 1977 and 1981 but is at approximately the same level as at other times since 1973.
- Severance taxes rose more than three times as fast as personal income between 1970 and 1982, primarily as a result of higher oil prices, but their revenue has plummeted since then. These taxes account for more than 10 percent of revenue in eight states.
- Revenue from other state taxes—primarily various excises such as on motor fuel, tobacco products, and alcoholic beverages—has grown relatively slowly, declining by about one-third as a proportion of personal income since 1970. Demand for many of the products subject to these taxes has grown relatively slowly, and revenue increases also have been depressed because many taxes are based on quantities rather than values and therefore do not respond to higher prices. However, in the 1980s, states were more willing to raise

Table 1.

State and Local Tax Revenue Per $100 of Personal Income, 1970 to 1987

Fiscal Year	Total	Local	State	State — General Sales	Personal Income	Corporation Income	Severance	Other
1987	$11.48	$4.48	$7.02	$2.26	$2.16	$0.59	$0.12	$1.89
1986	11.24	4.37	6.89	2.26	2.04	0.55	0.19	1.85
1985	11.28	4.34	6.97	2.25	2.06	0.57	0.23	1.86
1984	11.30	4.35	6.96	2.21	2.09	0.55	0.26	1.85
1983	10.68	4.25	6.46	2.02	1.88	0.50	0.28	1.78
1982	10.59	4.12	6.49	2.01	1.82	0.56	0.31	1.79
1981	10.85	4.20	6.67	2.07	1.82	0.63	0.28	1.87
1980	11.02	4.26	6.78	2.14	1.84	0.66	0.21	1.93
1979	11.37	4.46	6.94	2.19	1.81	0.67	0.16	2.11
1978	12.08	5.01	7.10	2.21	1.82	0.67	0.16	2.23
1977	12.15	5.17	7.02	2.14	1.77	0.64	0.15	2.32
1976	11.98	5.17	6.85	2.10	1.65	0.56	0.16	2.38
1975	11.74	5.09	6.68	2.07	1.57	0.55	0.15	2.34
1974	11.93	5.16	6.81	2.07	1.57	0.55	0.11	2.51
1973	12.41	5.43	7.01	2.04	1.60	0.56	0.09	2.72
1972	12.24	5.51	6.77	1.99	1.47	0.50	0.09	2.72
1971	11.50	5.26	6.27	1.88	1.24	0.42	0.09	2.64
1970	11.32	5.07	6.29	1.86	1.20	0.49	0.09	2.65

Note: Revenue for each fiscal year is divided by personal income in the calendar year that ended during it. District of Columbia taxes are included with those for local governments. Calculations involving state tax revenue exclude the District of Columbia's personal income.

Sources: For tax revenue, U.S. Census Bureau, *Governmental Finances* (Washington, D.C.: U.S. Government Printing Office, various years); U.S. Census Bureau, *State Government Finances* (Washington, D.C.: U.S. Government Printing Office, various years). For personal income, U.S. Department of Commerce, *Survey of Current Business* 67 (August 1987): 44.

13

the rates for these taxes than previously, so the long decline in reliance on them came to a halt. Between 1980 and 1987, the ratio between their revenue and personal income did not decrease, remaining at about 1.9 percent.

The national aggregate figures just discussed conceal a great amount of variation among the states. The articles in this book by Helen Ladd and Robert McIntyre include tables showing some of the differences in state tax structures, and *Reforming State Tax Systems* had further detailed information.[1]

Reasons for the Burst of Activity in 1987

At least three considerations explain the high level of tax reform activity in 1987.

By far the most important factor is the federal tax reform enacted in 1986, which paved the road for state tax reform in at least six ways:

- It virtually forced most states to reconsider their income taxes because they are closely tied to the federal income tax. If the states did not conform to the revised federal provisions that they previously had adopted, taxpayers would have been burdened with much greater compliance problems in calculating their state income tax. Administrative considerations also argued for conformity, since states rely heavily on IRS assistance in enforcing their own income taxes.
- It incorporated a number of important principles that states found attractive. If it was good policy and good politics for the federal government to remove the poor from the income tax rolls, boost personal exemptions and the standard deduction, and broaden the tax base while lowering nominal tax rates, then in many states it also made sense to consider such policies.[2]
- The so-called "windfall"—the increased revenue for states resulting from conformity—is another reason why states had to consider their income tax structure; some of them did not need the additional "windfall" revenue, so some action was required to avoid receiving it.
- The "windfall" associated with federal tax reform made it possible to raise the standard deduction and

personal exemption without raising nominal tax rates. Some state officials said that they had been contemplating such changes for years but had been stalled by the lack of available revenue.

- The redistribution of state income tax burdens resulting from conformity to the new federal tax base— especially the large increases at high income levels— also stimulated tax reform by making it possible to reduce marginal tax rates on the affluent without lowering their effective tax rates.

- The decrease in federal marginal tax rates induced states to reduce their own tax rates because the value of state income tax deductions on federal returns was not worth as much in terms of federal tax savings. This spurred on a previous trend in the 1980s for states with high marginal tax rates to reduce them.[3]

A second reason why there was so much tax reform activity in 1987 is that the ground had been prepared by an extended period of study of state tax systems. More than half of the states had conducted major tax studies earlier in the decade (usually stimulated by dissatisfaction with the existing tax structure),[4] and following a period for digesting and debating the ideas discussed in those studies, the situation was ripe for making major changes. High-tax states particularly had been sensitized to the desirability of reducing marginal tax rates on high-income households, and flat-tax proposals had been in the air for a number of years.

Although most of these tax studies had not borne fruit in terms of new legislation, there were two major exceptions. In 1985, Wisconsin enacted a far-reaching income tax reform, involving the elimination of numerous itemized deductions and other tax preferences, establishment of a large standard deduction that phased out as income increased, and reduction of tax rates.[5] The following year, New Mexico reformed its income tax, repealing the automatic linkage to federal taxable income (because of the dependence it implied on federal tax changes) and increasing tax rates. Less far-reaching reforms included targeted income tax relief for the poor in Massachusetts in 1986 and exempting inventories from the property tax in many states earlier in the 1980s.[6]

A third cause of 1987 tax reform is increasing awareness of major economic changes that are occurring. Concern about competitiveness, both domestic and international, is stimulating reconsideration of tax policies in many states (leading, for example, to efforts to reduce marginal tax rates). Another important economic change is the growing importance of the service sector. Because services are relatively lightly taxed, the elasticity of state sales taxes is being

eroded. Hawaii and New Mexico have taxed most services for decades, Iowa extended its sales tax to many services in 1967, and
South Dakota taxed most services beginning in 1979. Proposals for
similar action, however, had been rejected in many states earlier in
the 1980s. Sooner or later, states will be forced to tax services more
heavily if they are to avoid ever-higher sales tax rates, reduced
reliance on the sales tax, or a permanently diminished rate of revenue growth in total.

Tax Reform Activity Following Enactment of Federal Reform

In 1987, nearly every major category of state taxation was affected by changes in some states. The following year was relatively
quiet, but Kansas and Maine enacted major tax reforms (and those
states are included in the following tabulations, along with Ohio,
which responded to federal tax reform in November 1986). This
chapter, however, concentrates on the reforms involving the three
biggest state taxes—the general sales tax and the personal and
corporation income taxes. These taxes account for 71 percent of total
state tax collections (32 percent, 31 percent, and 8 percent, respectively).[7] Table 2 summarizes the major changes in these three taxes
following the enactment of federal tax reform. One area where several states made fundamental reforms that are not discussed here,
due to their complexity and space limitations, is taxation of telecommunications.[8]

Personal Income Tax

This tax has been the most important focus of recent state tax
reform activity. It is important to recognize that there is no such
thing as a "typical" state income tax. Enormous diversity exists
among states in the level and progressivity of tax rates and the size
of personal exemptions (or personal credits) and standard deductions. While most states define income subject to tax as the federal
government does and provide for itemized deductions that are similar or identical to those on federal returns, several states do not.
About half the states that are tied to federal adjusted gross income
or taxable income make such conformity automatic, while the other
half update conformity periodically by statute.[9]

Most states conformed to all or nearly all the federal reforms
that affected their tax structure, but they also went further:

- Sixteen states reduced tax rates (this tally includes Virginia, which raised the income level at which its top rate takes effect but did not reduce the rate itself);
- Thirteen of the states reducing the level of tax rates also decreased the number of tax brackets;
- Twenty states increased the personal exemption or personal credit;[10]
- Twenty-two states increased the standard deduction (and eight states emulated the federal government by removing the feature of their standard deduction that made it depend on income, thereby making its value equal for all returns that claim it);
- Fourteen states that formerly imposed an income tax on poor families no longer will do so;
- Many states eliminated special deductions or exclusions not in the federal tax code, including four states that terminated their deduction for federal income tax payments; and
- Seven states—Colorado, Kansas, Maine, Minnesota, Nebraska, New York, West Virginia—restructured their entire income tax.[11]

It is unusual for seven states to restructure their income tax in a two- year period. Although no two states are exactly alike, some similarities among most of them are notable:

- All seven states lowered their tax rates, with the maximum rate being cut at least 2 percentage points, and reduced the number of tax rates. Kansas, Minnesota, and New York emulated the federal government by adopting a two-rate tax structure (4.05 percent and 5.3 percent in Kansas,[12] 6 percent and 8 percent in Minnesota, and 5.5 percent and 7 percent in New York—after a four-year phase-in). Colorado went even further by adopting a flat 5 percent tax.
- Four of the states either conformed to federal taxable income or moved close to it. This entails adopting the federal itemized and standard deductions, personal exemptions, and exclusions from income. States that take this step thereby will exempt poor families and reduce the number of itemizers significantly. Colorado and Minnesota henceforth will base their taxes on federal taxable income (except that Colorado retains a $20,000 exclusion for pension income). Kansas' personal exemption and standard deduction are the same as those for the federal income tax in 1988, but they are not

Table 2.

Summary of Major Personal Income, Sales, and Corporation Income Tax Changes in 1987 and 1988

State	Personal Income Tax		Sales Tax	Corporation Income Tax
	Retained Windfall?	Changes Enacted		
New England				
Connecticut	No	e		
Maine	No	abc		Reduced*
Massachusetts	Yes			
Rhode Island	None	abc		
Vermont	None	abc		
Mid-Atlantic				
Delaware	Part	abc	N/A	
Maryland	Part	abe		
New Jersey	None			
New York	No	abc		Reduced*
Pennsylvania	None			Reduced*
Great Lakes				
Illinois	Yes			
Indiana	Yes	d		Increased rate
Michigan	Part	a		N/A
Ohio	No	c		Reduced*
Wisconsin	No	bce		
Plains				
Iowa	Part	bce		
Kansas	Part	abc		
Minnesota	No	abc	Increased base	Increased base
Missouri	Yes	b		
Nebraska	None	abd		
North Dakota	None	abd	Increased rate	
South Dakota	N/A		Increased rate	N/A
Southeast				
Alabama	Yes			
Arkansas	Yes	a		
Florida	N/A		Increased rate	
Georgia	No	ab		
Kentucky	Part	e		
Louisiana	Yes			
Mississippi	Yes			
North Carolina	Yes			Increased rate
South Carolina	None	abd		Reduced*
Virginia	No	abc		
West Virginia	No	ac		
Southwest				
Arizona	No			
New Mexico	Yes			
Oklahoma	Yes		Increased rate	
Texas	N/A		Increased rate and base	N/A

	Personal Income Tax			
State	Retained Windfall?	Changes Enacted	Sales Tax	Corporation Income Tax
Rocky Mountain				
Colorado	Part	abc		Reduced*
Idaho	Yes	abd		Increased rate
Montana	Yes	d	N/A	
Utah	Yes	ab	Increased rate	
Far West				
California	No	abc		Reduced*
Hawaii	No	ace		Reduced*
Oregon	Part	bc		Reduced*

Key to personal income tax changes:
a. Increased personal exemption or credit
b. Increased standard deduction
c. Reduced rates
d. Increased rates
e. Did not fully tax capital gains

Note: Alaska, Nevada, New Hampshire, Tennessee, Washington, and Wyoming do not impose a broad-based income tax and did not make changes affecting the other taxes. Ohio's actions were taken in November 1986. Kentucky did not hold a regular legislative session in 1987. The table includes an increase in a personal credit in Hawaii that is not counted in the text for technical reasons.

*States listed as reducing corporation income tax avoided receiving a "full" corporate "windfall" but did not generally reduce the effective tax rate.

N/A indicates that this state does not impose this tax. "None" indicates that a state did not receive an individual income tax "windfall."

Source: Steven D. Gold, "The Great Blizzard of 1987: A Year of Tremendous Tax Reform Activity in the States," *Publius* (August 1988); supplemented by information for states enacting legislation in 1988.

indexed to inflation. Maine established credits whose value for taxpayers in the lowest tax bracket is equal that of the federal personal exemption and standard deduction.

- New York moved in the direction of conformity with the federal tax code by repealing some of its unusual deductions and will have a $13,000 standard deduction for joint returns, thereby exempting most poor families.
- West Virginia cut its top rate from 13 percent to 6.5 percent while eliminating all deductions. It may be the only state where the progressivity of the income tax is less than in 1986.
- Nebraska's reform involved abandoning its previous practice of making its state income tax a percentage of federal tax liability (which is still the system in three states). Instead, it adopted a four-rate tax structure based on federal adjusted gross income with its own personal exemption and standard deduction. An important motivation for this change was to lessen the state's dependence on what was perceived as unstable federal tax policy.

Each of these seven states raised the personal exemption and standard deduction, except for West Virginia, which repealed its standard deduction along with all itemized deductions. In addition, 13 other states raised the personal exemption (or credit) and 16 others increased the standard deduction. These actions contributed to one of the major trends of 1987 and 1988—an increase in the progressivity of the state income tax because an increased personal exemption and an increased standard deduction reduce taxes proportionately more for taxpayers with relatively low income than for those with high income. (In addition, many high-income taxpayers receive no benefit from the standard deduction because they itemize.) The other major reason for increased progressivity is that states conformed to the federal changes that are expected to broaden the tax base much more at high income levels than at middle income levels. States could have prevented this increase in progressivity by lowering tax rates disproportionately at high income levels, but they did not do so.[13]

These increases in personal exemptions and standard deductions were the main devices for relieving taxes on the poor. Maryland and Pennsylvania adopted measures that targeted additional income tax assistance to the poor, and Maine, Ohio, and Vermont expanded property tax circuitbreakers for low-income households. Maryland became the second state to provide for an earned income tax credit piggybacked on the federal credit, which reduces taxes for low-income wage earners with children.

The federal reform eliminating preferential treatment for capital gains was adopted in most states, but there were six exceptions. Connecticut (which taxes capital gains, dividends, and interest but not other income), Iowa (with some qualifications),[14] and Wisconsin will continue to exclude 60 percent of capital gains from taxation. Maryland will exclude 40 percent, and Hawaii set a maximum rate of 7.25 percent on capital gains, although other income may be taxed as high as 10 percent. In addition, Kentucky retained a capital gains preference because it has not yet enacted legislation conforming to federal tax base changes.[15]

The post-federal tax reform activity accelerated the existing trend away from high marginal tax rates. All of the 15 states lowering their maximum tax rates had a top nominal rate of 7.9 percent or more before 1987. Only four of the other 25 states with broad-based income taxes have a higher maximum tax rate (Arizona, Idaho, Montana, and New Mexico).[16] Table 3 shows the maximum tax rate in each state once 1987 and 1988 reforms are fully in effect.

This summary has emphasized structural changes in income taxes rather than how states have dealt with the income tax "windfall" because the amount of the "windfall" retained was quantitatively insignificant. States retained about 20 percent of the potential "windfall" they would have received if they had conformed to federal reforms without changing tax rates ($1.1 billion out of $6.1 billion). This is a small amount in comparison with annual state income tax collections of $80 billion. In addition, five states reduced income tax revenue beyond what was necessary to avoid the "windfall," and six states increased revenue by more than merely retaining the "windfall."[17]

Corporation Income Tax

Much less attention was devoted to corporate tax issues in 1987 than to those involving the personal income tax. A considerably larger proportion of states retained the "windfall" from this tax than for the personal income tax. Only nine states (California, Colorado, Hawaii, New York, Ohio, Pennsylvania, Oregon, Maine, and South Carolina) took direct action to avoid at least a portion of the corporate "windfall," and two of these actions (in Colorado and South Carolina) were not scheduled to take effect immediately. On the other hand, Idaho, Indiana, and North Carolina raised the tax rate on corporations, and Minnesota increased corporate taxes by expanding the tax base.

One of the reasons for the relative lack of activity involving this tax was the high level of uncertainty surrounding the effects

Table 3.

Marginal Tax Rates for State Personal Income Taxes, Joint Returns, Once Currently Enacted Reforms Are Fully Phased In

State	Highest Nominal Rate (Percent)	Highest Rate Adjusted for Federal Deductibility (Percent)	Highest Rate Starts at This Level of Taxable Income* ($000)
New England			
Maine[b]	8.00	8.00	30
Massachusetts	5.00[a]	5.00	0
Rhode Island[b]	6.43[c]	6.43	30[c]
Vermont[b]	6.44[c]	6.44	30[c]
Mid-Atlantic			
Delaware[b]	7.70	7.70	40
Maryland	5.00	5.00	3
New Jersey	3.50	3.50	50
New York[b]	7.00	7.00	27
Pennsylvania	2.10	2.10	0
Great Lakes			
Illinois	2.50	2.50	0
Indiana[d]	3.40	3.40	0
Michigan	4.60	4.60	0
Ohio[b]	6.90	6.90	100
Wisconsin[b]	6.93	6.93	20
Plains			
Iowa[b]	9.98	7.19[e]	45
Kansas[b]	5.30	5.30	35
Minnesota[b]	8.00	8.00	19
Missouri	6.00	4.32[e]	9
Nebraska[d]	5.90	5.90	45
North Dakota[d]	3.92[c,g]	3.92	30[c]
Southeast			
Alabama	5.00	3.60[e]	6
Arkansas	7.00	7.00	25
Georgia	6.00	6.00	10
Kentucky	6.00	4.32[e]	8
Louisiana	6.00	4.32[e]	50
Mississippi	5.00	5.00	10
North Carolina	7.00	7.00	10
South Carolina	7.00	7.00[h]	14
Virginia[i]	5.75	5.75	17
West Virginia[b]	6.50	6.50	60
Southwest			
Arizona	8.00	5.76[e]	14
New Mexico[d]	8.50	8.50	64
Oklahoma	6.00[g]	6.00[g]	15

State	Highest Nominal Rate (Percent)	Highest Rate Adjusted for Federal Deductibility (Percent)	Highest Rate Starts at This Level of Taxable Income* ($000)
Rocky Mountain			
Colorado[b]	5.00	5.00	0
Idaho[d]	8.20	8.20	20
Montana[d]	12.10[f]	8.71[e,f]	44
Utah[j]	7.35	6.66	8
Far West			
California[b]	9.30	9.30	48
Hawaii[b]	10.00	10.00	40
Oregon[b]	9.00	9.00[h]	10

Notes: This table does not reflect the deductibility of state taxes on federal income tax returns. The omitted states either do not tax income at all or tax only dividends, interest, and/or capital gains.

*Income at which highest rate starts is rounded to nearest thousand dollars.

a. This is rate for earned income. Unearned income is taxed at 10 percent.

b. State reduced tax rates in late 1986, 1987, or 1988.

c. State tax is a percentage of federal liability. Highest rate is that percentage multiplied by 28 percent. This is the federal tax rate for income above $29,750, except that the rate is 33 percent over a certain range depending on number of dependents. For a joint return with two dependents, 33 percent rate applies from taxable income of $71,900 to $194,050 in 1988.

d. State increased tax rates in 1986 or 1987. (In Nebraska, state tax reform prevented rate from decreasing as much as it would have if previous tax structure had been maintained.)

e. Federal tax payments are fully deductible in computing state taxable income. Rates shown are calculated by multiplying nominal tax rate by 72 percent (i.e., 1 minus 28 percent). In the range where the federal rate is 33 percent, the state rate is 7 percent lower than indicated in table.

f. Rate shown includes 10 percent surcharge that is scheduled to expire in Montana after 1988.

g. Table reflects a rate schedule that does not permit deductions for federal taxes paid. Most taxpayers use this schedule because it results in lower tax liability than the alternative schedule with federal taxes deductible.

h. A limited amount of federal tax payments are deductible, but taxpayers with high income normally would pay a higher amount, so this provision does not affect tax rate at the margin.

i. State reduced tax rate in 1987 by increasing income level at which maximum rate takes effect.

j. State effectively increased tax rate in 1987 by repealing deductibility of federal tax payments without lowering tax rates. One-third of deductibility was restored in 1988, and the tax rate was reduced.

Source: National Conference of State Legislatures survey of states, updated 1988.

of federal tax reform. While estimates for the personal income tax were difficult to develop, the estimation problems were even greater for the corporation income tax because most states have much weaker systems for analyzing their corporate tax base and because federal tax reform incorporated features (such as fundamental changes of accounting rules) that have little precedent.

Robert Aten of the U.S. Treasury Department estimated that the state corporation income tax "windfall," if there were no countervailing adjustments, might be on the order of $3.4 billion,[18] that is, approximately half as large as the personal "windfall." Since states obtain only about 28 percent as much revenue from the corporation income tax as from the personal income tax, the potential "windfall" from corporations would represent (assuming the accuracy of Aten's estimate) a much larger proportion of total collections than from individuals.

As of mid-1988, there was no sign of the corporate windfall. In fact, many states had unexpectedly low corporate tax collections. The long-term significance of this trend was uncertain. It might mean that there was a temporary delay in the increase in corporate tax burdens due to uncertainty about new federal provisions, or it might indicate that behavioral responses would reduce revenue permanently below the level projected. In 1987, California attempted to anticipate one such behavioral response by imposing a 2.5 percent tax on Subchapter S corporations.[19]

States generally conformed to most of the federal tax base changes. But one area where relatively few states followed the federal lead was the new corporate minimum tax. Only 10 states now have such a provision, usually tying it in some manner to the federal Alternative Minimum Tax.[20]

One other development in 1987 merits mention. Montana and North Dakota repealed worldwide unitary combination, the final states to do so for all corporations. Several years ago a dozen states had the unitary approach in their statutes, but now only Alaska employs it, and only for oil companies.

The area of corporate taxation is one place where considerable activity may occur during the next few years, as the effects of federal reform become more apparent. Interstate tax competition could lead to tax reductions if increases in corporation tax burdens result from federal reform. On the other hand, states might take steps to increase revenue if behavioral changes reduce revenue below original expectations.

General Sales Tax

The most controversial tax development of 1987 was Florida's extension of the sales tax to a broad range of services, including not only most consumer services but also many business services such as accounting, legal, and advertising services. Florida briefly joined Hawaii, New Mexico, and South Dakota in having relatively comprehensive coverage of the service sector. Florida also went further than any other state has attempted by imposing a use tax on services, so that services imported into the state were taxed at the same rate as services produced in Florida. (All states with a sales tax on goods also impose a use tax designed to tax goods purchased outside the state for use within its boundaries, but no state had applied the same approach to services.)

The passage of Florida's legislation marked a break with the usual experience of proposals to impose the sales tax broadly on services. Many such proposals have been defeated in the 1980s, and, in fact, at least seven states rejected them in 1987—Arkansas, Indiana, North Dakota, Minnesota, Oklahoma, Texas, and Washington. Two of these states—Minnesota and Texas—did, however, moderately expand their coverage of the service sector this year.

Five states also raised the sales tax rate in 1987—North Dakota, Oklahoma, South Dakota, Texas, and Utah. It is noteworthy that all of them are west of the Mississippi River and suffer from depressed energy- or farm-based economies. Such states were also those most likely to increase the personal income tax.

Recent Reforms in Relation to Previous Trends

In *Reforming State Tax Systems,* five important underlying developments were identified.[21] To conclude this overview, it is worth reviewing them and speculating about whether they will be in force in the future:

> • *Reduced concern about the progressivity of the tax system.* This trend was reversed in 1987, as nearly all states increased the progressivity of their income taxes. As mentioned above, to some extent this occurred because federal reform broadened the tax base so much more at high income levels, but states accentuated the trend by the manner in which they avoided the "windfall."
>
> The riddle of why progressivity increased after diminishing previously is partly explained by the fact that it is much more difficult for a single state to

impose higher taxes on the affluent than it is for many states acting together at the same time. A second factor is that many state income taxes had relatively little progressivity in the first place, and the pressure to curtail progressivity mainly has been felt by the small number of states with the greatest degree of progressivity.[22] Third, much of the increase in progressivity occurred automatically as a result of conforming to federal tax reform, so most of the public (and probably many public officials) failed to appreciate what was occurring. Finally, the attention on the issue of taxation of the poor generated by federal reform contributed to the drive for progressivity at the lower end of the income scale.[23]

- *Intensified interstate tax competition.* Many observers have noted that states are competing fiercely to make themselves attractive to business investment and high-income individuals. The sharp reduction of marginal tax rates resulting from federal tax reform is likely to exacerbate this competition because it reduces the federal tax savings that result from payment of state or local taxes so that state-local taxpayers will have to bear a greater proportion of the cost of state-provided services.

This competition is one of the environmental factors that led many of the states with relatively high marginal tax rates to reduce them. Since states that already had relatively low tax rates were not at a competitive disadvantage, it is not surprising that they did not reduce their tax rates this year.

- *Erosion of tax bases.* The essence of much tax reform is broadening tax bases, so this is another previous trend that at least has been reversed temporarily, not only by income tax reform but also by the two states that moderately broadened their sales tax base. One of the great uncertainties about the course of future tax policy is whether it will be dominated by further state base-broadening or by a resumption of the trend toward erosion. Economic development incentives could entail renewed erosion of the corporation income tax base, regardless of what happens to the bases of the personal income and the general sales tax.

- *Reduction of the income elasticity of tax systems.* The chapter in this book by Harvey Galper and Stephen Pollock indicates that the 1987 changes in income taxes—particularly the decrease of marginal tax rates and the flattening in the structure of rates—will result in slower growth of state income tax revenue over time. On the other hand, taxing services is expected to raise the elasticity of the sales tax because demand for services tends to grow faster than demand for goods. Without Florida's reform, however, the broadening of the sales tax base in 1987 was trivial compared with the income tax changes that occurred.

- *Reduction of the stability of tax systems.* Lower marginal rates also may reduce the instability of state revenue because it will not be as sensitive to economic cycles. Likewise, taxing services reduces instability because the strong upward trend in demand for services tends to remain even during cyclical downturns.

To summarize, the situation regarding three of the five important trends changed in 1987. Progressivity was increased, and there were movements away from erosion of tax bases and greater instability of the tax system. Interstate tax competition not only remains but may intensify, and income elasticity continues to decrease. Whether the three reversals will turn out to be long-standing trends or short-term detours is one of the big questions yet to be answered over the next decade.

Notes

The author appreciates the helpful comments on an earlier version of this chapter by Robert Aten, Corina Eckl, Brenda Erickson, Robert Ebel, Hal Hovey, and Tom Severn.

1. Steven D. Gold, ed., *Reforming State Tax Systems* (Denver: National Conference of State Legislatures, 1986), Ch. 2. NCSL publishes annual updates on changes in state tax structures.

2. For a more extensive list of possible lessons for the states, see Steven D. Gold, "Themes of Federal Tax Reform for State Tax Policy," in *Reforming State Tax Systems,* pp. 177-184.

3. Steven D. Gold, "Developments in State Finances, 1983 to 1986," *Public Budgeting and Finance* 7 (Spring 1987): 10-15.

4. Robert Ebel, one of the leading participants in the state tax studies of the 1980s, suggests that the studies are important because "if well timed they pave the way for the legislature to make better decisions than they otherwise would." For discussions of some of these studies, see the articles from the session on state tax reform in National Tax Association-Tax Institute of America, *Proceedings of the Seventy-seventh Annual Conference: 1984* (Columbus: National Tax Association-Tax Institute of America, 1985), pp. 183-204; Steven D. Gold, "Discussion: State Tax Reform and State Tax Commissions," *Proceedings of the Seventy-eighth Annual Conference: 1985* (Columbus: National Tax Association-Tax Institute

of America, 1986), pp. 155-158; and Sharon Robinson and Astrid Merget, *A Service Sector Sampler: Case Studies of Seventeen States,* vol. 3, *Where Will the Money Come From?* (Washington, D.C.: Academy for State and Local Government, 1986).

5. Steven D. Gold, "Income Tax Reform—Wisconsin Style," *State Legislatures* (January 1986), pp. 8-9.

6. Massachusetts exempted all families with incomes under $12,000 from its income tax and established a 10 percent tax to phase them in to the regular income tax structure. (For single individuals, the exemption is $8,000.) At least 12 states exempted inventories in the first half of the 1980s. Steven D. Gold, "How the Taxation of Business Property Varies Among the States," *Assessment* Digest (January/February 1987), pp. 14-26.

7. Data on the composition of state revenue are from U.S. Census Bureau, *State Tax Collections in 1987* (Washington, D.C., 1988). For more details about state tax changes in 1987, see Steven D. Gold, Corina L. Eckl, and Brenda Erickson, *State Budget Actions in 1987* (Denver: National Conference of State Legislatures, 1987). The most comprehensive description of income tax changes is found in Steven D. Gold, *The Budding Revolution in State Income Taxes* (Denver: National Conference of State Legislatures, 1987). The text includes changes in Michigan in December 1987, and in Kansas and Maine in 1988.

8. See, e.g., Karl E. Case and Charles Zielinski, *The Challenge of Telecommunications State Regulatory and Tax Policies for a New Industry* (Washington, D.C.: Council of State Planning Agencies, 1986).

9. See National Conference of State Legislatures and National Association of State Budget Officers, *Federal Tax Reform: Implications for the States* (Washington, D.C., 1986).

10. Hawaii also provided a new refundable credit of $45 per person (intended to offset the sales tax on food), which is technically not a personal credit, although it is similar to one.

11. The seven states that are said to have "restructured their entire income tax" adopted wholly new rate structures and made major changes in standard deductions and personal exemptions, as well as other changes in most cases. The other states changing their income taxes can be arrayed on a continuum from those making major changes to those with relatively minor changes. California probably made the biggest changes, lowering its top rate 1.7 percentage points, reducing the number of rate brackets significantly, and making a large increase in its personal credit and a small increase in its standard deduction. Other states generally reduced their top tax rate by 1.1 percent or less, if at all, while increasing the standard deduction and usually the personal exemption. Ohio lowered its top rate 1.65 percentage points but retained its previous rate brackets and made no other changes aside from reducing rates.

12. The rates mentioned in the text for Kansas are for joint returns. The rates for single returns are 4.8 percent and 6.1 percent.

13. Ohio was one of the few states to reduce its top tax rate by a larger proportion than other tax rates, and even it is estimated to have increased progressivity because the rate reduction did not fully offset base-broadening at the top of the income scale. For illustrative statistics on how federal base-broadening affected the progressivity of the income tax in one state, see Philip M. Dearborn and Robert D. Ebel, "State Individual and Corporate Tax Alternatives," *Hamline Journal of Public Law and Policy* viii (Spring 1987): 157-172.

14. Iowa allows the 60 percent exclusion only for the first $17,500 of capital gains earned by a taxpayer and provides that the exclusion will be

pro-rated if it reduces aggregate state revenue more than a specified amount.

15. Kentucky is expected to a hold a special session before year-end, but at the time this chapter was written that session was expected to be limited to workers' compensation issues.

16. The tally of 15 states reducing their top rate does not include Virginia (where the rate was unchanged but the level where it takes effect was raised) or the District of Columbia. The comparison of marginal tax rates should take into account whether federal income tax payments are deductible. If they are, the tax rate that appears in official documents exaggerates the actual tax rate. For example, in a state with such deductibility, a 10 percent nominal rate corresponded approximately to a 5 percent rate for top-bracket federal taxpayers when the federal marginal tax rate was 50 percent; with a 28 percent top federal rate, it corresponds to a 7.2 percent rate. Two of the remaining three states with rates above 7.9 percent—Arizona and Montana—permit full federal deductibility. See Steven D. Gold, "Developments in State Finances, 1983 to 1986," *Public Budgeting and Finance* (Winter 1987), pp. 5-23.

17. The "windfall" tally does not count Kentucky, where the "windfall" is estimated to be $116 million. All estimates are for fiscal year 1988.

18. Robert H. Aten, "The Magnitude of Additional State Corporate Income Taxes Resulting from Federal Tax Reform," *Tax Notes* (August 3, 1987), pp. 529-534. Aten speculated that only about $1 billion of the potential "windfall" would be retained, once some states had taken action to avoid it. Robert Tannenwald of the Boston Federal Reserve believes that the corporate windfall is considerably smaller, according to estimates in his "State Response in New England to Federal Tax Reform," *New England Economic Review* (September/October 1987), pp. 25-44. For an earlier version of his analysis, see "The Effects of Federal Tax Reform on New England's Income Tax Revenues," *National Tax Journal* xl (September 1987): 445-459.

19. Subchapter S corporations are exempt from the corporate income tax. Some experts have predicted that many corporations would adopt the Subchapter S structure because the Tax Reform Act made personal income tax rates lower than corporate income tax rates.

20. Coopers & Lybrand, *Tax Topics Advisory: State and Local* (April 18, 1988) lists nine states with a corporate alternative minimum tax— Alaska, California, Florida, Iowa, Maine, Minnesota, New York, North Dakota, and Pennsylvania. Kansas enacted one shortly thereafter.

21. Steven D. Gold, "State Tax Policy: Recent Trends and Future Directions," in Gold, *Reforming State Tax Systems,* pp. 20-25.

22. In 1983, Feenberg and Rosen estimate that half of the 40 state income taxes had an elasticity of 1.5 or less, considerably less than the elasticity of the federal income tax of 1.72. Only 11 income taxes were more progressive than the federal tax. The elasticity in this study measures the average percentage income in tax liability when income increases 1 percent, using a uniform income distribution for all states. See Daniel R. Feenberg and Harvey S. Rosen, "State Personal Income and Sales Taxes: 1977-1983," in Harvey S. Rosen, ed., *Studies in State and Local Public Finance* (Chicago: University of Chicago Press, 1986), p. 142.

23. Steven D. Gold, *State Tax Relief for the Poor* (Denver: National Conference of State Legislatures, 1987). Michael Mazerov and Iris Lav, *The Fairest of Them All: A Rating of Personal Income Taxes for 1987 Returns* (Washington, D.C.: American Federation of State, County, and Municipal Employees, 1988) reveals that the trend toward increased progressivity was widespread but not universal. Using 16 measures of pro-

gressivity in each state, it found that 21 of 40 states had a decrease in progressivity according to at least one measure. In nearly all states, however, the majority of measures showed increased progressivity.

III

The Meaning of Balance for State-Local Tax Systems

by
Helen F. Ladd

The fiscal environment of state and local governments has changed markedly during the past decade and further changes are likely in the future. As evidenced by the tax and expenditure limitation movement, local voters have been increasingly vocal in their opposition to certain revenue and expenditure policies of state and local governments. At the national level, recent actions of the federal government in the areas of tax reform and grants-in-aid are likely to have profound impacts on state and local governments and to force them to reevaluate the adequacy of their tax structures.

To help states improve their tax structures, the U.S. Advisory Commission on Intergovernmental Relations (ACIR) has advocated, among other things, that states strive for "revenue diversification." To ACIR, revenue diversification means more than simply that a state should use all three broad-based taxes—income, general sales, and property; it also means that a state should raise approximately the same revenue from each tax.[1] That is, if a state collects about a third of its state-local tax revenue from each of the big three taxes, it has a diversified state tax structure; otherwise it does not. Throughout this chapter, the terms *revenue balance* or *balance among revenue sources* are used to refer to this ACIR concept of diversification. As elaborated below, very few states currently meet ACIR's criterion for revenue balance.

Upon first reflection, ACIR's call for revenue balance seems sensible and intuitively appealing. ACIR has argued, for example, that no one tax is ideal. By spreading the burden among tax sources, states are able to avoid the disadvantages of excessive reliance on a particular tax and to benefit from the strengths of all three broad-based taxes. Thus, by analogy to a three-legged stool, it seems to make sense for a state to use all three legs of its revenue-producing system—that is, its income tax, general sales tax, and property tax—and by analogy to the lengths of the legs of the stool, the state should use each of them in approximately equal proportions.

Significantly, however, most academic experts on tax policy do not include revenue balance explicitly as one of the requirements of a good tax system.[2] Instead, they list requirements such as fairness, minimal distortion of economic behavior, and revenue-raising potential. Moreover, these experts emphasize that policymakers often must make tradeoffs between conflicting policy objectives. According to this approach, states should strive for balance among competing policy goals, not necessarily for balance among revenue sources.

Of course, balancing competing policy goals could lead to more balanced revenue systems in the ACIR sense. If this were the case for most states, ACIR's call for balanced state tax systems could be interpreted as a means to the more subtle end of encouraging states to find an appropriate balance among the traditional goals of tax policy. Thus, a main purpose of this chapter is to determine the extent to which moving toward a more balanced revenue system would facilitate the achievement of each of several standard goals of tax policy in the various states. This review shows that revenue balance is consistent with some of the standard goals but not with others.

More important, this review indicates that moving to a balanced tax structure may make sense for some states but not for others. This conclusion simply reflects the diversity among states both in the structure of their economies and in the weights they attach to different objectives of tax policy. With respect to economies, some states have a lot of business property while others do not, and some have a lot of spending by out-of-staters compared with that of others. With respect to policy goals, some states place high value on the fairness of their tax structures while others put more weight on the competitive position of their state vis-à-vis other states. Some are concerned with the cyclical stability of their revenue systems; others are more concerned with secular growth.

These differences in economies and in the weights states attach to particular policy goals imply that states should not strive for similar tax structures. Instead, each one should strive for a tax structure that represents the best balance among its competing tax policy goals given the constraints imposed by and the opportunities provided by its economy. In some states, this balancing of policy goals may favor a more balanced tax system in the form advocated by ACIR; in other states, it may not.

Existing Tax Systems

Based on ACIR's concept of revenue balance, few states currently have balanced tax systems, and the number varies depending on whether attention is focused on all own-source revenues or on taxes alone. When balance is defined in terms of all revenues from own sources, ACIR typically argues that between 20 and 30 percent of such revenues should come from each of the three major taxes—income, property, and sales—and that the remaining 10 to 40 percent should come from charges and all other revenues.[3] Based on this strict criterion for balance, no state has a balanced revenue structure.

Based on a somewhat more liberal definition of revenue balance—namely, that at least 15 percent of all state and local own-source revenues come from each of the big three taxes—only eight states have balanced revenue structures. In this group are California, Georgia, Idaho, Indiana, New York, North Carolina, Ohio, and South Carolina.

Table 1 focuses on taxes alone. Even with this restricted focus, only 12 states meet the requirement for what might be called a *strongly balanced* tax system—that is, one in which each of the big three taxes accounts for at least 20 percent of the total tax revenues from these three sources. Another 10 states can be categorized as *relatively balanced,* but the striking conclusion is that more than half have tax systems that are out of balance according to ACIR's definition.

Table 1.

Balance Among State and Local Government Tax Sources, 1984

State	Percent Distribution		
	Property Tax Revenue	Income Tax Revenue	General Sales and Gross Receipts Revenue
United States	**40.9%**	**27.3%**	**31.9%**
Strongly Balanced			
Arkansas	27.8%	30.2%	42.0%
California	32.9	30.8	36.4
Georgia	34.6	30.4	35.0
Idaho	35.3	31.4	33.3
Indiana	36.5	25.1	38.3
Kentucky	28.5	38.1	33.3
North Carolina	31.3	39.6	29.1
Ohio	38.2	34.5	27.2
Oklahoma	30.0	20.9	40.1
Pennsylvania	39.4	34.3	26.2
South Carolina	33.2	33.3	33.5
Utah	33.9	25.1	41.0
Group Average	**33.4%**	**31.9%**	**34.6%**
Relatively Balanced			
Colorado	40.2%	21.7%	38.1%
Hawaii	21.7	30.3	48.0
Illinois	47.3	23.7	29.0
Iowa	48.5	26.6	24.9
Maine	47.0	24.1	29.0
Minnesota	35.2	42.1	22.7
Missouri	29.9	26.5	43.6
New York	38.9	36.9	24.2
Virginia	40.2	36.6	23.2
Wisconsin	40.6	36.4	23.0
Group Average	**38.9%**	**30.5%**	**30.6%**
Balanced **States' Average**	**36.0%**	**31.3%**	**32.8%**
Reliant on Property Taxes			
Alaska	88.0%	0.2%	11.8%
Connecticut	56.6	7.5	35.9
Kansas	49.3	24.5	26.1
Massachusetts	43.4	39.1	17.5
Michigan	47.7	32.4	19.9
Montana	74.0	26.0	0.0
Nebraska	52.6	19.7	27.7
New Hampshire	96.7	3.3	0.0
New Jersey	57.2	19.8	23.0
North Dakota	44.6	14.7	40.7
Oregon	55.6	44.4	0.0

State	Property Tax Revenue	Income Tax Revenue	General Sales and Gross Receipts Revenue
		Percent Distribution	
Rhode Island	50.3	26.6	23.1
South Dakota	57.9	0.0	42.1
Texas	59.5	0.0	40.5
Vermont	54.9	27.9	17.2
Wyoming	73.0	0.0	27.0
Group Average*	**58.2%**	**19.1%**	**22.7%**
Reliant on Sales Taxes			
Alabama	20.7%	30.8%	48.4%
Arizona	36.0	17.8	46.3
Florida	49.1	0.0	50.9
Louisiana	24.8	13.6	61.6
Mississippi	30.4	16.1	53.5
Nevada	39.8	0.0	60.2
New Mexico	22.2	7.9	69.9
Tennessee	35.1	1.9	63.0
Washington	36.2	0.0	63.8
West Virginia	24.0	25.4	50.6
Group Average	**31.8%**	**11.3%**	**56.8%**
Reliant on Income Taxes			
Delaware	25.1%	74.9%	0.0%
Maryland	33.1	47.2	19.8
Group Average	**29.1%**	**61.0%**	**9.9%**
Imbalanced			
States' Average*	**46.3%**	**19.3%**	**34.4%**

*Excludes Alaska

Source: U.S. Department of Commerce, Bureau of the Census, *Governmental Finances in 1983-84* (Washington, D.C.: U.S. Government Printing Office, 1985).

States with imbalanced tax structures—that is, those that obtain either less than 20 percent or more than 48 percent of their broad-based tax revenue from a single source—are further classified in Table 1 as being *reliant on property taxes* (16 states), *reliant on sales taxes* (10 states), or *reliant on income taxes* (2 states). For example, most of the New England states rely heavily on property taxes, many southern states on sales taxes, and Delaware and Maryland on income taxes.

Given the degree of imbalance in current state and local tax structures, it would be folly to recommend that states move quickly to achieve the revenue balance advocated by ACIR. Whether revenue balance should be a longer-run goal of state policy, however, depends on the extent to which such a tax system helps a state achieve the standard goals of good tax policy. The following sections address that issue for several specific goals of tax policy.

Revenue-Raising Potential

First, consider the basic goal of tax policy—namely, to raise revenue. With the decline in federal grants-in-aid, state and local governments increasingly are pressured to raise more money from their own sources. Would a balanced tax system make it easier for a state to raise revenue and, hence, to provide public services to its residents? The argument here might be that excessive reliance on a single tax might serve as a lightning rod for antitax and antispending sentiments, thereby making it difficult for a state with an imbalanced tax system to raise revenue.

One relatively crude, but still useful, way to shed light on this question is to look at the relationship between a state's per capita revenues or expenditures and the degree of balance of its tax system. This type of analysis indicates that a balanced tax structure is not a necessary condition for a state to raise a lot of tax revenue or to spend a lot on public services. Indeed, of the 10 states with the highest per capita tax revenues in 1984, only one has a strongly balanced tax system and five have imbalanced systems. With respect to expenditures, among the 10 states with the highest per capita general expenditures from own sources only, one has a strongly balanced system, while five have imbalanced tax systems.[4]

These findings imply that the case for revenue balance cannot be based on the argument that more balanced systems make possible greater revenues or expenditures. At the same time, however, the data suggest that excessive reliance on at least one of the broad-based taxes—namely, the general sales tax—may limit a state's ability to raise tax revenue. For example, the 10 states relying heavily on sales taxes raise less revenue per capita on average than states with other tax structures. Despite this observation that one form of tax imbalance may restrict revenue-raising capacity, the main point is that a strongly balanced tax system is not a prerequisite for high revenues.

Revenue Growth and Stability

The requirement that state and local governments balance their budgets forces policymakers to pay attention to the secular growth of tax revenues and to their instability over the cycle. To balance their budgets, state and local governments may want tax revenues to grow in line with income. This automatic growth allows state and local governments to satisfy demands for public services that typically rise at least as fast as income without imposing net taxes or increasing tax rates.[5]

Taxes vary in their responsiveness to changes in state income. Revenues from state and local income taxes typically grow faster than state income; revenues from sales taxes grow more slowly than income; and, over the long run, revenues from property taxes grow at about the same rate as income. These measures of responsiveness are only averages; the responsiveness of a particular tax in a specific state will depend on how the state defines the tax base. For example, a sales tax that includes services is likely to be more responsive to income growth than a more narrowly defined retail sales tax. And the revenue from an income tax with progressive tax rates is more responsive than that from a flat rate tax.

Empirical estimates of the responsiveness of state and local tax systems by state indicate the predicted result that balanced tax systems better achieve the policy goal of assuring that tax revenues grow in line with income than do unbalanced tax systems.[6] This makes sense because the slow growth of property or sales taxes is offset by the faster growth of the income tax. Of course, if the policy goal is revenue growth that exceeds that of state personal income, heavy reliance on a progressive personal income tax is called for.

Revenue sources that are responsive to income are a double-edged sword. As long as income is rising, they are fine, but when income falls, revenues also fall. This decline in revenues makes it difficult for states to balance their budgets during cyclical downturns in the economy. As a result, state officials may face a tradeoff between growth and cyclical instability in state tax revenues.[7] If a state has a strong preference for stability over revenue growth, then minimal reliance on income and certain types of sales taxes may make sense. Alternatively, if a state has a strong preference for revenue growth over stability, then heavy reliance on income taxes is warranted. For states that care equally about growth and stability, a relatively balanced tax system is probably needed, provided revenues from the different taxes do not move together over the business cycle.

Fairness

In addition to revenue-raising potential, other tax policy goals, such as distributing the burden fairly among taxpayers, are also important in designing tax systems.

One approach to fairness focuses on the line between taxes paid and benefits received. That is, a tax system is deemed fair to the extent that taxpayers contribute in line with the benefits they receive from public goods and services. This concept of fairness is useful in narrowly defined program areas where the direct beneficiaries of public programs can be identified and taxed. The most common example is gasoline taxes for highway uses but this principle offers limited guidance for the broad-based taxes considered here.

A second, more useful approach to fairness states that taxpayers should be taxed in line with their ability to pay. Horizontal equity requires that taxpayers with equal ability to pay face similar tax burdens, while vertical equity requires that taxpayers with greater ability contribute more than those with lesser ability. By one interpretation of the ability-to-pay principle, a state that is concerned exclusively about equity would choose the best measure of ability to pay (typically taken to be personal income) and then rely solely on this base for all its tax revenue. This interpretation would lead to a very imbalanced tax structure.

Disagreement about what constitutes the best measure of ability to pay complicates the picture. Persuasive arguments can be made for consumption or wealth, in addition to income, as appropriate measures of taxpaying ability. This disagreement could justify a diversified tax structure even if the tax structure were designed exclusively with fairness in mind. Diversification would reflect a state's attempt to distribute tax burdens in line with the various measures of ability to pay.

States also may be concerned with the vertical equity of their state-local tax structures. Such tax structures are typically regressive—that is, tax burdens as a fraction of income are higher for low-income than for high-income households. The question here is how the balance among tax sources affects the distribution of tax burdens across income classes.

Sales taxes are generally regressive, since the proportion of household income spent on taxable consumption is typically higher for low-income than for high-income households.[8] In addition, from the perspective of local governments, property taxes are also regressive.[9] Only the income tax can introduce progressivity into the state-local tax structure. Thus, the relative reliance on each individual tax source combined with the state-specific characteristics of each tax determines the overall degree of regressivity or progressivity of a state's tax structure.

Among the five categories of states listed in Table 1, states that rely heavily on sales or property taxes have the most regressive tax systems on average.[10] Moving toward greater revenue balance in such states would reduce the regressivity of the state-local tax burden. The effect of diversifying revenues is reversed for states that currently rely heavily on income taxes; in these states, revenue diversification would reduce reliance on the relatively progressive income tax in favor of regressive sales and property taxes. According to the data, states with relatively—but not strongly—balanced tax systems have the least regressive tax systems on average.

These findings imply that some use of the income tax is desirable if a state is concerned with vertical equity, but that a strongly balanced tax system need not be better than a relatively balanced system or one that relies heavily on income taxes.

Behavioral Distortions

Tax systems also may have unintended side effects. In particular, a tax system may create incentives for firms and households to change their behavior in undesirable ways to avoid bearing the burden of the tax. For example, if a state has a particularly high tax rate—say, a sales tax rate of 7 percent—people may shop outside the state to avoid the tax. Similarly, if a state's property or income tax rates are above those in competing states, firms and households may alter their location decisions to avoid the state's high taxes.

Remember, however, that firms and households respond to the level of tax rates, not to tax revenues, and that heavy reliance on a particular tax need not mean that a state imposed an above-average tax rate for that tax. A low overall level of taxes could lead to an average or below-average tax rate on the heavily used tax. Or a state may have a larger-than-average base for that tax that would allow it to collect above-average revenues without above- average rates. Whether states that rely heavily on a particular tax impose above-average tax rates for that tax is an empirical question.

Rough data from the states with imbalanced tax structures suggest that states that make heavy use of particular taxes do tend to use above-average tax rates.[11] The two states that rely heavily on income taxes, for example, have average income tax rates that are approximately double the average in all other states. Similarly, states that rely heavily on sales taxes tend to have higher rates than other states. And states that rely heavily on property taxes impose property tax rates that exceed those in other states by about 75 percent. Moreover, the states that rely heavily on property taxes also tend to tax business activity at above-average rates, where the tax rates on business include eight types of taxes that have an initial impact on business. The higher tax burden on business in these states probably reflects the fact that property taxes account for a large portion of the tax on business firms; if these states reduced their property tax rates, they also would be lowering the tax rates on business.[12]

To the extent that differential tax rates distort the location decisions of households or firms, the data suggest that if the states with imbalanced tax systems shifted away from reliance on the overused tax in favor of more balanced tax systems, behavioral distortions would be reduced. In this sense, moving toward more balanced state tax systems would be a positive step.

Competitive Tax Rates

It is one thing to argue that it might be better (at least in terms of the goal of reducing distortions) for states that rely heavily on a particular tax to reduce reliance on that tax in favor of other taxes—that is, on other legs of the revenue-producing stool. It is quite another thing to argue that states should aim for equal revenues from each tax—that is, that the legs of the stool should all be the same length.

Assume for a moment that policymakers are concerned particularly about the competitive position of their state vis-à-vis other states. That is, they want to make sure that their tax rates are not out of line with those of other states. This concern about competitive tax rates is understandable given the increasing mobility of firms and households across the nation. Although an extensive body of literature generally suggests that taxes have little impact on the location decisions of firms, most state officials apparently believe the contrary—namely, that taxes do influence location decisions, especially if a state's tax rates are far out of line with those in competing jurisdictions. Considerations of this sort might lead officials to strive for a tax system in which the tax rates of major taxes are comparable to those in competing states.

But the policy goal of competitive tax rates need not be compatible with the idea of revenue balance because the composition of tax bases differs across states. For example, a state such as Nevada has a much larger sales tax base than other states relative to its potential property and income tax bases. If it were to apply competitive tax rates, defined crudely for this analysis as national average tax rates, to each of its bases, Nevada would end up with more than 50 percent of its tax revenue from the sales tax.

Similarly, 19 other states, including Connecticut, Hawaii, Louisiana, and Utah, all have disproportionately large property tax bases relative to potential income and sales tax bases. This observation means that these states have an opportunity to collect disproportionately large amounts of revenue from the property tax without charging above-average tax rates. Such states probably should take advantage of that revenue-raising potential, despite the fact that by doing so they may end up with imbalanced revenue systems according to ACIR. No compelling reason exists for states not to capitalize on their favorable economic situations.

Intergovernmental Dimension of Balance

The three-tiered federal structure of the U.S. fiscal system underscores the importance of considering the roles and responsibilities of different levels of government in assessing the desirability of balance among tax sources. Typically, state governments use income and sales taxes while local governments rely more heavily on property taxes. Hence, states that rely heavily on the property tax tend to be the most decentralized in terms of spending responsibilities.

To argue that such states should balance their revenue systems is in effect an argument either for strengthening the states' fiscal role in the state and local government system or for permitting greater use of income and sales taxes at the local level. In states with strong traditions of local control, political accountability at the local level argues for devolution of revenue responsibility to the local level. This devolution justifiably may be limited in practice, however, by the existing structure of fragmented governmental units. Hence, in some states, the goal of a balanced state-local tax system in the ACIR sense may conflict with a state's chosen distribution of responsibilities among levels of government.

Conclusion

This brief review of standard criteria for evaluating tax policy shows that a balanced tax structure as advocated by ACIR facilitates the achievement of some of the standard goals of tax policy but hinders the achievement of others. For some states, the movement toward more balanced tax systems could reduce tax rate differentials, could lead to a tax system in which taxes grow more closely in line with incomes, and could lead to a fairer distribution of tax burdens. But these benefits would not necessarily materialize in all states. Moreover, in some states, the movement to revenue balance might conflict with the goal of competitive tax rates and with the state's values about the appropriate degree of fiscal decentralization. Nor does revenue balance appear to be a requirement for raising large amounts of revenue. Thus, the desirability of revenue balance as defined by ACIR will vary from state to state depending on a state's economic situation and its policy goals. For many states, ACIR's concept of revenue balance will not make sense.

In one sense, ACIR's logic is similar to the logic presented here—namely, that a good tax structure is one that balances conflicting policy goals. Recognizing that no single tax is ideal based on standard criteria, ACIR argues that states should spread the burden among tax sources. This spreading helps states avoid the disadvantages of excessive reliance on a particular tax and allows them to garner the benefits of all three broad-based taxes.

In a recent paper, the former director of ACIR, John Shannon, argues further that a balanced revenue system also achieves an important political balance between liberals and conservatives.[13] For example, use of all three taxes balances the desires of conservatives for more use of sales and property taxes with those of liberals who favor progressive income taxes. And it balances the conservative desire for revenues that grow more slowly than income with the liberal desire for revenues that grow faster than income. Finally, the balanced revenue concept represents a middle-of-the-road course between those who favor a centralized state-local fiscal structure and those who favor a decentralized fiscal structure.

This chapter differs from ACIR in emphasizing the variation across states in the composition of their potential tax bases and by granting more legitimacy to the variation across states in policy goals. Together, these differences among states call for variation in state tax structures rather than the more uniformly balanced tax structures advocated by ACIR.

Notes

The chapter is based on joint work with Dana Weist, Department of City and Regional Planning, University of North Carolina. Our paper "State and Local Tax Systems: Balance Among Taxes vs. Balance Among Policy Goals" (Cambridge, Mass.: Lincoln Institute of Land Policy Research, forthcoming) provides a more detailed discussion of many of the points made here.

1. For the ACIR's position on revenue diversification, see *State and Local Roles in the Federal System,* Report A-88 (Washington, D.C.: U.S. Advisory Commission on Intergovernmental Relations, 1982), especially Ch. 3, "The State Role and State Capability." Interpretations of this position are found in Robert J. Cline and John Shannon, "The Property Tax in a Model State-Local Revenue System," in *The Property Tax and Local Finance,* ed. by C. Lowell Harris (New York: Academy of Political Science, 1983), pp. 42-56; and Robert J. Kleine and John Shannon, "Characteristics of a Balanced and Moderate State-Local Revenue System," in *Reforming State Tax Systems,* ed. by Steven D. Gold (Denver: National Conference of State Legislatures, 1986).

2. See, for example, Richard A. Musgrave and Peggy B. Musgrave, *Public Finance in Theory and Practice,* 4th ed. (New York: McGraw-Hill, 1984), Ch. 10, "Introduction to Taxation"; Edgar K. Browning and Jaquelene M. Browning, *Public Finance and the Price System,* 2nd ed. (New York: McGraw-Hill, 1984), Ch. 10, "Introduction to Taxation"; Edgar K. Browning and Jaquelene M. Browning, *Public Finance and the Price System,* 2nd ed. (New York: MacMillan, 1983), Ch. 1, "Introduction"; Bernard P. Herber, *Modern Public Finance,* 5th ed. (Homewood, Ill: Richard D. Irwin, 1983), Ch. 5, "Fiscal Principles and Concepts"; or David N. Hyman, *Public Finance: A Contemporary Application of Theory to Policy,* 2nd ed. (New York: Dryden Press, 1987), Ch. 11, "Introduction to Government Finance."

3. These other sources of revenue include interest earnings, rent, royalties, donations, fines, forfeits, sale of property, and other minor sources of revenue not previously classified.

4. The 10 states with highest revenue per capita from the property, sales, and income taxes in 1984 were California, Connecticut, Hawaii, Massachusetts, Michigan, Minnesota, New Jersey, New York, Wisconsin, and Wyoming. The 10 states with the highest per capita spending were Alaska, California, Delaware, Hawaii, Minnesota, Nevada, New Mexico, New York, Wisconsin, and Wyoming.

5. In a review of much of the empirical research measuring the demand for local public services, Inman found that the income elasticity of demand for housing and urban renewal, parks and recreation, welfare, and investments in future public services exceeded unity, while the income elasticity of demand for most other local services was generally less than one. See Robert P. Inman, "The Fiscal Performance of Local Governments: An Interpretative Review," in *Current Issues in Urban Economics,* ed. by Peter Mieszkowski and Mahlon Straszheim (Baltimore, Md.: The Johns Hopkins University Press, 1979), pp. 270-321.

6. This conclusion is based on careful estimates of income elasticities for personal income taxes and general sales taxes calculated by Feenberg and Rosen (1986), and for property taxes cited by ACIR (1979). Feenberg and Rosen developed a synthetic data series based on a stratified random sample of federal income tax returns. Information on state tax rate structures and base definitions then was incorporated into this data series to characterize the structures of state tax systems. Although the elasticities cited therein assume a uniform distribution of income across states, they do reflect the diversity in tax structures and sales and income elasticities across states. Due to a lack of recent data measuring the elasticity of the property tax with respect to income, it was necessary to rely on national average estimates of property tax elasticities cited by ACIR (1979). As a result, the weighted estimates do not fully measure the variability in income elasticities across states.

7. In considering this tradeoff, White has introduced the notion of an efficiency frontier for tax structures that provides the highest possible growth rate in tax revenues for any degree of tax instability or the lowest possible degree of tax instability for any given growth rate in tax revenues. See Fred C. White, "Trade-off in Growth and Stability in State Taxes," *National Tax Journal* 36 (September 1983): 103-114.

8. This statement assumes that the sales tax is borne by consumers in the form of higher prices. The amount of regressivity also is affected by what is included in the tax base. A sales tax, for example, will be less regressive if food and drugs are excluded from taxation and if some types of services are included in the tax base.

9. This conclusion is based on the "local view" of the incidence of the property tax. The "new view" of the property tax is a tax on capital, which results in a progressive tax burden. This "new view" considers the incidence of the property tax from a national perspective. Since state and local policymakers will be concerned most with the impact of their tax structures on their jurisdictions, the "local view" of property tax incidence is more appropriate in this context.

10. This conclusion is based on estimates of the average income elasticity and the Suits index on progressivity, presented in Donald Phares, *Who Pays State and Local Taxes?* (Boston, Mass.: Oelgeschlager, Gunn and Hain, 1980), pp. 133-134, 142-143. See also "The Role of Tax Burden Studies in State Tax Policy," *Reforming State Tax Systems* (Denver, Colo.: National Conference of State Legislatures, 1986), pp. 67-88.

11. This conclusion is based on tax rates calculated as follows. The income tax rate in each state is calculated as personal income tax revenue divided by state personal income; the property tax rate is calculated as property tax revenue divided by an estimate of the full market value of property. For sales taxes, the statutory rate is used, both adjusted and unadjusted for local sales tax rates.

12. The business tax rates are those reported in William C. Wheaton, "Interstate Differences in the Level of Business Taxation," *National Tax Journal* 36 (March 1983).

13. John Shannon, "State Revenue Diversification—The Search for Balance," paper prepared for the Lincoln Institute Tax Roundtable, Cambridge, Mass., May 1, 1987, forthcoming in conference volume.

References

Atkinson, Anthony B., and Stiglitz, Joseph E. *Lectures on Public Economics*. New York: McGraw-Hill, 1980.

Feenberg, Daniel R., and Rosen, Harvey S. "State Personal Income and Sales Taxes, 1977-1983." In *Studies in State and Local Public Finance*. Edited by Harvey S. Rosen. Chicago, Ill.: University of Chicago Press, 1986, pp. 135-186.

Cline, Robert J., and Shannon, John. "The Property Tax in a Model State-Local Revenue System." In *The Property Tax and Local Finance*. Edited by C. Lowell Harris. New York: Academy of Political Science, 1983, pp. 42-56.

Inman, Robert P. "The Fiscal Performance of State and Local Governments: An Interpretative Review." In *Current Issues in Urban Economics*. Edited by Peter Mieszkowski and Mahlon Straszheim. Baltimore, Md.: The Johns Hopkins University Press, 1979, pp. 270-321.

Kleine, Robert J., and Shannon, John. "Characteristics of a Balanced and Moderate State-Local Revenue System." In *Reforming State Tax Systems*. Edited by Steven D. Gold. Denver, Colo.: National Conference of State Legislatures, 1986.

Mieszkowski, Peter, and Toder, Eric. "Taxation of Natural Resources." In *Fiscal Federalism and the Taxation of Natural Resources*. Edited by Charles E. McLure and Peter Mieszkowski. Lexington, Mass.: DC Heath and Co., 1983, pp. 65-91.

Mikesell, John L. "The Cyclical Sensitivity of State and Local Taxes." *Public Budgeting and Finance* 4 (Spring 1984): 32-39.

Musgrave, Richard. "The Nature of Horizontal Equity and the Principle of Broad-based Taxation: A Friendly Critique." In *Public Finance in a Democratic Society,* Vol. 1. New York: New York University Press, 1986, pp. 301-315.

Musgrave, Richard, and Musgrave, Peggy B. *Public Finance in Theory and Practice,* 4th Ed. New York: McGraw-Hill, 1984.

Phares, Donald. *Who Pays State and Local Taxes?* Boston, Mass.: Oelgeschlager, Gunn and Hain, 1980.

Shannon, John. "State Revenue Diversification—The Search for Balance." Paper presented to the Lincoln Institute Tax Policy Roundtable, Cambridge, Mass., May 1, 1987. (Lincoln Institute conference volume, forthcoming.)

U.S. Advisory Commission on Intergovernmental Relations. *Significant Features of Fiscal Federalism*. 1982-83 Ed. Washington, D.C.: ACIR, 1984.

_____. *State and Local Roles in the Federal System*. Report A-88. Washington, D.C.: ACIR, 1982.

_____. *State and Local Finances in Recession and Inflation*. Report A-70. Washington, D.C.: ACIR, 1979.

U.S. Department of Commerce. Bureau of the Census. 1982 Census of Governments. *Compendium of Government Finances,* Vol. 4. Washington, D.C.: U.S. Government Printing Office, 1984.

_____. *Governmental Finances in 1983-84*. Washington, D.C.: U.S. Government Printing Office, 1985.

_____. *1986 Statistical Abstract,* 106th Ed. Washington, D.C.: U.S. Government Printing Office, 1986.

_____. Bureau of Economic Analysis. *Survey of Current Business.* August 1986.

Wheaton, William C. "Interstate Differences in the Level of Business Taxation." *National Tax Journal* 36 (March 1983): 83-94.

White, Fred C. "Trade-off in Growth and Stability in State Taxes." *National Tax Journal* 36 (March 1983): 103-114.

IV

Principles of a High-Quality State Revenue System

State tax systems have gone through a tumultuous period over the past decade, and the future does not appear as if it will be easy either. The Lincoln Institute of Land Policy and the National Conference of State Legislatures (NCSL) brought together a group of state legislators and staff with considerable leadership experience in developing their states' tax policies. This chapter is the result of their deliberations during which they reflected on what constitutes a high-quality state-local revenue system. These ideas represent the consensus of this group of legislators and staff but not necessarily the positions of the legislative bodies to which they belong, NCSL, or the Lincoln Institute.

The group hopes that this chapter will assist legislators as they grapple with the difficult task of shaping tax and revenue policy in the 1980s and 1990s. States are in the midst of a period of extensive review of their tax systems. To an important extent, this review has been stimulated by federal tax reform, which has demonstrated the feasibility of achieving far-reaching change in tax policy and has altered fundamentally the fiscal environment in which states operate. But many legislators were calling for a review of state tax policy even before federal tax reform occurred.

It is a good idea to reconsider periodically how a tax system has evolved and whether it is meeting the needs of a changing economy and changing ideas about the appropriate role of government.

Those who prepare a set of principles of this type are indebted to others who have made similar attempts before them. We acknowledge in particular the contribution of John Shannon, former director of the U.S. Advisory Commission on Intergovernmental Relations, and Robert Kleine, whose 1985 paper on characteristics of a balanced revenue system helped spark interest in this subject.[1] We drew not only on their work but also on the ideas developed by several recent state tax study commissions.

This statement of principles is idealistic in the sense that it describes what state tax policy should be like, even though formidable if not insurmountable political obstacles stand in the way of making a state's policies fully consistent with these principles, especially in the short run. We believe, however, that there is value in setting out certain standards against which progress can be measured. We hope that this statement will stimulate discussion about the attributes of a high-quality revenue system and thereby help build momentum for improving state tax systems.

While good state revenue systems have certain elements in common, they also differ in many respects because of differences in state economies, resource endowments, demographics, history, and the values of citizens, among other factors. It is impossible to develop a single blueprint that sets out in detail what a high-quality tax system looks like. This statement spells out a number of specific principles, but tradeoffs are inevitably present among them. The resolution of these tradeoffs is inherently a political decision to be decided on a state-by-state basis.

Two important aspects of the scope of this statement should be noted:

- Although the major source of revenue for state and local governments must be taxation, most of the principles are discussed in terms of a *revenue* system rather than a *tax* system, in recognition of the fact that fees and charges play a major role in financing states and localities.
- A state tax system should be viewed in terms of not just state but also local taxes. Local governments raise about 40 percent of total state-local revenue, so local taxes are highly significant. While many aspects of local taxation usually are left to the discretion of localities, the state is responsible for creating the system in which localities must operate.

The division of responsibility for financing services between state and local governments varies greatly among states. However that responsibility is divided, states should be certain that local governments have sufficient fiscal capacity to carry out their duties. States have a responsibility to monitor and referee how local governments finance themselves within the total state-local fiscal system.

While this statement covers a large number of issues, some important aspects of state tax policy are not covered, such as earmarking of revenue, the treatment of family units, tax and expenditure limitations, lotteries, and special provisions for particular groups, such as senior citizens.

The 10 basic principles of a high-quality state revenue system are as follows:

1) A high-quality revenue system should be composed of elements that function well together as a logical system, including the finances of both local and state governments.

2) A high-quality revenue system should produce revenue in a reliable manner. Reliability involves stability, certainty, and sufficiency.

3) A high-quality revenue system should have substantial diversification of revenue sources over reasonably broad bases.

4) A high-quality revenue system should be equitable. Minimum aspects of a fair system are a) that it shields genuine subsistence income from taxation, b) that it is not regressive, and c) that all households with a certain income should pay approximately the same tax.

5) A high-quality revenue system should be understandable, raise revenue efficiently, minimize compliance costs for taxpayers, and be as simple to administer as possible.

6) A high-quality revenue system should have accountability.

7) A high-quality revenue system should be administered professionally and uniformly—both throughout the state and within individual jurisdictions.

8) A high-quality revenue system should result in enough equalization of the resources available to local governments that they are able to provide an adequate level of services.

9) A high-quality revenue system should minimize interstate tax competition and business tax incentives.

10) A high-quality revenue system should not be used as an instrument of social policy to encourage particular activities, although it is appropriate to discourage some actions through tax policy.

1) A high-quality revenue system should be composed of elements that function well together as a logical system, including the finances of both local and state governments.

The parts of the revenue system should be complementary rather than contradictory. Too often the tax system develops incrementally without an overall vision of how all parts relate to one another, and one segment of the system tends to cancel out another segment of the same system. Some inconsistency of provisions is inevitable because a tax system must pursue multiple objectives, but conflicts should be recognized consciously and minimized to the extent possible.

One of the major areas where states often fail to consider the revenue structure as a system involves local taxes and charges. The state is responsible for determining the functions of local governments and the taxes that they may employ, and it should recognize that its actions may interfere with or enhance the effective and equitable financing of local services. Usually, local governments are financed primarily through regressive taxes and fees, tending to undermine the equity of the state tax system.

2) A high-quality revenue system should produce revenue in a reliable manner. Reliability involves stability, certainty, and sufficiency.

Reliability encompasses a number of desirable characteristics. First of all, revenue should be relatively *stable*. A considerable degree of instability is inescapable because of the volatility of the economy, but states can design their revenue systems so that this instability is mitigated, for example, by establishing well-endowed Rainy Day Funds and by levying taxes on bases that do not fluctuate any more than the economy as a whole. A second aspect of reliability is *certainty*. Taxpayers should not have to cope with perpetual changes in tax rates and bases. This characteristic goes hand in hand with the previous one: If revenue is highly unstable, frequent changes in tax rates will be necessary. If revenue is stable, citizens can have greater certainty about the taxes they will have to pay from one year to the next. Finally, the system must produce *sufficient* revenue to fund the level of spending that citizens want and can afford. This requires not only that revenue be adequate to balance the state budget in the short run but also that revenue should grow at approximately the same rate as desired state spending; in other words, taxes whose revenue grows relatively slowly should be offset by taxes that tend to grow more rapidly than income.

3) A high-quality revenue system should have substantial diversification of revenue sources over reasonably broad bases.

A diversified revenue system normally would raise substantial revenues from six sources—the general sales tax, the personal income tax, the property tax, excise taxes (particularly on tobacco, alcoholic beverages, gasoline, and motor vehicles), business taxes, and user charges. Reliance on each of these revenue bases makes it possible to keep tax rates on each particular object of taxation at a relatively low level. This is desirable because every tax has some undesirable effects, and they are magnified when rates are high. Every tax is unfair in some respects, but if a variety of taxes are levied, the biases of each tax tend to cancel out; and every tax can distort individual and business behavior, but if rates are low, the disincentives produced by taxes are minimized.

Each of the six revenue sources has a role to play. Certain user charges, selected business taxes, some excise taxes, and a portion of the property tax can be justified on the benefit principle—that those who benefit from government services should pay for them. This principle is appropriate in many instances but can be extended too far, for example, if low-income people cannot afford certain necessities. Several other taxes are related to ability to pay, and the rationale for some excise taxes is that they discourage consumption of products that have social costs.

Broad tax bases are desirable for many of the same reasons as a diversified revenue structure. In fact, a broad base may be viewed as diversification of burdens for a particular tax. Avoiding exemptions makes it possible to maintain lower rates and also contributes to fairness (a narrow base tends to cause people with similar incomes to pay different amounts of tax).

A diversified revenue structure with broad tax bases also tends to be considerably more stable than an undiversified structure with narrow bases. In other words, fluctuations and shifts in the economy will not have as great an impact on the level of revenue if a variety of taxes are levied.

The proper balance among the six major revenue sources will vary from state to state depending on a state's natural resource and economic endowments. For example, if a large amount of revenue is easily obtainable from taxes on mineral production or tourism, that is a practical reason for having a somewhat unbalanced tax system. Excessive taxation of such activities, however, may have negative economic effects in the long run.

Sales, personal income, and property taxes should raise considerably more revenue than the other three revenue sources. Balance does not require that the three leading taxes raise exactly the same amount of revenue, but if one of them brings in more than 50 percent as much as one of the others, consideration should be given to restoring a more equal balance. (Fifty percent is an arbitrary level that may be used as a guidepost.)

4) A high-quality revenue system should be equitable. Minimum aspects of a fair system are a) that it shields genuine subsistence income from taxation, b) that it is not regressive, and c) that all households with a certain income should pay approximately the same tax.

Because fairness is a subjective concept, we have framed this principle in terms of its minimal characteristics to allow wide latitude for differences in personal attitudes. Some persons may have more expansive concepts of equity, incorporating the idea of progressivity (that is, the principle that taxes should represent an increasing proportion of income as household income rises). Since nearly all state-local tax systems are currently regressive (taking a smaller proportion of income as income rises), moving to a proportional tax system and one in which all tax burdens on subsistence income are eliminated would represent a substantial change from the status quo. We also call attention to the importance of horizontal equity—the idea that families with similar income should be taxed uniformly.

Exempting those with poverty-level income from income taxation was achieved by the federal government as a result of the 1986 tax reform. Most states, however, continue to impose substantial tax burdens on low-income households, particularly through sales, property, and excise taxes. States have a variety of means available for relieving the poor of tax burdens, such as exemptions, credits, and rebates.

The progressivity or regressivity of *any particular tax* is not of great importance. What is significant is how the burden of *the entire tax system* is distributed (global incidence). Thus, levying some regressive taxes is not inconsistent with good tax policy, provided that the overall tax system is proportional.

A qualification to the principle that global incidence is more important than the incidence of each tax is that if particular tax burdens are much higher than in neighboring states, this may affect the movement of some high-income individuals and certain economic activities, especially in communities near a state's border. If this effect is large, it may constrain the burdens that a state can impose on some high-income individuals. The federal government is in a far better position to redistribute income than states because it does not have to be concerned, as states must, about citizens "voting with their feet" and moving from high-tax to low-tax jurisdictions.

5) A high-quality revenue system should be understandable, raise revenue efficiently, minimize compliance costs for taxpayers, and be as simple to administer as possible.

While avoiding reliance on an overly complex maze of taxes, forms, and filing requirements is clearly desirable, some level of complexity and some expenses are inevitable. These principles sometimes will conflict with others discussed in this statement and are probably less important than some of those other principles. For example, shielding poverty-level households from taxes while maintaining broad tax bases requires provision of tax credits targeted at those with low incomes, even though provision of such credits necessarily entails a degree of complexity.

One important aspect of simplicity is not to levy more different taxes than necessary. Many states impose special taxes on specific industries (such as telecommunications, banking, and insurance) for reasons that may not be particularly persuasive. It would make sense to consider repealing such taxes and levying a single business tax in their place.

Policymakers often have not paid sufficient attention to the difficulty of administering tax provisions and to compliance burdens, particularly on business. Provisions of existing taxes should be reexamined to eliminate complexities whose costs outweigh their benefits, and administrative and compliance problems should be given serious consideration in future tax reforms. Tax provisions should be unambiguous, so that their meaning does not have to be negotiated by taxpayers and tax collectors.

6) A high-quality revenue system should have accountability.

The essence of accountability is that tax policy should be explicit. Hidden tax increases should be avoided. If a government wants to increase the tax burden, this should result from explicit action rather than an automatic process. Likewise, decisions about tax breaks should be overt rather than obscure.

One means of enhancing accountability is truth-in-taxation policies for the property tax. Such policies inform property owners in clearly written statements about reasons for proposed changes in their tax bills and provide an opportunity through special public hearings for the public to challenge proposed tax increases. Truth-in-taxation policies can help make members of the public better informed about why their tax bills are rising, for example, by distinguishing between higher valuations and increased tax rates.[2]

A second way to improve accountability is to require that assessments of property be based on full value rather than on a fraction of value. Fractional assessments are confusing and detract from accountability for assessors.

Tax expenditure budgets are another method of enhancing accountability. These documents measure the tax revenue lost as a result of tax preferences such as deductions, exemptions, and exclusions from the tax base. Sunsetting tax expenditures (that is, allowing them to expire if they are not renewed by legislation) forces periodic review of whether their benefits are commensurate with their cost in terms of foregone revenue.

Accountability often is taken to imply that a personal income tax should be indexed because, if it is not, effective rates will increase due to inflation, even though no increase had been legislated. A possible problem with such a conclusion is that it could cause total state tax revenue to lag behind the growth of expenditures. Many state taxes increase more slowly than inflation, and the above-average growth of the income tax pulls up the total revenue increase.

Accountability is also important in policies affecting local governments. State mandates that increase the cost of providing local services may lead to higher local taxes. State officials should consider these repercussions of existing and prospective mandates carefully.

7) A high-quality revenue system should be administered professionally and uniformly—both throughout the state and within individual jurisdictions.

Many states have considerable room to improve the administration of their tax systems, especially at the local level. Poor tax administration results in unjustified inequalities in the distribution of taxes. If tax payments increase for those not paying their rightful share, the level of taxation can be reduced for others.

An important but often neglected aspect of tax administration is compiling and distributing reports that show how the tax system is operating—which income groups and industries are responsible for paying taxes.

8) A high-quality revenue system should result in enough equalization of the resources available to local governments that they are able to provide an adequate level of services.

While all states recognize a responsibility to equalize education resources, most states do relatively little to assist cities, counties, and other taxing jurisdictions unable to finance services that they are mandated or expected by the state to carry out. The virtues of fiscal decentralization should be preserved, but states should not be blind to the difficulties of poor communities with excessive burdens. This does not mean that resources have to be equalized completely but rather that extreme inequalities should be avoided. This issue is particularly important in the current period as the federal government is reducing its aid to local governments.

9) A high-quality revenue system should minimize interstate tax competition and business tax incentives.

Businesses are adept at playing one state off against another to extract tax concessions. Lobbyists for businesses invariably emphasize the least attractive aspects of a state's tax system for lobbying purposes, ignoring the positive aspects.

Interstate tax competition is depleting state resources without enhancing job creation significantly because tax concessions offered by one state generally are countered by similar tax reductions elsewhere, resulting in little if any net advantage for either state.

Admittedly, if a state's tax system imposes burdens that are far out of line with those of neighboring states, it runs the risk of hurting its economy. That is a different matter, however, and does not imply that every tax incentive offered by a neighbor must be matched. In comparison with factors such as labor costs, access to markets, and availability of capital, taxes are not a particularly important factor in most business location decisions. The total package of business and personal taxes should be considered, not any specific provision in isolation.

Taxes should provide a "level playing field" with similar treatment for all industries and all firms within each industry. This implies avoidance of industry-specific tax incentives or special taxes on selected industries.

10) A high-quality revenue system should not be used as an instrument of social policy to encourage particular activities, although it is appropriate to discourage some actions through tax policy.

The main purpose of a state tax system is to raise the revenue needed to finance government expenditures, not to promote social goals. The reason taxes are more appropriate as a means of discouraging rather than encouraging actions is that taxes are inherently a negative tool—taking away resources and income. Tax incentives are an inefficient means of stimulating desirable actions because a large proportion of the tax savings go to people and businesses for doing what they would have done in any case. These criticisms apply to federal tax policy, but they are even more valid at the state level because state tax rates are much lower than federal tax rates, and the magnitude of the incentive provided is proportional to the level of the tax rate. In contrast with direct outlays, tax expenditures tend to be invisible and to grow annually without careful review of their costs. In many cases, the value of a tax expenditure is directly related to a taxpayer's marginal tax rate, which increases with income. These drawbacks of using tax policy to encourage certain actions are not counterbalanced by their advantages, such as not requiring a government bureaucracy to administer them. Promotion of social objectives is best pursued through nontax policies, involving either direct expenditures or regulations.

On the other hand, taxes are sometimes a good mechanism for discouraging socially undesirable activity, such as air and water pollution, smoking, and consuming alcoholic beverages to excess. Some studies suggest, for example, that teenage consumption of cigarettes can be reduced substantially by increasing their price.[3] In some situations, taxes are a better method of discouraging activity than outright prohibition because they preserve a degree of freedom of choice. Another benefit of levying heavy taxes on such activity is that it enables the state to recover a portion of the social costs incurred as a result of the problems this activity causes.

As noted at the beginning of this chapter, this statement of principles is intended to serve as a stimulus for additional discussion, not as the last word on the subject. Because we believe that the principles discussed in this statement are essential attributes of a high-quality revenue system, we feel that the burden of proof must be on those who advocate departures from these principles.

> C. Gilmore Dutton, Kentucky Legislative Research Commission
> Representative Linda Emmons, Connecticut
> Senator Wayne Goode, Missouri
> Representative Dan Grimm, Washington
> Senator Laurence Levitan, Maryland
> Frank J. Mauro, former secretary, New York Assembly Ways and Means Committee
> Representative Karen McCarthy, Missouri
> Senator Dawn Clark Netsch, Illinois
> Representative Jeffrey Neubauer, Wisconsin
> Gary Olson, Michigan Senate Fiscal Agency
> Representative Paul Schauer, Colorado
> Representative Bill Schreiber, Minnesota
> Representative Delwyn Stromer, Iowa

Notes

Three persons served as staff to this group of legislators and legislative staffers: Steven Gold (director of Fiscal Studies for the National Conference of State Legislatures), Will Knedlik (former director of Legislative Programs for the Lincoln Institute of Land Policy), and Corina Eckl (senior staff associate in the Fiscal Affairs Program of the National Conference of State Legislatures).

1. Robert J. Kleine and John Shannon, "Characteristics of a Balanced and Moderate State-Local Revenue System," in Steven D. Gold, ed., *Reforming State Tax Systems* (Denver: National Conference of State Legislatures, 1986), pp. 31-54.

2. Local officials sometimes claim that they have not increased taxes because the tax rate has been stable even though revaluation of property may be causing increases in property tax bills and the effective tax rate. Florida and Utah are among the states with the strongest truth-in-taxation provisions.

3. See evidence cited in Thomas F. Pogue, "Excise Taxes," in *Reforming State Tax Systems,* pp. 270-272.

Appendix
Checklist of Characteristics of a Good State Revenue System

by
Steven D. Gold and Corina L. Eckl

The chapter "Principles of a High-Quality State Revenue System" provides a useful framework for developing proposals to reform state tax systems. To facilitate implementation of the principles, the following checklist was derived from it. The 23 questions on the checklist can be employed by legislators and citizens in each state to evaluate their existing tax systems.

Every state tax system is deficient according to many if not most of the questions on the checklist. This is not surprising in view of the authors' recognition that their statement of principles is an idealistic one. No state can move overnight to having a perfect tax system, but the checklist suggests standards toward which a state may aspire and approach incrementally.

1) Do the parts of the revenue system function well together as a logical system, including the finances of both local and state governments? (Principle 1) To answer this question, one must have an overall view of the state-local revenue system. Such a view requires, among other things, analysis of the following information:

- The distribution of tax burdens among income groups;[1]
- The impact of taxes on various types of businesses;[2]
- The variation in tax effort and tax capacity in jurisdictions throughout the state; and
- The incentives created by the tax system.

Usually this information is unavailable. Since policymakers lack the information they need to obtain a systematic view of how the tax system operates, it is extremely unlikely that it does operate in a logical manner, so most states fall far short of conforming to this principle.

2) Is the revenue produced by the tax system relatively stable, or is it highly sensitive to economic fluctuations? (Principle 2) Among the factors that increase instability are heavy reliance on a) a sales tax with a narrow base (e.g., one that exempts food, services, and perhaps clothing) and b) the corporation income tax. The demand for food and services is not as cyclical as the demand for many other products, particularly durable goods, and profits fluctuate considerably over the course of the business cycle.

3) Is there a well-endowed Rainy Day Fund? (Principle 2) While more than half the states have such funds, most of them hold significantly less than 5 percent of General Fund revenue. These inadequately funded reserves would not provide much protection in the event of an unexpected revenue shortfall.

4) Does the revenue system exhibit stability in the sense that tax rates and other provisions are not subject to frequent changes? (Principle 2) By changing provisions every year or two, some states create confusion and interfere with planning by businesses and individuals.

5) Does the revenue system produce sufficient revenue to fund the level of spending citizens want and can afford? (Principle 2) The overall growth of revenue roughly should match the growth of state and local spending. States with highly inelastic tax systems do not meet this criterion since they are prone to periodic revenue shortfalls. On the other hand, a highly elastic tax system also might be criticized because it produces large revenue increases without explicit decisions to increase tax rates, perhaps making it "too easy" to increase taxes. A highly restrictive formal tax limitation measure also could interfere with achievement of this principle.

6) Does the revenue system have adequate diversification of revenue sources? (Principle 3) As Helen Ladd explains in her chapter of this book, diversification is not an end in itself. The statement of principles does not dispute her contention; instead it argues that reliance on a variety of tax bases is desirable because it fosters stability and facilitates keeping tax rates low, which is desirable on equity and efficiency grounds. According to the statement, there is insufficient diversification if the sales, personal income, or property tax generates more than 50 percent as much as one of the other major taxes.

7) Are the income and sales tax bases broad? (Principle 3) This principle is violated if a state allows income tax deductions that are more generous than those allowed on the federal income tax, or if the sales tax does not extend to a broad range of services.

8) Are households with subsistence income shielded from taxation? (Principle 4) Approximately a third of the states with personal income taxes exempt the poor, as the federal government does, and many states provide some property tax relief for low-income households, especially senior citizens. But, as Robert Greenstein and Frederick Hutchinson point out in their chapter in this book, most states are a long way from eliminating the total tax burden of the poor, especially when sales, property, and excise taxes are considered.

9) Is the tax system either proportional or progressive in its incidence among income groups? (Principle 4) No up-to-date studies are available for most states, but as of 1976 it appeared that only four states did not have a regressive tax system, that is, one which claims a higher share of income from low- and moderate-income households.[3]

10) Are families with similar income taxed relatively uniformly? (Principle 4) The best way to move toward conformity with this principle is to have broad tax bases, since exemptions tend to produce unequal tax burdens depending on how income is earned or spent.

11) Have tax provisions been sufficiently simplified so that any remaining complexities are necessary to achieve important goals that cannot be attained in some other manner? (Principle 5) The chapters in this book by Harley Duncan and Richard Pomp provide examples of complex provisions of doubtful value.

12) Are the telecommunications, utilities, and financial industries treated in the same manner as other industries as much as is feasible? (Principle 5) To provide a level playing field, it is generally desirable to avoid industry-specific taxes.

13) Is there a truth-in-taxation process designed to maximize public understanding of changes in property taxes, including written notification of changes to individual taxpayers before local government budgets are approved? (Principle 6) Most of the truth-in-taxation provisions in effect require newspaper notices and a special public hearing, but unless customized notices are sent to taxpayers, this process is not as effective as it could be.

14) Are property tax assessments based on 100 percent of a property's full value? (Principle 6) Most states unnecessarily confuse taxpayers by requiring that assessments be a fraction of full value.

15) Is a tax expenditure budget published regularly, and are tax expenditures subject to a requirement that they be reviewed periodically? (Principle 6) Tax expenditures are provisions (exemptions, exclusions, and deductions) that reduce tax revenue. They should be reviewed periodically to see whether their benefits are commensurate with the revenue they sacrifice.

16) Are mandates on local governments reviewed carefully prior to their imposition? (Principle 6) If they are not, accountability is undermined.

17) Are taxes administered professionally and uniformly, both at the state and local levels? (Principle 7) State tax agencies and local assessors often lack adequate budgets to enforce tax laws as they are written. Low levels of performance are frequently a particular problem for property assessment.

18) Are reports prepared regularly showing how the tax system is working—which groups and industries are paying taxes and at what rates? (Principle 7) Most states do not comply adequately with this relatively simple principle.

19) Does the state government have aid programs to assure that poor jurisdictions have sufficient resources to provide an adequate level of services? (Principle 8) The validity of this principle has been questioned on the grounds that a state should not have to "prop up" small local governments that are not viable. This objection, however, does not apply to aiding large cities or counties that have small tax bases and heavy service burdens.

20) Does the state avoid offering special tax concessions to business in cases where those concessions do not have much effect in generating new jobs and investments? (Principle 9) Useful procedures are to monitor the cost of tax breaks, to evaluate their effectiveness in terms of job creation and new investment, and to require that they be reauthorized periodically.[4]

21) Does the state have a system for evaluating how its total package of business and personal taxes compares with those of its neighbors with whom it is competing? (Principle 9) Such a system for business taxes is outlined by Michael Vlaisavljevich in his chapter in this book.

22) Does the state avoid using its revenue system as an instrument of social policy to encourage particular activities when a direct spending program would be more efficient? (Principle 10) Tax preferences often result in the loss of large amounts of revenue, necessitating higher tax rates, even though preferences are often an inefficient means of achieving a desirable goal.[5]

23) Does the state impose heavy taxes to discourage socially undesirable activity, such as emitting pollution and consuming excessive amounts of alcoholic beverages and tobacco products? (Principle 10) A tax is inherently a negative instrument, so it can be used properly to reduce negative "spillover effects" that may occur when an activity adversely affects other persons.[6]

Notes

1. See Donald Phares, "The Role of Tax Burden Studies in State Tax Policy," in Steven D. Gold, ed., *Reforming State Tax Systems* (Denver: National Conference of State Legislatures, 1986), pp. 67-88.

2. Examples of such information are provided by the AFTAX model developed by Professor James Papke of Purdue University and the article by Michael Vlaisavljevich in this book.

3. Phares, "Tax Burden Studies," pp. 80-81.

4. See Larry C. Ledebur and William W. Hamilton, "The Failure of Tax Concessions as Economic Development Incentives," in *Reforming State Tax Systems,* pp. 101-118.

5. For a critique of such measures, see the article by Richard Pomp in this book and also his "Simplicity and Complexity in the Context of a State Tax System, in *Reforming State Tax Systems,* pp. 119-141.

6. Thomas Pogue, "Excise Taxes," in *Reforming State Tax Systems,* pp. 259-275.

Checklist

1) Do the parts of the revenue system function well together as a logical system, including the finances of both local and state governments? (Principle 1)

2) Is the revenue produced by the tax system relatively stable, or is it highly sensitive to economic fluctuations? (Principle 2)

3) Is there a well-endowed Rainy Day Fund? (Principle 2)

4) Does the revenue system exhibit stability in the sense that tax rates and other provisions are not subject to frequent changes? (Principle 2)

5) Does the revenue system produce sufficient revenue to fund the level of spending citizens want and can afford? (Principle 2)

6) Does the revenue system have adequate diversification of revenue sources? (Principle 3)

7) Are the income and sales tax bases broad? (Principle 3)

8) Are households with subsistence income shielded from taxation? (Principle 4)

9) Is the tax system either proportional or progressive in its incidence among income groups? (Principle 4)

10) Are families with similar income taxed relatively uniformly? (Principle 4)

11) Have tax provisions been sufficiently simplified so that any remaining complexities are necessary to achieve important goals that cannot be attained in some other manner? (Principle 5)

12) Are the telecommunications, utilities, and financial industries treated in the same manner as other industries as much as is feasible? (Principle 5)

13) Is there a truth-in-taxation process designed to maximize public understanding of changes in property taxes, including written notification of changes to individual taxpayers before local government budgets are approved? (Principle 6)

14) Are property tax assessments based on 100 percent of a property's full value? (Principle 6)

15) Is a tax expenditure budget published regularly, and are tax expenditures subject to a requirement that they be reviewed periodically? (Principle 6)

16) Are mandates on local governments reviewed carefully prior to their imposition? (Principle 6)

17) Are taxes administered professionally and uniformly, both at the state and local levels? (Principle 7)

18) Are reports prepared regularly showing how the tax system is working—which groups and industries are paying taxes and at what rates? (Principle 7)

19) Does the state government have aid programs to assure that poor jurisdictions have sufficient resources to provide an adequate level of services? (Principle 8)

20) Does the state avoid offering special tax concessions to business in cases where those concessions do not have much effect in generating new jobs and investments? (Principle 9)

21) Does the state have a system for evaluating how its total package of business and personal taxes compares with those of its neighbors with whom it is competing? (Principle 9)

22) Does the state avoid using its revenue system as an instrument of social policy to encourage particular activities when a direct spending program would be more efficient? (Principle 10)

23) Does the state impose heavy taxes to discourage certain undesirable activity, such as emitting pollution and consuming excessive amounts of alcoholic beverages and tobacco products? (Principle 10)

State Tax Expenditure Budgets— And Beyond

by
Richard D. Pomp

All governments use their tax systems for more than just the raising of revenue. Tax laws typically contain provisions intended to subsidize favored economic activities or to relieve personal hardships. These provisions accomplish their goals by granting a tax reduction to selected taxpayers. A trivial but illustrative example of a relief measure would be an exemption from a state's sales tax for items bought for seeing-eye dogs. This exemption is not a necessary part of the structure of a sales tax but is intended to help subsidize the special costs of the blind. The provision is essentially tantamount to a spending measure, equal in cost to the sales tax revenue that otherwise would have been collected.[1]

Because these "subsidy" or "relief" measures are spending programs implemented through the tax system, they commonly are known as tax expenditures.[2] A tax expenditure can be viewed as if the taxpayer had actually paid the full amount of tax owed in the absence of the special provision and simultaneously had received a grant equal to the savings provided by the special provision. Characterized in this manner, a tax expenditure is just one of a number of ways of providing governmental assistance and should be reexamined periodically using traditional budget and funding criteria: How much money is being spent; how is this money being distributed; is the expenditure achieving its intended goal; and is the expenditure the best means of achieving such a goal?

The concept of a tax expenditure is a powerful analytical tool that has revamped traditional ways of viewing a tax system. One application of the concept has been the compilation of a tax expenditure budget, which identifies "subsidy" or "relief" provisions and estimates their cost in forgone revenue.[3] In 1968, the Treasury Department published a tax expenditure budget[4] analyzing the federal personal and corporate income taxes. In 1974, the Congressional Budget Office began publishing its own annual tax expenditure report, and in the same year the Office of Management and Budget began including a tax expenditure analysis with the President's annual budget request to the Congress. No doubt inspired by these federal actions, the concept of a tax expenditure budget spread to the states. By 1985, 19 states prepared some form of tax expenditure budget.[5]

An unusually voluminous and fertile literature exists on the concept of a tax expenditure.[6] That literature makes a convincing case that "unless attention is paid to tax expenditures, a country does not have either its tax policy or its budget policy under full control."[7] The state of New York provides dramatic evidence of the correctness of this warning. In 1969, New York adopted an investment tax credit—a quintessential tax expenditure— without any revenue estimate of its cost. By 1983, more than $660 million of investment-related tax credits had been claimed by corporations. In 1983, the most recent year for which data are available, two corporations used nearly 40 percent of the total amount of credits used that year.[8] Until a 1985 report by New York's Legislative Tax Study Commission,[9] the investment tax credit—which costs more than the budgets of most state agencies—received less review and analysis than did explicit spending programs that cost a million dollars or less. It is inconceivable that had the investment tax credit been implemented as an explicit spending program, 16 years would have elapsed before any rigorous study was undertaken.

Because most state tax expenditure budgets have been adopted only recently —11 states, for example, have implemented them only in the last few years—it is perhaps too early to evaluate their success. What evidence exists, albeit tentative, suggests that state tax expenditure budgets have not yet had any serious impact on the legislative process. A report prepared by the National Conference of State Legislatures concluded that "tax expenditure budgets are unlikely to produce any meaningful policy changes except under special circumstances."[10] In evaluating a 1984 questionnaire prepared by the U.S. Advisory Commission on Intergovernmental Relations, another commentator concluded that "although state budget officials indicate that they are optimistic about the process, they concede that there are few solid examples where tax expenditure reporting has contributed to tax decisions."[11]

While many "solid examples" may be difficult to identify, it is possible, of course, that tax expenditure budgets have had an impact on increasing the sensitivity and consciousness of legislators in ways that may be difficult to measure.[12] Even in a state in which new tax expenditures have been added despite the existence of a tax expenditure budget, the number of new provisions still might have been less than what otherwise would have occurred.[13] In any event, approaches can be suggested at the state level that have the potential of increasing the effectiveness of the concept of a tax expenditure.

Part I of this chapter discusses a way of reducing the problem of defining a tax expenditure—a problem that needlessly has undermined the value of the concept. Part II suggests that rather than (or in addition to) a full-fledged tax expenditure budget covering the major taxes, a state should conduct a rigorous cost-benefit analysis of selected provisions. Part III recommends identifying by name the major corporate beneficiaries of selected tax expenditures, along with the amount of their tax savings.

I. Avoiding Definitional Quicksand

Any tax consists of a series of provisions that can be characterized as falling on a continuum. At one end of the continuum are those provisions whose only purpose is to implement traditional tax policy criteria. These provisions are unambiguously part of the normative structure of a tax. One example would be a deduction in an income tax for the cost of goods sold. At the other end of the continuum are those provisions that are intended solely to favor certain types of economic activities, for example, an investment tax credit, or to relieve personal hardships, such as a property tax circuitbreaker.

Most tax provisions, however, cannot be characterized as falling neatly on either end of the continuum. Consider, for example, the dependency exemption in an income tax. Using traditional tax policy criteria, the dependency exemption has been defended as implementing the goal of a fair distribution of tax burdens. From this perspective, the exemption would be part of the normative structure of an income tax and should not be analyzed as a tax expenditure. The exemption, however, also has been defended on the grounds that the support of children is partially a community responsibility that should be subsidized by the government. Stated in these terms, the exemption implements a spending goal and should be evaluated according to budget criteria rather than tax policy criteria.[14]

Because most tax provisions cannot be located easily on the continuum, substantial controversy has surrounded the compilation of a tax expenditure budget. Those who oppose the characterization of a particular provision in a tax expenditure budget as a subsidy or relief measure muster tax policy arguments for why the provision should be viewed as part of the normative structure of the tax. Those who defend the provision's inclusion might posit a different normative model of the tax; might emphasize the spending or budget arguments used to rationalize the existence of the provision; or might rely on the grounds that the provision's characterization as a tax expenditure is acceptable to most tax policymakers and specialists.[15] The result often has been a spirited, disputatious, and ultimately inconclusive debate over the definition of a tax expenditure. This definitional quagmire has helped undermine the legitimacy of the tax expenditure concept and perhaps has discouraged some states from compiling a budget.

The controversy that has surrounded the definition of a tax expenditure is unfortunate because it can be avoided, or at least mitigated. As a leading commentator has proposed,[16] one approach to resolving the definitional problem is to determine why the question of whether a provision is a tax expenditure is being raised at all. The answer to this question will affect how a tax expenditure is defined and even can render the issue moot.

Suppose, for example, that a newly appointed state commissioner of energy is reviewing all of that state's energy-related tax expenditures, that is, those provisions that affect the use or production of energy, or which subsidize the cost of energy. The commissioner's goal is to determine whether the money now being spent through tax expenditures would be better used to finance a new set of programs. In the context of this goal, the commissioner, in drawing up a list of tax expenditures, would include any state tax provision that has been justified in energy-related terms. Such a list might include an income tax credit for home insulation; a sales tax exemption for heating oil; and an income tax deduction for intangible drilling costs. Each of these provisions would be evaluated using traditional budget criteria.

Some legislators might well challenge the commissioner on the inclusion of certain provisions. They might argue, for example, that the commissioner misunderstood the rationale for deducting intangible drilling costs. The purpose of the deduction, these critics might assert, is to better measure net income. Hence, the deduction properly should be viewed as part of the normative structure of an income tax and not as a tax expenditure.

No unnecessary battles need be fought over whether the commissioner or his critics were "correct." Rather, the weight of the tax policy arguments made by supporters of the deduction has to be balanced against the weight of the commissioner's tax expenditure analysis. This approach of evaluating both the tax policy and tax expenditure arguments recognizes that certain provisions in a tax can be described as implementing both tax policy goals and spending goals. A decision whether such a provision should be continued, eliminated, or replaced with an explicit spending program will involve balancing one set of arguments against another. Debate should be focused properly—not on the abstract question of whether a provision is a tax expenditure—but on the relative weight that should be given to the tax policy analysis and the tax expenditure analysis. If, for example, the tax policy arguments on behalf of the state deduction for intangible drilling costs were problematic, and if a tax expenditure analysis identified weaknesses with the provision, serious consideration should be given to the commissioner's proposal for replacing the deduction with an explicit spending program.

As another illustration, suppose a state were considering a bill proposing a graduated corporate income tax. The bill was introduced on behalf of the small business community and was defended both as implementing a concept of ability to pay and as subsidizing low-income corporations. Which legislative committee should have jurisdiction over the bill—the committee on ways and means or the committee on small business? Applying an orthodox tax expenditure approach, debate would center on whether a graduated corporate rate were part of the normative structure of the tax. The answer to this question, however, has no relationship to why the question is being asked, which is to determine the committee that should exercise jurisdiction over the bill. The appropriate committee is the one that has the relevant skills needed to evaluate the arguments made by the bill's supporters. Because the bill is being defended using both tax policy goals—implementing a concept of ability to pay—and spending goals—the subsidization of low-income corporations—both committees should have concurrent jurisdiction. Ways and means should analyze the bill using traditional tax policy criteria and assess how well a graduated corporate tax implements a concept of ability to pay. The committee on small business should conduct a tax expenditure analysis and determine whether a graduated rate is an efficient subsidy for low-income corporations.[17]

Differences between the committees obviously would have to be reconciled. The point is not that the suggested approach is a panacea, but only that it shifts the analysis to the appropriate issues. The definitional quagmire of whether to characterize a graduated corporate rate as a tax expenditure is avoided.

II. Analyzing Selected Tax Expenditures

As the examples above suggest, applications of the tax expenditure concept extend beyond the compilation of a tax expenditure budget. In the context of a tax expenditure budget, however, the suggested approach to resolving the definitional imbroglio requires determining why a legislature has requested the compilation of such a budget. Since most states intend the budget to be informational only, the definitional problem is handled easily. Provisions whose classification is subject to legitimate disagreement can be included in a tax expenditure budget with an appropriate caveat that alerts readers to the provision's dual characterization. By proceeding in this manner, analysts would provide legislators with the maximum information possible.[18]

While this approach would save analysts from sinking in a definitional bog, another problem remains. Many state tax expenditure budgets are broader than the federal endeavors and can include not only the personal and corporate taxes but also taxes on sales, property, motor vehicles, motor fuel, banks, insurance companies, cigarettes, horse racing, alcohol, inheritance, natural resources, utilities, soft drinks, telephone companies, and lodging. Minnesota, for example, includes 17 state and local taxes. State tax expenditure budgets can overwhelm policymakers with information that they usually cannot use or do not understand, which raises the risk of discrediting the entire concept or of obfuscating information that should be of value.[19]

To be sure, this problem of information overload is manageable if the analysts who draw up the budget have the authority to highlight items of priority. A more serious obstacle to the use of state tax expenditure budgets, however, is the integrity of the revenue estimates. The research capacity needed to generate reliable and meaningful estimates of revenue forgone from tax expenditures is exceedingly scarce in most states.[20] Several years of experience may be necessary to develop the required methodologies and data. Information may be needed that never has been collected previously or tabulated; new sampling or other collection techniques may have to be developed and implemented.[21]

State legislators often underestimate the amount of time needed to produce a quality tax expenditure analysis whose revenue estimates can be relied upon for serious decision making. The former head of the Tax Analysis Division of the Congressional Budget Office assumed as a rule of thumb that it easily could take a good analyst six months to do an in-depth examination of one major tax expenditure.[22] Moreover, he also warns legislators not to

> ask for more tax expenditure information than you can reasonably use, and don't expect analytic staffs to regularly provide good information that is not regularly used....Don't expect good staff people to spend their time providing information you are not going to use, think carefully in advance about what you need, and then ask just for that....If, for example, you do not anticipate any legislative action...on the state inheritance tax, you may decide that information on tax expenditures in that tax has a lower priority than information on some other taxes.[23]

Although the adoption of a tax expenditure budget of limited scope is probably a worthwhile undertaking in many states, provided a legislature is willing to commit sufficient resources so that the necessary research and analytical skills are available, it is but a first step. A tax expenditure budget identifies only how much money is being spent through a particular provision; it is not intended to answer traditional budget and spending questions regarding how this money is distributed among beneficiaries, whether the expenditure is achieving its intended goal, and whether the expenditure is the best means of achieving that goal. To answer these questions, an additional level of analysis is needed on a subset of those provisions listed in a tax expenditure budget.[24]

This subset could be selected by identifying those tax expenditures that:

> 1) Result in substantial amounts of forgone revenue;
> 2) Are amenable to a cost-benefit analysis;
> 3) Generally are regarded as subsidy or relief provisions;
> 4) Have a skewed distribution of benefits; and
> 5) Are politically vulnerable.

Depending on the number of provisions that satisfy these criteria,[25] some or all can be selected for a rigorous tax expenditure analysis.

The last two criteria might be difficult to assess prior to a detailed study. Whether a provision is politically vulnerable may depend on the results of a tax expenditure analysis. Similarly, the cost and distribution of benefits also may not be known until after the study. Nevertheless, policy analysts probably can make a reasonable assessment of which provisions are likely to satisfy these criteria based on their own experience, based on that of other states, or through a preliminary investigation.

This intensive analysis of a selected number of provisions is a viable strategy in a state that does not have a tax expenditure budget. This strategy might require fewer resources than would the compilation of a full-fledged tax expenditure budget and so may be the only approach available in some states. A state with scarce analytical and research capacity, however, may not have the financial resources for even this limited approach. In these states, a legislature may be willing to commit the necessary resources only as part of the adoption and implementation of a broader tax expenditure budget; but such resources then could be used for a cost-benefit analysis of selected provisions.

To have an effect on decision making, the information generated by a tax expenditure analysis should be integrated and coordinated with a government's normal budgetary process. The literature contains ample suggestions for accomplishing this, including establishing a budget subcommittee or task force to review tax expenditures; delegating to budget subcommittees the responsibility for reviewing tax expenditures falling within their jurisdictions; requiring a governor to submit a tax expenditure budget to the legislature recommending those provisions that warrant special review; requiring that a selected number of tax expenditures be placed in the appropriate functional areas in the budget; sunsetting tax expenditures; applying any existing statutory constraints on spending to take tax expenditures into account; requiring that tax expenditures be reduced by a specified amount; and treating tax expenditures like any other spending program in determining the budget of various agencies.[26]

No state yet has implemented any of these proposals in a manner that has yielded significant results, although it is probably premature to sound the death knell.[27] A cynic might observe, however, that the most costly tax expenditures have significant and influential constituencies. The very feature of tax expenditures that makes an accounting of them so necessary— the hidden, backdoor spending that occurs implicitly through the tax system— also may make it more difficult for a well-meaning legislator to garner the political support needed to battle well-entrenched constituencies. This same cynic might note further that limited to informational purposes only, a tax expenditure budget or report may remain a fairly innocuous document that legislators can parade forth to show their commitment to "good government" without having to take any further action that might offend powerful interest groups. Although there have been some minor successes attributed to state tax expenditure budgets,[28] California's Governor Deukmejian claimed in 1984 that "special interest groups have been too effective in maintaining their special privileges to achieve any significant reform."[29]

III. Truth in Taxation: Disclosing the Identities of Corporate Beneficiaries

Whether a pessimistic view of state tax expenditure budgets is merited or premature, the political and public relations value of a tax expenditure analysis probably would be enhanced if in addition to determining the aggregate revenue loss of particular provisions, and the distribution of those benefits, the major corporate beneficiaries of such provisions were identified along with the amount of their tax savings.[30] Identifying corporate beneficiaries by name is consistent with the philosophy underlying the concept of a tax expenditure. The major corporate tax expenditures tend to be investment-related subsidies, like an investment tax credit. If these expenditures took the form of an explicit spending program, the identity of the recipients most likely would be public information either as part of the application process for the subsidy or through freedom of information laws. Information that sensibly would be made public as part of a spending program similarly should be disclosed as part of a tax expenditure analysis. The public's right to know which corporations are receiving public funds should not be undercut simply because benefits are being offered through the tax system rather than through direct spending programs.

Moreover, to evaluate whether tax expenditures are serving their ostensible purposes, policymakers must know, at the least, what corporations are receiving what types of incentives and in what amounts. Only then can it be determined whether the benefits of these subsidies justify the forgone revenue, whether the benefits are distributed equitably among the corporate community, and whether such incentives need to be enhanced, reduced, or redirected.

The disadvantage of not identifying corporate beneficiaries by name is suggested by New York's report on its investment tax credit.[31] Adopting a traditional tax expenditure analysis, that report revealed that in 1982 nearly 4,000 corporations used the state investment-related tax credits to reduce their corporate income tax to the minimum of $250. This group included corporations having New York sales in excess of $1 billion and New York property in excess of $2 billion. In that same year, one corporation claimed an investment tax credit in excess of $25 million; two corporations used nearly 40 percent, or $86 million, of the total amount of investment and employment tax credits used by all corporations. These were startling statistics that initially caused a stir in the New York press.[32] But the New York study did not have access to actual returns and could not identify by name which corporations were receiving the lion's share of these credits. The press soon lost interest, which in turn reduced the pressure on the legislature to address this subsidy program.[33]

In order to spark interest in an issue—certainly one as complicated as taxation—it must be made real and human. A cold statistic is just that—cold. Eyes glaze and interest wanes. Policymakers and other concerned citizens cannot have a dialogue with a statistic. To learn that one corporation claimed an investment tax credit in New York in excess of $25 million (information that would be unavailable in a traditional tax expenditure budget) probably would not have the same potential impact on the legislative process as would revealing the identity of that corporation. Certainly any attempt to determine whether the program of investment tax credits should be continued is stymied without being able to identify the major beneficiaries.

The difference between cold statistics and warm bodies was demonstrated graphically during debate over federal tax reform. One of the major catalysts for the corporate reforms made by the Tax Reform Act of 1986 was the disclosure by Citizens for Tax Justice (CTJ) of the nominal amount of income tax paid by some of the largest corporations in the country.[34] Working with data from annual reports to shareholders and Securities and Exchange Commission (SEC) reports, CTJ revealed, for example, that General Electric earned $6.5 billion in pretax domestic profits during a three-year period and paid no federal taxes; indeed, the company claimed tax refunds of $283 million. Six other companies—Boeing, Dow Chemical, Tenneco, Santa Fe Southern Pacific, Weyerhaeuser and DuPont—received net benefits or refunds in excess of $100 million, despite profits totaling $9.8 billion. Moreover, nearly 30 percent of 250 major U.S. corporations paid no federal income tax in a recent year. CTJ's study had a profound effect on educating the public and on shaping public opinion, unlike previous studies relying only on statistical aggregates.

Any proposal to identify by name the major beneficiaries of selected tax expenditures along with their tax savings can be expected to meet vehement opposition. Undoubtedly, claims will be made that disclosing the names of beneficiaries will violate constitutional rights to privacy.[35] If the courts view tax expenditures as spending programs, constitutional claims to privacy evaporate. The Supreme Court has never held that a constitutional right to privacy attaches to information in the hands of government—indeed, freedom of information laws embody exactly the opposite philosophy. Furthermore, even if the courts do not view tax expenditures as spending programs, no constitutional rights to privacy have ever been extended to corporate income tax returns. Corporations are publicly created entities with rights derived from, and circumscribed by, public policy. The Supreme Court has said that while corporations "may and should have protection from unlawful demands in the name of public investigation . . . [they] can claim no equality with individuals in the enjoyment of a right to privacy.[36] SEC regulations and general principles of accounting already require corporations to disclose a wide range of information about their financial and tax affairs, and identifying the major beneficiaries of tax expenditures and the amount of their savings would be consistent with these practices.

A proposal to disclose the identity of major recipients of tax expenditures is also likely to be opposed as undercutting a state's business climate. Disclosure, it will be argued, will reflect or exacerbate an antibusiness climate, antagonize the business community, and merely inflame the public. It will detract from the aura of goodwill that creates a positive business climate and will provide one more weight in the balance of factors that ultimately may influence a corporation to locate its business in a friendlier state.

On a general level, this argument proves too much. Any legislation that the corporate community opposes can be characterized as poisoning the business climate. In considering any legislative proposal, the intended benefits obviously must be weighed against possible deleterious effects.

Evaluating this argument on a more specific level is difficult because the factors that comprise a state's business climate elude easy analysis. Many considerations affect a particular corporation's view of a state's business climate, and the issues important to one corporation may be unimportant to another. Factors that might contribute to a specific corporation's perception include the cost of energy, land, labor, or transportation; zoning regulations; restrictions on construction; the attitude of those public officials with whom a firm most often deals; the speed with which telephone calls are returned from the public sector; the degree of government regulations; the way businesses are treated by a tax department's auditors; the level of civility that characterizes interaction with government personnel; the amount of red tape that exists; the number of forms and permits required; and the governmental assistance provided to a new firm and its employees in relocating. Perceptions of business climate also are based on intangibles and imponderables that defy easy analysis or quantification (e.g., personal idiosyncracies of executives).[37] Unlike many of the above factors, however, identifying the major recipients of tax expenditures would not affect the cost of doing business or a corporation's bottom line.

Any legislative proposal to withdraw, albeit slightly, the cloak of secrecy that protects the confidentiality of tax expenditure recipients will be controversial. But all businesses might not resist such a proposal. Indeed, some might respect, if not welcome, legislative efforts directed at examining an important component of a state's revenue and tax structure.[38]

IV. Conclusion

The tax expenditure concept has generated extraordinary insights into the taxing and spending processes. The concept has provided a powerful analytical tool, although regrettably policymakers often have been drawn into needless definitional battles.

Nineteen states have embraced the concept by compiling a tax expenditure budget. A state tax expenditure budget can serve to highlight and publicize defects in the tax system. The next step, either independent of or in conjunction with such a budget, is for a state to apply a tax expenditure analysis to a manageable number of carefully selected provisions. Part of this analysis should include disclosing the names of major corporate beneficiaries of these selected tax expenditures, along with the amount of their tax savings.

Notes

The author would like to thank Steve Gold, Rob Plattner, and Mike McIntyre for their helpful comments on this article. Professor McIntyre developed the conceptual framework upon which this article draws. See infra note 6.

1. See Stanley Surrey and Paul McDaniel, "The Tax Expenditure Concept and the Legislative Process," supra note 1, in Henry Aaron and Michael Boskin, eds., *The Economics of Taxation* (Washington, D.C.: The Brookings Institution, 1980).

2. The tax expenditure concept was first developed in the United States by the late Professor Stanley S. Surrey of Harvard Law School.

His work in this area reflected his experiences as assistant secretary of tax policy under Presidents Kennedy and Johnson as well as the insights gained through his other academic and scholarly pursuits. The tax expenditure concept has been described as the "major innovation in tax and public finance during the last twenty or thirty years." See Richard Pomp, "The Mortgage Interest and Property Tax Deduction: A Tax Expenditure Analysis," 1 *Can. Tax* 23 n. 1 (1979). The concept of a tax expenditure was developed further by Paul McDaniel, a former professor of law at Boston College Law School and a long-time collaborator of Surrey's.

3. The estimates are made on the assumption that a taxpayer's behavior would remain unchanged if the tax expenditure were eliminated. While this assumption might be unrealistic in some circumstances, a similar assumption is implicit in stating the cost of explicit spending programs. For example, a job retraining program that spends $100 is described as "costing" $100, even though if the program were eliminated, the amount spent on some other program, such as welfare, might increase.

4. Secretary of the Treasury, *Annual Report on the State of the Finances, Fiscal Year 1968,* pp. 326-340.

5. Steven Gold and Dale Nesbary, "State Tax Expenditure Review Mechanisms," *Legislative Finance Paper,* No. 47 (Denver: National Conference of State Legislatures, 1985).

6. For a small sampling of the literature on tax expenditures, see Stanley S. Surrey, *Pathways to Tax Reform: The Concept of Tax Expenditures* (Cambridge: Harvard University Press, 1973); Surrey and McDaniel, "The Tax Expenditure Concept and the Legislative Process," supra note 1; Michael McIntyre, "A Solution to the Problem of Defining a Tax Expenditure," 14 *U.C. Davis Law Review* 79 (1980); Surrey and McDaniel, *Tax Expenditures* (1985); Paul McDaniel and Stanley Surrey, eds., *International Aspects of Tax Expenditures: A Comparative Study* (1985). For a concise summary of the issues raised by the tax expenditure concept and an extensive citation of the literature, see Stanley Surrey, Paul McDaniel, Hugh Ault, and Stanley Koppelman, *Federal Income Taxation I* (Mineola, N.Y.: Foundation Press, 1986), pp. 232-254.

7. Surrey and McDaniel, supra note 1 at 124.

8. See Richard Pomp, "Reforming a State Corporate Income Tax," *Albany Law Review* (forthcoming, 1988).

9. See Legislative Commission on the Modernization and Simplification of Tax Administration and Tax Law, *The New York Investment and Employment Tax Credits,* March 11, 1985; Pomp, supra note 8.

10. Supra note 5 at 16.

11. Karen Benker, "Tax Expenditure Reporting: Closing the Loophole in State Budget Oversight," 39 *National Tax Journal* (December 1986), pp. 403, 414. See also note 27 infra.

12. The increasing use of tax credits, which avoids the well-known upside-down effect of tax exemptions or tax deductions, is perhaps directly traceable to the influence of the tax expenditure concept.

13. Governor Deukmejian recommended that California's tax expenditure budget be eliminated because "the report seems to have had little impact, since a number of tax expenditures have been adopted over the last decade." Cited in Benker, supra note 11, at 414. Characterizing a provision as a tax expenditure is not equivalent to recommending that it necessarily should be eliminated or replaced with a spending program. An increase in the number of new tax expenditures is not necessarily bad, unless these new provisions are ill-founded. Without more information, it is difficult to know what conclusion should be drawn from a

statistic indicating that the number of tax expenditures has increased in California, other than underscoring the need for accountability and scrutiny that should accompany any spending program.

14. See McIntyre, "A Solution to the Problem of Defining a Tax Expenditure," supra note 6, pp. 94-96.

15. Ibid., p. 82.

16. Ibid., p. 6.

17. For exactly such an analysis of a proposal to adopt a graduated corporate tax rate in New York, see Pomp, supra note 8. See also McIntyre, "A Solution to the Problem of Defining a Tax Expenditure," supra note 6, pp. 89-90; remarks of U.S. Senator Edward Kennedy, *Congressional Record*, Sec. 5203-09 (Daily ed., April 17, 1978).

18. See Carl Shoup, "Surrey's Pathways to Tax Reform—A Review Article," 20 *Journal of Finance*, pp. 1329, 1334 (1975). For other approaches that can be adopted in drawing up a tax expenditure budget that avoid the definitional bog, see McIntyre, supra note 6 at 89.

19. Many times, for example, the greatest revenue losses identified by a tax expenditure budget are from broad-based exemptions, which are the least desirable (or impossible) for legislators to alter. The author has seen key legislators quickly lose interest in a state tax expenditure budget after focusing on the items having the largest revenue losses and realizing that these were untouchable.

After the author had delivered the speech that is reprinted in the text, two prominent legislators in the audience, each from a different state having a tax expenditure budget, shared their own experiences, which indicate how a tax expenditure budget can be abused. One legislator said that he uses the document to obtain campaign contributions by "reminding constituents how I ignored the advice of the analysts to repeal these provisions." (But see note 13 supra). In a variation on the argument, he "shows them how much I've done for them in the past by getting these provisions adopted." The other legislator described how "various interest groups use the budget to show how they were getting shortchanged because the amount of their tax expenditures was less than everyone else's."

For a discussion of how the tax expenditure concept might have had the perverse and unintended effect of legitimizing the proliferation of new tax subsidy provisions, see Robert McIntyre, "Lessons for Tax Reformers from the History of the Energy Tax Incentives in the Windfall Profit Tax Act of 1980," 22 *Boston College Law Review* 705 (1981).

20. See Benker, "Tax Expenditure Reporting," pp. 410-413.

21. According to a former government official, the reason the U.S. Treasury has been able to provide good tax expenditure data on an annual basis is that it uses the same information it has to prepare regularly for executive decision making. Testimony of James Verdier, former head of the Tax Analysis Division of the Congressional Budget Office, before the Massachusetts legislature, Oct. 9, 1986. In many states, however, the information needed for a meaningful tax expenditure budget would have to be specially prepared because it is not normally available.

22. Ibid.

23. Ibid.

24. The suggestion in the text to deal with a limited number of carefully selected provisions is echoed elsewhere: "Many tax exemptions have a broad-based impact and significant constituencies. If your state legislature is contemplating the sunset review process to deal with tax exemptions, I would recommend that the process first be applied to a few exemptions which have demonstrably outlived their usefulness. Es-

tablishing a process is the most important thing. The issue of whether to terminate specific exemptions can be dealt with later." Statement of Matthew J. Coyle, deputy director of the Washington State Department of Revenue before the National Association of Tax Administrators Conference, 1983, cited in Benker, "Tax Expenditure Reporting," pp. 417. "Don't be too ambitious at the outset; building a useful tax expenditure budget takes time. Don't try to list all tax expenditures in the law, unless the law is easy to change." Verdier, supra note 21.

The criteria in the text also might be useful in deciding which provisions should be sunsetted. See Michael McIntyre, "The Sunset Bill: A Periodic Review for Tax Expenditures," *Tax Notes* (August 9, 1976), p. 3.

Consistent with the approach suggested in the text, the California Legislative Analyst reviewed in detail a limited number of that state's tax expenditures and recommended that these be discontinued or restricted. Jon Vasche, "Tax Expenditure Reporting—A Comment," 40 *National Tax Journal* 255 (1987); see also Statement of Peter W. Schaafsma, Principal Program Analyst, California Legislature, to the Senate and Assembly Revenue and Taxation Committees, May 17, 1986.

25. Part III suggests an additional possible criterion: provisions whose beneficiaries could be disclosed without frustrating any legitimate expectations of privacy.

26. See supra note 5 at 16; supra note 11 at 414-416; supra note 1; George Break, "The Tax Expenditure Budget—The Need for a Fuller Accounting," 38 *National Tax Journal* 261 (1985); McIntyre, supra note 6.

27. The federal experience is also discouraging. See supra note 1. Some commentators have suggested that the 1986 tax reform is evidence of the success of a tax expenditure budget and proof that similar state efforts can be worthwhile. These commentators apparently assume that because many provisions eliminated in the sweeping 1986 reforms were identified in one of the federal tax expenditure budgets, a causal relationship exists.

The role played by the tax expenditure budget in the 1986 reforms is unclear. On the one hand, the publication of a budget certainly increased congressional awareness and sensitivity to the issues underlying the concept of a tax expenditure. The tax expenditure budget may have focused attention on provisions that otherwise might not have been politically vulnerable. On the other hand, many of the provisions eliminated were on a "hit list" long before their inclusion in a tax expenditure budget. The nature and extent of the 1986 changes were exceptional, and the philosophical underpinnings of the Tax Reform Act extend well beyond the concept of a tax expenditure. The driving force behind the act was rate reduction. Attention was fixed on the distributional implications of the rate reduction and base-broadening, not on whether the provisions being eliminated should be replaced with explicit spending programs. Writing after the Tax Reform Act, Paul McDaniel, one of the architects of the tax expenditure concept (see supra notes 1, 2, and 6), concluded that tax expenditure analysts should "remain agnostic on the impact of the analysis on actual legislative outcomes." Neil W. Brooks, *The Quest for Tax Reform* (Toronto, Canada: Carswell, 1988), p. 395.

But even if the Tax Reform Act is considered a testament to the value of a tax expenditure budget, the fact is that most states rarely engage in sweeping tax changes, and, as the recent Florida debacle with its sales tax on services suggests, most states find it easier to raise rates than to broaden the base. Unlike the 1986 act, rate reduction is not a motivating force behind most state reforms, perhaps because state rates are generally low. The political dynamics are quite different at the state level when a rate reduction is from, say, 8 percent to 6 percent.

The clearest example of a state where rate reduction was a motivating force behind tax reform is New York, which recently restructured its personal income tax and reduced its top rate in stages from 13 percent to 7 percent (effective in 1991). This reduction in rates was accompanied by sweeping changes in the taxation of unearned income and the taxation of married couples. This major revamping of the personal income tax was accomplished without the benefit of a tax expenditure budget. As part of this reform, however, New York did eliminate some tax expenditures that had been the subject of the kind of selective cost-benefit analysis suggested in the text. See Reports by the Staff of the New York Legislative Tax Study Commission, *The New York State Personal Income Tax: An Overview* (May 29, 1985); *The New York State Personal Income Tax: Provisions Affecting the Determination of Gross and Adjusted Gross Income* (July 25, 1985); *The New York State Personal Income Tax: The Itemized Deductions* (February 18, 1986); Richard Pomp, "Simplicity and Complexity in the Context of a State Tax System," in Steven D. Gold, ed., *Reforming State Tax Systems* (Denver: National Conference of State Legislatures, 1986).

28. See Benker, "Tax Expenditure Reporting," p. 414.

29. Cited in Ibid. The California Department of Finance noted that "even the sunsetting recommendation, partially adopted, has proved to be ineffective since a tax expenditure once enacted is easily reenacted upon its expiration. Special interest groups have been too effective in maintaining their special privileges to achieve any significant reform." Gold and Nesbary, supra note 5, *Tax Expenditure Review Mechanisms,* p. 15.

30. The argument in this part is developed more fully in a paper prepared by the author for the New York Tax Study Commission. See Report by the Staff of the Legislative Commission on the Modernization and Simplification of Tax Administration and Tax Law, *Public Disclosure of Corporate Tax Information* (forthcoming, 1988).

31. See Report by the Staff of the Legislative Commission on the Modernization and Simplification of Tax Administration and Tax Law, *The New York Investment and Employment Tax Credits,* March 11, 1985; Pomp, supra note 8.

32. See, e.g., *Knickerbocker News,* March 18, 1985, at p. 1, col. 4.

33. The staff of the New York Tax Study Commission was able, however, through its own efforts, to keep the issue alive. The legislature eventually modified the credits, though it seems likely that more radical changes in the law might have been made if the identity of the major beneficiaries of the credit were publicly disclosed. For a detailed analysis of the New York investment credits and the changes recently made as part of that state's restructuring of its corporate tax, see Pomp, supra note 8.

34. See Citizens for Tax Justice, *Corporate Income Taxes in the Reagan Years* (1984).

35. In all states except Wisconsin, state statutes prevent the public disclosure of the taxes paid by either a corporation or an individual. Wisconsin allows its residents to obtain the amount of any individual's or corporation's personal income taxes or corporate income taxes merely by filing a request with the state. See Staff Report, supra note 30.

36. U.S. v. Morton Salt Co., 338 U.S. 632, 652 (1949).

37. Richard Pomp, "The Role of Tax Incentives in Attracting and Retaining Existing Business," 29 *Tax Notes* 521 (1985); reprinted in *Multi-State Tax Commission Review* (1985); *Colorado Municipalities* (March-

April 1986); *New York Economic Development Working Papers,* No. 4 (Rockefeller Institute of Government, 1987); excerpted in 13 *People and Taxes* (September 1985).

38.   If the cynical view of a tax expenditure budget is justified (see the last paragraph in Part II), a legislature is unlikely to endorse a proposal to disclose the identity of corporate beneficiaries and the amount of their tax savings. Disclosure might be accomplished, however, through public interest litigation, the nature of which would depend on the state involved.

VI

State Legislators and Tax Administrators: Can We Talk?

by
Harley T. Duncan

When asked to write a chapter on "why legislators should pay more attention to administrative considerations in passing tax legislation," my first reaction was, "You mean they don't listen to every word I say?" My second thought was, "Do I really have anything worthwhile to tell them?" More serious reflection quickly leads to the conclusion that effective tax administration can be fostered by well-designed legislation. Legislators and administrators both can be well served by a thorough assessment of the administrative implications of legislation while it is under consideration.

This chapter attempts to identify and explain the benefits that can accrue to state tax policy, tax administration, and the state as a whole when tax legislation is considered in an environment where administrative issues are understood and recognized as an integral component of state tax policy. The chapter begins with a definition of tax administration and the type of information tax administrators routinely should provide during the legislative process. It then discusses the types of benefits that can be realized (or pitfalls to be avoided) if tax legislation is passed in a form making it simple to administer. The chapter concludes with some thoughts on the need for administrators to listen to and learn from legislators in the tax policy process.

Defining Tax Administration

Historically, tax administration has been viewed as a rather arcane part of state government. It was considered to be inhabited largely by "eyeshade and armband" bureaucrats involved in accounting and auditing, lawyers drawing distinctions without a difference in making determinations on taxability, and a few economists talking about horizontal and vertical equity. Tax administration has enjoyed a renaissance of sorts in recent years for several reasons.

First, the 1981-82 economic recession, the subsequent modest and uneven recovery, and the collapse in the farm and energy sectors placed a great deal of fiscal stress on many states. As a result, states put a variety of tax administration techniques, such as tax amnesties, computer matching, increased penalties for tax evasion, and stepped-up collection of tax delinquencies to good use in improving compliance with existing tax laws and increasing revenue collections from the current tax base.[1] As governors, legislators, and others came to realize that enforcing existing tax laws and collecting delinquent taxes could substitute for tax increases, the perception of tax administration in state government changed markedly.

Second, the debate leading to passage of the federal Tax Reform Act of 1986 highlighted the relationship between simplicity in the tax laws and a variety of desirable attributes such as economic growth, tax equity, and compliance.[2] As states have responded to federal reform, tax simplicity, compliance, and administration have become discussion topics in many state capitols. Finally, states are competing intensely in the areas of economic development and growth. A number of states have examined their tax structures to insure that they do not impede economic growth. Interestingly, many of these discussions have focused not on tax incentives to promote development, but on the need for broad-based, low-rate taxes that are conducive to economic growth and, at the same time, foster tax compliance and cost-effective administration.

Generally, tax administration may be defined as the process of planning, developing, implementing, and evaluating the policies, procedures, and systems necessary to collect the taxes and fees imposed by the legislature in accord with its expressed intent. Tax administration encompasses a wide variety of activities and functions including: a) definition of the information to be submitted by the taxpayer and the manner and form in which it is to be submitted; b) design of remittance and deposit procedures and documents; c) development of taxpayer accounting systems; d) notification of taxpayers and provision of policy guidance regarding the responsibilities imposed on them; e) identification of non-filing and delinquent taxpayers; f) audit of taxpayer returns, books, and records and assessment of disclosed deficiencies; g) collection of delinquent or otherwise unpaid liabilities through various collection and legal mechanisms; and h) evaluation of the policy and administration as implemented to determine necessary and desirable changes. Similar responsibilities attend to those refund or expenditure programs sometimes administered by tax agencies. In short, tax administration should be construed broadly in the context of this chapter to include all the functions and activities associated with the implementation of tax legislation from the design of tax forms through the collection of delinquent liabilities.

Information Provided to Legislators

If we assume that legislators should listen to what tax administrators are saying when they consider tax bills, then we must assume further that tax administrators have something worthwhile to say. Tax administrators routinely should provide three general types of information to legislative committees—fiscal, administrative, and policy.

Fiscal Implications

The primary data that administrators should (and in virtually all states do) provide to the legislature is the fiscal impact of the proposed bill or its effect on state revenues.[3] The fiscal note should address not only the near-term (one- to two-year) impact, but where a significant change in the revenue implications is identifiable at some point in the future, those longer-term effects should be identified and estimated where possible. In addition to the macro-level revenue impact, the agency should attempt to provide data on the impact of the proposed change across groups of affected taxpayers. In other words, legislators ought to know who is affected, how much they are affected, and how the proposed change alters relationships among relevant groups of other taxpayers.

For their part, legislators must understand that the fiscal impacts presented are estimates. Pinpoint precision and accuracy are simply not possible. The fiscal estimate should be based on the best data available, with all underlying assumptions clearly stated. It should present the most reasonable range of expected impact. In many cases, it simply will not be possible to present precise estimates for several reasons—the lack of data in the tax agency files, the need to rely on national data or data not exactly on point, and factors that cannot be projected accurately, such as taxpayer behavior. Uncertainty was extremely prevalent in forecasting the state-level impact of the 1986 federal Tax Reform Act since it depended on data not normally available, macro-economic changes, and individual taxpayer behavioral changes.

Administrative Implications

The tax agency also should routinely provide information to the legislature on the administrative implications and costs of the proposed bill. When information of this sort is presented, it commonly focuses internally on the changes the bill will cause in tax department operations and the additional personnel that will be required to implement the bill. While these matters are important, there are other types of administrative information that also should be supplied.

First, the agency should identify points within the bill where modifications or clarifications are necessary if it is to be understood by the taxpayer and accomplish its intended effect. Second, the information provided should include an examination of the burden or changes the bill will cause for the taxpayers (or in the case of retail sales and similar excise taxes, tax collector/retailers) as well as the department. In particular, efforts should be made to identify where the bill will complicate the task of collection from the perspective of both the taxpayer and the department. Methods of reducing that complexity should be proposed. Finally, the agency should present the legislature with a realistic estimate of the resources necessary to administer the proposed enactment.

Policy Implications

Finally, administrators should provide legislators with their assessment of the tax policy aspects of significant tax proposals. This does not mean that the administrator routinely must regale the legislature with his or her opinion of the desirability of each proposal. Neither, however, should administrators feel they have fulfilled their obligation by saying that it is the job of the legislature to determine policy and the job of the administrator to implement it. Rather, the administrator should raise for the legislature general policy questions regarding the effects of the proposed change and its potential effectiveness and impact. These discussions should include items such as the effect of the proposed change on horizontal and vertical equity, groups or transactions similar to those addressed by the bill that may not come within its reach, and any unnecessary or undesirable deviations from established practice contained in the bill.

Administrators also need to place a renewed emphasis on providing the legislature with an evaluation of whether the proposed measure can be administered and enforced effectively and efficiently and whether other options that could be administered more simply should be considered. Tax proposals should be evaluated against a standard of whether they promote a simple, broad-based tax system that promotes easy compliance and fair administration. Too often in the past, administrators and legislators have concentrated on making a particular proposal work, regardless of its complexity. Administrators should aid legislators in recognizing that significant complexity has a variety of undesirable attributes that argue for simpler approaches to taxation.

Benefits To Be Realized

Several types of benefits to taxpayers, tax administrators, and the state as a whole can be realized by considering and recognizing the administrative aspects of a bill before enactment. First, legislatures should be able to avoid passing laws that, at worst, are unadministrable, and at best, are needlessly complex and fail to achieve the purpose for which they were enacted. Second, the state should be able to avoid imposing unreasonable compliance burdens on taxpayers. Third, if tax administrators are not devoting effort to administering complex features, they can concentrate on enforcing compliance with current tax laws. Finally, the thought process involved should improve the tax policies enacted by the legislature.

Avoiding Unintended Consequences

Discussions of simplicity and complexity in tax administration invariably revolve around tax expenditures, or special treatment via credits, exemptions, or deductions of certain income or transactions. The special treatment commonly is not for revenue-generating purposes but, rather, is directed at some other goal.

The question is not whether tax expenditures add complexity to the tax code; they are by definition complex because they call for treatment of a particular item in a fashion different from the norm. Rather, the question is whether the tax expenditure is so complex that the costs of administration outweigh any benefits from the special treatment. It is the author's view that state tax expenditures often become so complex that they fail to achieve the goal at which they were directed or to provide any demonstrable benefits.

This is often the fate of state tax incentives designed to promote economic development. Such laws tend to follow Richard Pomp's second law of tax thermodynamics, becoming inordinately complex over time. This occurs because the drafters of such measures often attempt to target the incentives to particular types of enterprises and to avoid subsidizing activities and development that would occur without them. They also are drafted with an eye on the state treasury and a concern about potential cost. The result is often legislation so complex that it produces a variety of unintended, undesirable consequences. For example, the legislation may be so limiting that only a few taxpayers qualify, and "desirable" projects are not brought within the scope of the legislation. Or, the record-keeping requirements are such that the benefits are overwhelmed by the costs of compliance. The net result is legislation that fails to achieve its intended goal.

The 1976 Kansas Legislature passed the Job Expansion and Investment Credit Act[4] to provide income tax credits to firms and individuals establishing "new," "expansion," or "replacement" business facilities and providing additional employment opportunities through the creation of at least two "new" jobs. These credits later were increased and augmented with a refund of sales and use taxes paid on machinery, equipment, and other personal property associated with such facilities when located in an enterprise zone. The amounts of the credits are $100 per $100,000 of investment and $100 per employee ($350 in an enterprise zone), subject to a limit of offsetting not more than 50 percent of the tax associated with the income from the facility. They may be taken in each of 10 years following the commencement of operations at the facility. Limits are placed on the types of firms that qualify for the credits and on the relationship between the taxpayer and the predecessor operator of the facility to avoid a churning of corporations to obtain tax benefits.

While sounding straightforward, administration of this act has proved to be anything but. Innumerable efforts have been made to define new, expansion, or replacement facilities, and each application virtually has had to be treated individually. Further, because it focuses on building and operating facilities, the act does not cover "retooling" efforts that retain jobs, nor does it deal well with holding companies as a financing vehicle for facility development and operation. Frequent complaints also were received that record-keeping requirements for the sales tax refund were onerous and that the refund was diminished seriously in value because it was paid without interest after the facility began operation. The act, however, did work well for new plant locations hiring new employees; unfortunately, the number of such instances was few.

The result was that by 1986 the Job Expansion and Investment Credit and Enterprise Zone acts were more a source of frustration in the business community than an incentive for development. Annual costs (revenues foregone) amounted to only $1.2 million, and the acts had proved useful to only about three major manufacturing projects. Many taxpayer claims were being disallowed on "technicalities" after taxpayers thought they qualified. Many taxpayers were concerned only with receiving the sales tax refund and not with what they considered inconsequential income tax credits, particularly when looking ahead 10 years. Further, the Department of Revenue was devoting an auditor and an attorney nearly full-time to administering the act at an annual cost of $75,000.

To make the law more administrable and of greater utility to the taxpayers, the 1986 legislature made two significant changes.[5] It deleted virtually all references to facilities, whether they be of the new, expansion, or replacement variety and instead keyed the availability of tax credits to "investment." Second, the sales tax refund was converted to an exemption with exemption certificates issued on a project-by-project basis. The effect has been to remove considerable uncertainty in the minds of the taxpayer. No determination regarding a qualifying facility is necessary; only demonstrations of increased investment and increased employment are required. The 1986 amendments also simplified the sales tax component of the program and made it financially more attractive to taxpayers. The staff effort required by the department has been cut in half.[6]

Similar circumstances occurred with the passage in 1986 of several bills aimed at improving the availability of risk and venture capital in Kansas by allowing taxpayers an income tax credit equal to 25 percent of their investment in a qualified risk or venture capital fund.[7] To limit the revenue impact, however, taxpayers could take only 25 percent of the available credit in any one year, and the credit could offset only 25 percent of their liability for the tax year. But, to make the credit more useful to the taxpayers, the legislature allowed them to carry unused credits back for three years and forward until used fully.

By attempting to balance the potential revenue loss with the desire to stimulate the capital investment, the legislature created an unnecessarily complex set of credits. In particular, the carryback feature introduced such complexity that few taxpayers or their preparers could figure it out, and the required forms and instructions constituted four pages. Further, this complexity was required for a credit that would affect very few taxpayers, that was likely to average about $2,000 to $3,000 in total for those who were affected, and that could offset fewer than $1,000 in annual liability on average for those likely to claim it.[8] In short, the law failed to achieve its goal of stimulating investment because it was so complex it was not used.

These complexities were eliminated by 1987 legislative amendments.[9] The carryback feature was eliminated, and taxpayers were allowed to use the credit available in any one year to offset all the liability for that year and to carry any unused credit forward until used fully. While this may increase the near-term revenue loss somewhat, the credits are now understandable and usable.

In short, it has been the Kansas experience (and most likely that of many other states) that well-intended features of many tax expenditures have rendered them so complex that they have been of limited utility. While making them simpler may have contravened the intent of their designers, they have become at least understandable and usable.

Avoiding Unreasonable Compliance Burdens

Legislators also should remain mindful that complexity commonly flows through to the taxpayer as well as the tax agency. This is particularly important at the state level where the retail sales tax is a major revenue source in 45 states. Here, the burden of complexity does not fall necessarily on the taxpayer who is the ultimate purchaser or consumer,[10] but rather on an often unreimbursed tax collector— the retail merchant who collects and remits the tax from the consumer to the state.[11]

With apparently little thought or attention, states have imposed what can be considered unreasonable requirements on some retailers through various sales tax exemptions passed in pursuit of one worthwhile social goal or another. Some are straightforward. Prescription drugs are a popular sales tax exemption, and because of their nature present no particular administrative problem. A majority of sales tax states now exempt food for home consumption. By linking the definition of qualifying food to U.S. Department of Agriculture food stamp guidelines, problems have been reduced even though what constitutes nontaxable fruit juice as opposed to taxable fruit drinks and other questionable distinctions remain.

When one gets into the nonprescription drug and clothing exemptions in some states, however, the complexity changes markedly.[12] For example, running or jogging bras are exempt in Massachusetts, but running outfits are taxable on a theory that the running bra can be worn as part of normal attire, but the running suit is primarily for recreation. In the nonprescription medicine and drug area, baby powder is not taxable in Massachusetts, but baby oil is. Similar distinctions are drawn in New York, where regular shampoo is taxable, but dandruff shampoo is not; and sterilized cotton is exempt, but nonsterilized cotton is taxable. The difficulty states impose on retailers is significant as witnessed by a New York survey that found that 82 percent of pharmacies and 52 percent of food stores were charging tax on some exempt items.[13]

In Kansas, the common practice is to exempt certain purchases of certain organizations. For example, purchases of medical supplies and equipment by skilled and intermediate care nonprofit nursing homes are exempt from the sales tax, provided that such supplies and equipment are not used customarily for human habitation.[14] Our definition of medical supplies and equipment and human habitation is such that a nursing home bed is taxable, but the "pull-up" bar is not; a chair is taxable, but a walker is not.

The points to be understood here are several. First, it is entirely unreasonable to expect a retailer to be able to comply fully with such laws. It is simply not practical to expect retailers and their clerks to be aware of, much less appreciate, comprehend, and apply the distinctions required to abide by all tax agency rulings. Second, the complexity makes it difficult for one to perceive the tax system as fair especially when one not only is confronted with a Herculean compliance burden but also can be audited and held liable for past taxes, penalties, and interest for inappropriately applying what may or may not be written tax agency rulings and guidelines. A tax system that taxpayers perceive as unfair and unreasonable breeds further intentional noncompliance.

Finally, when complexity of this sort is imposed on taxpayers, states ought to question seriously the utility of the tax expenditure. They should ask whether the social goal sought is worth pursuing, and if so, can the complexity be reduced in some fashion. Obviously, tradeoffs are involved, and some of the exemptions mentioned as examples could be replaced with direct rebate/expenditure programs or simpler, fixed value income tax credits. Alternatives might involve less precision in the amount of tax benefits provided (i.e., the benefit will not equate exactly to the tax paid on the subject items), but greater simplicity is certainly of some value. In any event, tax benefits are not actually matched to expenditures on the subject items at present because of the inability to apply the law as written.

Opportunity Costs

Administration of complex tax laws carries with it two types of costs. The first is direct, or the actual dollars expended on forms, systems, and staff to implement and administer the law. The second is of greater magnitude and is the opportunity cost of the additional revenues forgone because resources are devoted to activities other than pursuing the collection of taxes due and owing, but unpaid, under current law.

The direct costs of administering areas of complexity, primarily tax expenditures, can be significant. The sheer magnitude of the task imposed at times is witnessed by the fact that administering the sales tax exemption for nonprescription drugs in New York requires the creation and maintenance of a list of over 6,000 exempt items with some medical attribute. Beyond this, administering tax expenditures often can take tax agencies out of their realm of expertise. For example, the solar energy, energy conservation, and related credits and deductions passed in the 1970s caused tax agencies to acquire expertise in engineering, physics, and construction, talents not common among the accountants, auditors, and lawyers that populate tax agencies. Similar problems are posed by laws that exempt materials and utilities "consumed" in the production of goods. Effective administration requires personnel that understand and can measure consumption during the production process.

The largest cost to administering complex laws and tax expenditures is not the direct cost of administration, but the opportunity cost of the revenue foregone because resources are diverted from pursuing the collection of taxes that are due and owing, but unpaid. As mentioned at the outset, a number of states in recent years have implemented aggressive, successful enforcement programs aimed at improving compliance with the tax laws. The programs have included a variety of efforts such as automated collection systems, property seizures, and additional collection personnel to pursue delinquent taxes; computer matches, license reviews, and information exchanges to detect nonfiling taxpayers; and enhanced field audit capacity, particularly in the corporation income tax and sales and compensating use tax areas.

The success of these enhanced enforcement programs has been staggering, and the return on investment has been substantial. Michigan estimates that from October 1985 to June 1987, an investment of $7.6 million in enforcement and compliance programs (primarily increased audit resources and an automated collection system) has yielded nearly $110 million in new revenues, a return of 13:1. New enforcement programs now are budgeted as a profit center within the revenue agency. Funds from the increased enforcement are recycled to finance the effort, and the revenue commissioner is required to generate at least $25 million annually in excess of the amounts expended.[15] In 1986, the Minnesota Legislature appropriated $3 million and enacted eight new statutory tools to assist in collection, based on an estimated $25 million return to the state treasury. Actual increased collections amounted to $30 million. Based on this result, the 1987 legislature appropriated $22 million for additional systems and personnel to support the enforcement and compliance function.[16] In Kansas, collections on field audit activity regularly yield a return on investment of about 7:1 for sales and use tax activity and over 15:1 for corporation tax activity. A personal income tax compliance program has returned over $10 million in its first three years on expenditures of less than $750,000. While all administrators agree there is a point where the rate of return on additional enforcement investments begins to decline, few would say they have approached that point. The revenue opportunities in increased enforcement are amply evidenced by the results of the tax amnesty programs run in a number of states. Over $750 million was collected in the 25 state tax amnesties authorized as of 1986.[17]

Beyond the direct revenues from enhanced compliance efforts, states also should expect increased receipts from additional voluntary compliance with the tax code. That is to say, good enforcement breeds higher levels of voluntary compliance. Massachusetts estimates that revenue from increased voluntary compliance in the three years following its major enforcement initiatives totalled $1.0 billion.[18]

In short, complexity has its costs: not only the direct costs of administering the tax expenditures or other features of the code that contribute to complexity, but also the larger costs through revenue foregone as a result of diverting resources from tax enforcement. On the other hand, avoiding complexity increases voluntary compliance.

Improved Tax Policy

The issues of simplicity and complexity aside, both administrators and legislators gain materially from engaging in the type of dialogue outlined at the beginning of this chapter because it leads to improved tax policy. First, there is improved knowledge of the expected effects of the actions under consideration, not only from a revenue perspective but also from an administrative, compliance, and enforcement standpoint. Second, the dialogue generates consideration of alternative methods of achieving the desired policy end and the pros, cons, and tradeoffs associated with those alternatives. Third, legislatures begin to recognize the opportunity costs accompanying certain enactments.

Fourth, the legislature is able to address an estimate of the direct administrative costs necessary to implement effectively the measure under consideration. Legislatures in the past have tended to ignore such costs. They presume that the administrative agency can absorb the additional workload because of "fat" in the budget or that a change is "just another line on the return." Failure to provide for administrative costs generally yields two results. First, resources are diverted from other areas, often those devoted to enforcement and delinquent tax collection, which translates into a direct revenue loss. Second, the administration of the new law is usually inadequate because of the lack of resources.

For their part, tax administrators commonly have been their own worst enemy in this regard. That is, they have exaggerated the expected costs of administration in an attempt to protect themselves or to "kill the bill." Administrators tend to prepare for the worst. When a measure is implemented with fewer resources than requested, their requests for funding are viewed as "crying wolf." What is necessary, of course, is cooperation between the legislature and the administrator to prepare a reasonable estimate of the administrative costs and to engage in a reasoned discussion of that estimate and the consequences of failing to provide for the proper administration.

Finally, the discussion that should occur will reduce subsequent policy disputes between the legislature and the tax agency regarding the legislature's intent. Communicating also should minimize instances of administrative interpretation or practice and should reduce the need for legislation by regulation or policy directive.

The Tradeoff: Simplicity and Other Tax Policy Goals

If simplicity is so virtuous, why then are state and federal taxes so complex? One obvious reason is that pursuit of simplicity often conflicts with other legitimate tax policy goals. Simplicity will conflict with many perceptions of equity when it affects sales and income tax expenditures aimed at low-income citizens. It also will compete with interests targeted to limit revenue losses. Finally, it will conflict with those interested in promoting some type of behavior or development through the tax code if it argues against further tax expenditures.

To all outward appearances, the advocates of simplicity have lost consistently in their efforts to avoid additional tax expenditures or simplify those currently in law. Several inherent features of state tax systems, however, imply that states could err on the side of simplicity in considering tax expenditures without doing great disservice to other tax policy goals, including equity, targeting benefits, and revenue protection.

First, state tax rates tend to be relatively low, particularly compared with federal rates for the individual and corporation income tax. Thus, the actual effect of any tax expenditure, regardless of the intended goal, is likely to be minimal. It is doubtful that a state income tax expenditure will cause a taxpayer to do other than what is in his or her economic interest under the federal tax code, with rates of 30 to 35 percent, when state rates are commonly below 10 percent.

Relatively low rates also mute any effect from a tax expenditure when it does not conflict directly with federal law. For example, Kansas allows individual taxpayers to exclude from income the lesser of $500 or 50 percent of the costs of insulating a single-family residence. With a maximum tax savings of approximately $30 (9 percent marginal rate with a 30 percent federal offset), the energy conservation effect seems minimal and the complexity of verifying figures for which no federal tax form counterparts exist is substantial.

In a similar vein, a growing body of literature outlines a rationale for states to strike a blow for simplicity with respect to tax expenditures aimed at stimulating economic growth. Richard Pomp, for example, has identified nine reasons such incentives are ineffective.[19] The literature suggests three general themes regarding the ineffectiveness and, therefore, needless complexity of such incentives:

- State tax costs tend to be an insignificant factor in site location decisions and business operating costs when compared with wages, transportation, and the like;
- State programs of improving capital availability and training tend to be more influential and helpful to new and expanding firms; and
- Relatively few industry groups are sufficiently "foot-loose" to be in a position to avail themselves of the incentives.

Based on this ineffectiveness, researchers have argued that the road to simplicity lies in the repeal of the incentives. For a variety of political reasons, this is not likely to occur. The Kansas experience cited earlier indicates, however, that states can simplify their incentives and, at the same time, make them more useful and consistent with the economics of job creation. States would be well advised to develop incentives that are simple to understand, certain in their application, and focused directly on reducing the cost of capital investment. In this manner, administration and compliance do not compete with use of the incentive, and the taxpayer should have a greater certainty about qualifying for it. The tradeoff is simplicity and utility on the one hand and targeting and focus on the other. Experience has shown that the latter approach leads to complexity and ineffectiveness.

Finally, it seems that the case for simplicity in the state retail sales tax is strengthened when one considers the costs certain tax expenditures impose on retail merchants acting as tax collectors for the state. It is reasonable to impose a sales tax collection responsibility as a part of doing business. States, however, must be reasonable in this imposition, and the impact at the retail level should be part of the calculus in assessing the costs and benefits of tax expenditures and whether simplicity has merit in a particular case.

Cited earlier were several examples of the complexity caused for both the retailer and the state by the exemption of clothing, food, and nonprescription drugs. On simplicity grounds alone, serious consideration should be given to providing compensation in some other form, such as an income tax credit or direct expenditure/rebate program. Also, policy grounds argue for this approach, such as disproportionate tax relief to upper-income households and the fact that complexity interferes with providing relief as it was intended.

For example, rather than exempting food items, Kansas limits its relief to low-income persons and provides that relief through a direct payment to individuals.[20] Similar examples can be found in many states' property tax credit and rebate programs.[21] Such procedures obviously forgo the immediacy of the tax relief and the precision accorded by an exemption (i.e., the amount of relief is tied to a schedule based on purchases but the program cannot reimburse each citizen for each purchase). The simplicity afforded the retailer and the state, however, certainly argues for an examination of this approach if one believes the tax relief is warranted.

In short, all tax expenditures in state law have their supporters, and undoubtedly, a rationale exists for the existence of each. When viewed in isolation, each item of complexity can be defended. However, when the tax expenditure is viewed in its entirety and when it is considered against the factors just outlined, the tradeoff involved in repealing or simplifying it is likely to be less serious than originally thought.

Conclusion

The issues of simplicity versus complexity are not new, and they will never be resolved with finality. It is not the author's purpose to argue that each and every tax expenditure or complicating feature of a state tax code should be repealed. This will not and should not happen. The issue of simplicity in the state tax code, however, does deserve renewed attention. It is the responsibility of the tax administrator to raise the issue and that of the legislature to give it serious, continuing attention.

Certain inherent benefits can accrue to states from simplified tax laws. When taken together, these benefits alter the perceived cost-benefit ratios of many tax expenditures in the tax code. The benefits also make the necessary tradeoffs between simplicity and other legitimate tax policy goals much less significant and more favorable toward the goal of simplicity than traditionally has been the case.

Postscript

This chapter's underlying presumption has been that tax administrators can provide valuable advice to legislators in discharging their duties. The reverse is also true. There are several general areas in which administrators can learn from legislators.

- Constructive dialogue and listening should help the administrator in understanding the legislative intent;

- Legislators often have firsthand knowledge of the businesses affected by the tax changes and can help administrators understand specific impacts on taxpayers; and
- Legislators may be more sensitive to the impact of complexity on taxpayers because they hear from them directly. Often the tax administrator has contributed to complexity out of fear of an open-ended raid on the state treasury and a belief that if a form can be devised, a law can be administered.

Notes

1. For discussion of one such program, see Ira A. Jackson, "Tax Administration," in Steven D. Gold, ed., *Reforming State Tax Systems* (Denver: National Conference of State Legislatures, 1986), pp. 333-346.

2. For a discussion of tax simplicity, its benefits, and its role in tax reform, see U.S. Department of the Treasury, *Tax Reform for Fairness, Simplicity, and Economic Growth: The Treasury Department Report to the President,* Volume 1, *Overview* (Washington, D.C.: U.S. Government Printing Office, November 1984), pp. 1-20.

3. Practice varies among the states in terms of who submits the fiscal note to the legislature. In some cases, it is the administering agency, but more commonly, final fiscal notes are the responsibility of the executive budget agency or the legislative staff. In most states, however, the fiscal note necessarily must rely on information provided by the tax agency.

4. Codified as Kansas Statutes Annotated, Chapter 79, Article 32, 153 et seq.

5. Chapter 385, 1986 Session Laws of Kansas.

6. This discussion does not address whether such credits are effective in promoting development but on whether they can be administered. See later discussion regarding their utility in stimulating investment.

7. Chapter 332, 1986 Session Laws of Kansas.

8. Example assumes a $40,000 to $50,000 investment, a 25 percent credit, and an average liability of $3,000 to $4,000 for taxpayers with an adjusted gross income of about $75,000 and over.

9. Chapters 319, 320, and 321, 1987 Session Laws of Kansas.

10. Some states do impose the retail sales tax as a gross receipts tax on the vendor for the "privilege of doing business." While the vendor properly would be considered the taxpayer in this situation, the sales tax basically operates as if it were imposed on the consumer. The latest count shows that 13 states impose their sales tax as a vendor tax, 17 as a consumer tax, and 15 with a mix of the two types of taxes. The nature of the tax does not affect the discussion here. For a review, see John F. Due and John L. Mikesell, *Sales Taxation: State and Local Structure and Administration* (Baltimore: The Johns Hopkins Press, 1983), pp. 24-25.

11. Ibid. The latest tally shows that 25 states provide some form of compensation to the retailer for collecting the sales tax, while 20 do not. See Due and Mikesell, *Sales Taxation,* pp. 327-328.

12.   For a review of the states exempting food, prescription drugs, nonprescription drugs, and clothing, see John L. Mikesell, "General Sales Tax," in Gold, *Reforming State Tax Systems,* p. 215.

13.   Richard D. Pomp, "Simplicity and Complexity in the Context of a State Tax System," in Gold, *Reforming State Tax Systems,* p. 136.

14.   Chapter 64, 1987 Session Laws of Kansas.

15.   Telephone conversation with Susan W. Martin, Commissioner of Revenue, State of Michigan, October 8, 1987.

16.   Telephone conversation with Tom Triplett, Commissioner of Revenue, State of Minnesota, October 7, 1987.

17.   John L. Mikesell, "Amnesties for State Tax Evaders: The Nature and Response to Recent Programs," *National Tax Journal* XXXIX, no. 4 (December 1986): 507-525.

18.   Correspondence from Ira A. Jackson, Commissioner of Revenue, Commonwealth of Massachusetts, August 25, 1987.

19.   See Richard A. Pomp, "Simplicity and Complexity in the Context of a State Tax System," pp. 132-134. See also Larry C. Ledebur and William W. Hamilton, "The Failure of Tax Concessions as Economic Development Incentives," in Gold, *Reforming State Tax Systems,* pp. 101-118.

20.   Codified as Kansas Statutes Annotated, Chapter 79, Article 36, Section 32 et seq.

21.   For a review of such programs, see Steven D. Gold, *State Tax Relief for the Poor* (Denver: National Conference of State Legislatures, April 1987).

VII

Suggestions for Improving the Administration of State Taxes

by
Robert C. Witzel

Taxes are the price citizens pay for their democratic society. Taxes are necessary to fund government. Nevertheless, in extracting money for governmental services from the public's pocketbook, a heavy reliance is placed on "self-assessment" by each taxpayer. State legislators should consider the attitude that must be cultivated, nurtured, and constantly maintained in the taxpaying public's collective mind if state tax systems are to operate successfully.

To be truly efficient, a state revenue system must maintain the confidence of its citizens. They must view it as fair and evenhanded. It must be considered as nonintrusive in their everyday lives. It must be efficient in its ability to amass large amounts of revenue from many sources. Its integrity must be unmarked. These elements must be monitored closely by state legislators and not left solely to the revenue officials charged with administering the tax system.

This chapter points out several areas where the fairness, equity, and integrity of tax systems may be lacking. The administrative areas of tax statutes will be the focal point. As elected officials, legislators have as good a feel for the public's perception of the tax system as anyone. Moreover, the instincts of fairness, integrity, and credibility are not forfeited simply because they hold public office.

Interest

The payment of interest should represent the "time value of money"—no more and no less. Thus, the setting of statutory interest rates is most important. If interest rates are set too low, the state inadvertently becomes a low-interest bank/lender through the administration of its tax laws. Moreover, if interest rates are set too high, the state effectively is levying *hidden* penalties in addition to its statutorily authorized penalties. Neither imbalance of interest rates is proper.

A second principal point regarding interest rates is the parity that should be maintained for both the taxpaying public and the state. Payments flow both ways in any revenue system: Assessments are issued and refunds are granted. Thus, the interest rates set by statute should be applicable equally to assessments and refunds.

Currently, there are far too many examples where nominal or no interest is paid to taxpayers on refunds or overpayments, while a reasonable rate of interest is charged on assessments. Likewise, some instances exist where reasonable interest is paid on refunds, but inordinately high rates of interest are charged on assessments.

The period of time when interest is applicable is the final example of where disparity can exist. The tolling of interest from the date a refund claim is *filed* completely ignores the state's prior use of such funds. If the refund is to be granted properly, the entire time (other than a reasonable grace period for administrative purposes) of such use of funds should be compensated.

Statutorily setting a *reasonable* rate of interest and applying this rate equally to *both* sides is the solution most appropriate to maintaining the revenue system for what it is intended to be.

Statutes of Limitation

Statutes of limitation should exist for one reason: to set the time frame within which an act must be completed. Applying this premise to a revenue system, time frames are needed to help taxpayers comply with and authorities enforce revenue laws and then bring *finality* to these matters for both the taxpayers and the state. No state should have the threat of audit adjustments pending for inordinately long periods of time after the close of the tax period or tax year.

Equally important, the time frame for the state and its taxpayers should be balanced, not skewed in favor of the revenue authorities. It is not uncommon today to find statutes of limitations wherein the taxpayer's right to claim a refund is a short period of time, while the state's period of time for issuing assessments extends much longer.

In a few revenue systems, imbalance also is found between the time frames applicable to domestic (in-state) taxpayers versus foreign (out-of-state) taxpayers. The practice of creating separate classes of taxpayers solely along geographical lines is of questionable legal validity (under the U.S. Constitution) at its best and inept favoritism codified in law at its worst.

Federal and State Waivers

While a statute of limitations is meant to bring finality to the matters at hand, the existence of waivers allows for extending the period of time when such extensions are mutually agreeable to the taxpayer and the state. The key element is the *mutual* agreement.

Most common is the practice of automatically extending by statute the time period for both assessments and refunds when the taxpayer correspondingly extends the time frame with the Internal Revenue Service for federal income tax purposes. Although this practice is unique to income taxes, it generally remains fair and balanced for both the state and the public. It is appropriate when the state's income tax base is coupled to the taxpayer's federal income tax base.

To maintain equity, it is critical that only adjustments (up or down) to federal taxable income be entitled to the extended time frame for appropriate assessment of additional tax by the state or the filing of a refund claim by the taxpayer. Currently, a few state statutes hold that federal waivers open the entire tax year of the taxpayer for assessment purposes, regardless of IRS adjustments, thus rendering a complete nullity the original statute of limitations' efforts at setting finality to the matter. The existence of federal waivers is far too common in the corporate world of federal income taxation to have entire tax years (as opposed to just the adjustments themselves) held open for such extended periods of time.

Penalties

Penalties are an integral part of every state's revenue code, necessary to enforce compliance. The application of penalties, however, often extends into areas where statutes or case law render the taxable status of a transaction, property, or certain types of income highly questionable. Taxpayers taking a position of nontaxability face the added burden of penalties when the state adheres to a contrary position. The stage thus is set for administrative and judicial review, sometimes not on the merits that have been conceded subsequently, but solely for relief from the penalties assessed.

This situation is most aggravating when the state levies automatic penalties on any assessment of additional tax. This practice currently exists in some states. The administration of revenue laws, still relying heavily on voluntary taxpayer compliance, has no place for such an unnecessary irritant, which undermines the public's confidence in the fairness of the tax system.

The final concern regarding penalties results from "amnesty aftermath." In the last few years, many states have completed amnesty programs successfully, bringing many noncomplying taxpayers up-to-date and on the tax roll for the future. Although this is most commendable in enacting amnesty programs, legislatures always enhance the enforcement process with more and tougher penalties. Thus, long after the amnesty program has expired, the revenue authorities continue to *have and use* these enhanced penalties while forgetting their original target. The taxpayer who has filed his taxes for decades, never needing to avail himself of amnesty forgiveness, now faces felonies (instead of misdemeanors), 25 percent penalties (versus 10 percent), and sometimes additional (penal) interest charges. The enforcement sanctions enacted toward delinquents now become applicable to reputable taxpayers.

Legal Fees/Audit Charges

A small number of states maintain the practice of charging audit expenses to the taxpayers, regardless of the outcome of the audit. Is the taxpayer paying for the *privilege* of being audited? This practice aggravates the taxpayer, prostitutes the audit function, and embarrasses the revenue agents innocently involved.

Similarly, the state's legal fees are added to a favorable verdict under one state's system. This approach is *not* reversed when the taxpayer prevails in court. A balance would be better, but abolishment would be best.

Administrative Review

Whether it be on a refund claim or an assessment protested, the administrative review process is a vital element to any state's tax system. It can accomplish the desired goals of quick and inexpensive resolution of disputes, or it can aggravate tax disputes to the point of many unnecessary lawsuits being filed.

In the current era of rapid and substantial changes in federal and state tax codes, it first must be recognized that disputes do arise based on *legitimate* grounds from both sides' perspectives. A process, therefore, must exist for the quick, efficient resolution of a majority of these matters, leaving only a few significant issues for the already overburdened judicial systems.

First to be addressed is the period of time in which a protest or refund claim is to be filed. Fairness dictates that such period be reasonable, commencing with receipt (as opposed to mailing date) of the assessment. Thirty to 60 days appears to be the accepted norm, as opposed to the extremes in a few states of 10 days or 120 days.

The period for filing refund claims is determined easily under fairness principles by paralleling the same period that the taxpayer is open for adjustment by assessment. *In all cases,* the refund claim period or the assessment protest period should be identical for domestic and foreign taxpayers.

Next in order is the abolition of all *prepayment* requirements to the taxpayer's right to review. It is simply alien to the American tradition that one must pay in full what is perceived as an improper or illegal assessment *prior* to and as a prerequisite for one's opportunity for review by the appropriate authorities.

The prepayment requirement is particularly egregious where

overaggressive applications of penalties have occurred. The fear that taxpayers will abuse the review procedures by bringing spurious protests to stall ultimate payment is curable by setting reasonable, compensating interest rates as previously discussed. Likewise, in those few instances where the taxpayer's financial condition is such that future payment is questionable, limited use of bonding or escrow accounts may be appropriate.

The final area of concern is the effect to be given the decisions rendered under the administrative review process. Such decisions should be binding on the state, the protesting taxpayer, and all open tax years and not on a *prospective* basis only.

It is far too common today to have a tax declared unconstitutional, in whole or part, but the invalidity then is applied *prospectively only* due to the perceived hardship on the state that would be caused if taxes already collected were to be refunded. What about the hardship on the taxpayers forced to pay an illegal tax? Should the wrongdoer profit from its illegal acts? As states persist with taxing methods that push the outer limits of constitutional standards, should they not tread these paths at great risk? The risks must be great if a balance of power between the people and their government is to be maintained.

In conclusion, the issues of what to tax and to what degree are debated at length in every state capitol. The issues of *administrative* fairness and equity, however, seldom are addressed in such debates but certainly should be if public confidence and credibility are to be maintained in state revenue systems.

VIII

Models of State Income Tax Reform

by
Harvey Galper
and
Stephen H. Pollock

$\mathbf{T}$he dominant issue in domestic public policy in recent years, at both the federal and the state levels, has been tax reform. Tax policy, moreover, has not been removed from the public agenda. Many states have not completed or are just undertaking reviews of their fiscal systems, and the questions of whether and how to raise federal taxes still are being vigorously debated. Such reviews and debates ideally should make use of the most rigorous analytical tools available to elevate the level of public understanding of the effects of the current and any proposed new tax rules. The central message of this chapter is that the use of computer-based simulation models of state tax systems can contribute greatly to the discussion and evaluation of alternative tax policy options.

The models that we shall consider can be used most effectively when policymakers have a clear understanding of the goals that they are trying to achieve. Thus, section one of this chapter discusses the goals of tax reform. These goals include both the traditional objectives of tax reform—equity, efficiency, and simplicity—as well as other practical considerations such as developing a revenue system that is not unduly affected by shocks to a state's economy and yet is capable of generating increases in revenues as that economy grows.

As an introduction to the use of simulation models for evaluating tax systems, section two briefly describes what these models are and section three considers how these models can be used for policy analysis. The next two sections then illustrate how these models can be used by analyzing the federal and selected state individual income tax systems before and after the Tax Reform Act of 1986 and associated state tax reforms. The tax systems of five states were selected for analysis: California, Colorado, Nebraska, Oklahoma, and Virginia. Of these states, only Oklahoma did not directly change its income tax system in response to federal tax reform, but linking the state's measure of income to federal definitions changes the effect of its system nonetheless.

Section four discusses each of these tax systems, and section five presents the simulation results. Each tax system is examined with respect to its progressivity, its elasticity (or revenue responsiveness) with respect to real economic growth, and its treatment of low-income taxpayers. The general findings are that tax reform made the federal individual income tax and each state tax system more progressive but also less elastic with respect to real economic growth. Also, changes in both the federal and state income tax laws removed thousands of taxpayers from the tax rolls and, except for Oklahoma, reduced the number of taxpayers with higher state than federal income tax liabilities. The more general conclusion is that computer-based simulation models are an extremely useful tool for tax policy analysis.

I. Goals of Tax Reform

The traditional goals of tax reform—equity, efficiency, and simplicity—have almost lost their meaning through overuse. Nonetheless, since these standards still represent some of our highest aspirations, if not our noblest achievements, in tax policy, a brief discussion of each may be in order.

Equity or fairness is the goal that is probably the most often cited and least often agreed upon in the formulation of tax policy.

In part, disagreements arise because there is no accepted definition of what is fair; in part, disagreements reflect the fact that various aspects of fairness may be in conflict. For example, new tax rules may appear to be fair, but at the same time they may impose what may be considered unduly large additional burdens on those who relied on the old tax rules. As a result of such disagreements, more art than science may be needed to implement the two common views of tax equity: horizontal equity, or taxing equally those in equal economic circumstances; and vertical equity, or taxing unequally those in unequal economic circumstances.

Each of these notions of equity raises almost as many questions as it answers. In the case of horizontal equity, the following questions arise: What constitutes equal economic circumstances? How are extraordinary situations such as being disabled or having large medical expenses to be treated for tax purposes? What is the unit for measuring equal circumstances, the individual or the family; and if the family, how should the tax law treat families of different size? Further, how is noncash income, such as subsidized housing or employer-provided medical insurance, to be treated? Similar issues arise with respect to vertical equity. Of even greater importance, the answer must be found to an essentially unanswerable question: *How much* differently should taxpayers in unequal circumstances be treated?

It is often asserted that vertical equity is satisfied if the tax system is progressive. A progressive system is one in which taxes as a share of income increase as income itself increases (that is, the effective or average tax rate rises with income). But a tax system can be mildly progressive (that is, high-income taxpayers can have just slightly higher tax burdens than low-income taxpayers); or it can be steeply progressive. Furthermore, progressivity can be achieved in various ways, for example, by a system of graduated marginal tax rates or by a system with a single tax rate and a substantial tax-free allowance. In the former case, progressivity is achieved by subjecting additional increments of income to higher tax rates; in the latter case, it is achieved by subjecting a greater fraction of one's total income to tax as income rises, even though the income that is taxed faces a single rate.

Thus, notions of equity provide at best rough guides for evaluating a tax system. At bottom, a value judgment must be made that the progressivity of the system satisfies social norms. Furthermore, such value judgments themselves are subject to change over time as various other goals become more important or as economic conditions change. An economy with few low-income households may want to be (or can afford to be) more generous to such taxpayers than an economy with many such households.

The level of government levying the tax also affects one's evaluation of the importance of tax equity. It often has been asserted that progressivity is more important for the federal income tax than for state income taxes. The reason is that taxpayers can move much more freely from one state to another to avoid high state taxes than they can move out of the country to avoid high federal taxes. Tax competition among states is a fact of life that constrains what state tax systems can do.

Efficiency is a more rigorously defined goal, at least to economists if not to policymakers. From an economic point of view, the standard for evaluating tax systems is how the market would allocate resources in the absence of taxation. The presumption is that the market allocation best satisfies consumer preferences and should not be tampered with unless compelling evidence exists that the market is not working. (According to this criterion, the mere fact that a policymaker may want a different outcome does not constitute compelling evidence.) An efficient tax system is, therefore, one that does not change taxpayer behavior; thus, the output of goods and services, investment across industries and sectors, and saving and investment depart as little as possible from the allocation that would occur in a world with no taxes. Another term for an efficient tax system is a neutral tax system.

But the goal of efficiency also has its qualifications. First, the standard that the tax system should not change resource allocation is virtually impossible to achieve in practice. Any real-world tax regime will inevitably change individual behavior and, hence, the allocation of resources. Are all tax systems to be rejected as a result, or are there ways of determining that some are better than others? How much of a distortion in resource allocation is to be permitted, and how are distortions of one type—say, in the pattern of consumption across goods and services—to be compared with distortions of another type—say, in the decision to work or not to work or in the decision to consume rather than to save. While economic measures of the degree of distortion of various taxes and tax systems can be made, they depend upon assumptions that are not universally accepted and can be highly controversial.

Furthermore, the assumption that in the absence of taxes resources would be optimally allocated is surely far too sanguine a view of the operation of the economy. There are numerous instances of concentrations of economic power such that consumer satisfactions are not maximized, and other situations where externalities such as pollution require that market allocations be changed. On the other hand, the fact that the economy does not conform to the economist's models cannot be an adequate justification for complete anarchy in tax policy. The market economy operates sufficiently well to avoid tax rules that seriously distort economic decisions regarding consumption, investment, and work effort.

The goal of simplicity is also not an absolute, but rather a recognition that attention also must be given to developing tax rules that taxpayers can understand and tax administrators can enforce. This goal, unfortunately, has received insufficient attention in recent years, at least at the federal level. Although the economy and economic transactions are growing ever more complex, the tax system has done little to slow down this trend. Instead, as several aspects of the 1986 act have made us painfully aware, the complexity of the tax treatment of quite common transactions, such as buying household appliances on credit, is threatening to overwhelm the system. The reason for this result is the unwillingness of policymakers to make the appropriate tradeoffs among goals. To obtain a less complex system of income taxation, it may be necessary to allow some kinds of income to slip through the cracks or to make other practical compromises.

In addition to these traditional goals, states must be sensitive to other aspects of their economic environment in designing their tax systems. In recent years, the U.S. economy, and thus the economies of individual states, seem to have been buffeted by changes and shocks to an extraordinary degree. It would be difficult and even foolish to resist forces such as the increasing integration of the world economy. But one major implication is that developments around the world affect the United States as never before. The outbreak of hostilities in the Persian Gulf can affect the livelihood of Texas wildcatters at least as much as changes in domestic policies. As the U.S. economy remains open to flows of goods and capital from all over the world, American workers and businesses also are affected by fluctuations in the exchange rate, labor costs in South America and Asia, and interest rates in Europe. Such changes cannot always be anticipated or prevented, but it is necessary to remain flexible in responding to them.

Similarly, technological change continues as a major economic force, creating new industries and destroying old ones. Competition on an international scale may mean that new technologies come on line more quickly, subjecting the national economy and states to further uncertainty. At the same time, the U.S. economy is becoming more service oriented, with financial services, information processing, communications, and the like replacing manufacturing as the major source of employment growth.

Some states are thriving as a result of these changes, and others are doing less well, but for every state the implications for tax policy are significant. First, it may be more important now than in the past for states to have broader tax bases that are less dependent upon particular sectors and industries. States that traditionally have depended on energy-related taxes are perhaps most aware of this new reality. Of course, a state is in better shape if its underlying economy itself is broadly based. But for all states, tax systems can be structured to reach as much economic activity as possible.

Second, the robustness of the tax revenues may be a new consideration in state tax policy in addition to revenue elasticity. In other words, there may be a tradeoff between a robust tax system, or one that is less likely to yield revenue shortfalls in times of rapid economic change, and an elastic tax system, or one that is more attuned to generating large revenue increases in times of economic growth.

Third, a concern with robustness may mean that issues of tax mix may become more important: A progressive income tax may have greater elasticity, but a broad-based sales tax may be more robust. Perhaps a mix of taxes best combines the advantages of each. In a similar vein, if flexibility becomes more valued in periods of economic change, multiple revenue sources may provide the state with more options. Within the area of sales taxation, serious consideration should be given to taxing services to capture as much economic activity as possible in the tax base. Since the income tax captures income generated in the production of services, the sales tax should equally capture the consumption of services.

In sum, aside from achieving traditional goals of equity, efficiency, and simplicity, tax systems also should be broad based, robust, and flexible. In analyzing many of those characteristics of state tax systems, micro-simulation models have been found to be extremely useful tools. The next section describes these models in some detail and illustrates their use in tax policy analysis.

II. What Is a Micro-Simulation Tax Model?

The effects of tax reform proposals often are described in terms of the change in the tax liability of a "typical" family (for example, a married couple with two children, a mortgage, and $30,000 in income mostly from wages). While these "representative taxpayer" studies are popular and can provide an intuitive feel for changes in tax law, they are clearly insufficient for thorough policy analysis. However, such simple examples may be all that is available to policymakers in the absence of more sophisticated analytical tools.

A micro-simulation tax model combined with an analytical data base is based on the same intuitive principle of simulating the tax calculations of individual taxpayers. The micro-simulation model, however, calculates tax liabilities for thousands of families and individuals (the "micro" units in the economy) who are representative of the entire tax-filing population of a jurisdiction. It is the scope and quality of the underlying data base along with their ability to simulate quickly and accurately the effects of major structural tax changes that distinguishes micro-simulation tax models from the simple representative taxpayer approach.

The analytical data base in its simplest form is a statistically drawn sample of tax returns with each return weighted so that the sample represents the entire tax-filing population. A sample is used as a lower cost but still highly accurate alternative to a data base composed of every tax return filed in the jurisdiction. Ideally, tax returns showing very low and very high levels of income are sampled more heavily and thus have lower weights.

The state income tax models developed by Peat Marwick's Policy Economics Group make use of tax return data taken from one of two sources: the Internal Revenue Service's Statistics of Income file on federal tax returns, or the states' own income tax returns. Tax returns contain a wealth of information, such as marital status, number of dependents, amount and sources of income, amount and type of deductions and credits claimed, amount of income tax withheld, and the taxpayer's residence, by state and sometimes even by zip code.

As comprehensive as a data base derived from tax return information may be, it nonetheless has two major drawbacks. First, while it is adequate for simulating the tax law in place when the tax returns were filed, it cannot capture the effects of a whole range of new policy scenarios. For example, such a data base contains no information on nonfilers and, hence, cannot be used to examine policy changes affecting them. Moreover, since it takes a minimum of about two years to process and make publicly available an entire set of returns, any tax return data will be at least two years out of date and, thus, less representative of the current population. Compounding this problem is the fact that states are usually interested in the effects of a policy change for some future year when the policy will be put in place. Projections of data bases, perhaps three to five years beyond the year of the original data base, are needed in these cases.

Both of these problems can be dealt with effectively in the development of micro-simulation tax models. The first problem of limited information can be corrected by enhancing the data base through a variety of approaches. First, data from state and federal tax returns can be combined, thereby generating a data set that contains more information than each data source individually.

A second way of adding information to the file is through a statistical match of tax data with census data. In this procedure, a linear programming computer algorithm is used to merge the two data sets, resulting in a file that contains significant demographic and economic information. Such information includes income from nontaxable sources (such as transfer payments), an indicator of pension coverage, and an indicator of the dependent status of family members. The census file also contains information on individuals and families that do not file tax returns.

Also, the file can be enhanced further by the direct imputation of information gathered from independent sources. Variables that typically are imputed include consumption by type of good or service, itemized deductions for nonitemizers, industry in which the taxpayer is employed, and student status. During the imputation process, consistency checks are employed to assure that the totals for each of the imputed items match the aggregate data.

The problem of the timeliness of the data base is dealt with by extrapolation. The data base is extrapolated to reflect how the jurisdiction's economy will look in years beyond the base year from which the data have been taken. The resulting data base can have as many as 750 variables for each of the thousands of sample tax returns on the file and will be fully consistent with the economic and demographic profile of the taxing jurisdiction.

Given this data, the tax model itself is a procedure for simulating how the tax forms are filled out by each taxpayer. The computer will read the information for one taxpayer, calculate his or her tax liability, store the information, and proceed to the next taxpayer. The model simulates both federal and state tax law and computes tax liability just as the taxpayer would. Federal tax liability is calculated first so that, where necessary, items from the federal return can be entered onto the state return. After all the records have been processed, the information is tallied and summary tables are prepared.

III. The Use of Micro-Simulation Tax Models

The primary use of micro-simulation tax models at all levels of government is for estimating the revenue and distributional effects of alternative tax policy proposals. At the state level, the most prevalent recent applications have been to estimate the likely changes in tax revenue due to changes in federal tax law, i.e., the so-called revenue windfalls to states from the Tax Reform Act of 1986.[1] The models are ideally suited for this purpose because they can accurately capture the complex linkages between federal and state tax law and thus the magnitude of the state windfalls. The models also can be used to determine how state tax laws can be modified to return to state taxpayers whatever share of the windfall policymakers may want.

With respect to distributional analysis, many tax changes may be acceptable only if the distribution of the tax burden is altered in some predetermined fashion or if tax relief is given to particular groups such as low-income taxpayers. Although such distributional analyses are important applications of micro-simulation tax models, caution must be exercised when using a simple model based solely on tax return data for such purposes. The distributional results can be very sensitive to the choice of income definition used and to the choice of the unit of analysis. The simplest models and data bases are restricted to definitions of income that can be measured only from tax return information, such as adjusted gross income (AGI). This definition of income, however, is quite limited and omits income from nontaxable sources, adjustments to income, and many tax preferences.

Similarly, the unit of analysis is restricted to the tax return or the tax-filing unit in simple models. While this unit presents no problem for revenue estimation, the more appropriate unit for analysis of distributional effects is the household or family. For example, the Tax Reform Act of 1986 eliminated the personal exemption for those taxpayers who also are claimed as dependents on another tax return. Simulation of this provision based on tax units showed that this change primarily affects low-income taxpayers. However, when the simulation is done on a family basis, the increased tax burden is spread much more evenly across income classes. Even though the dependent taxpayers themselves have low income, they are often members of middle-income and upper-income families.

The tax models of the Policy Economics Group can be simulated with a variety of income definitions. The merge and imputation procedures have added information on other income sources that can be used to approximate an economic definition of income. Furthermore, with the use of census information, families can be used as the unit of analysis, rather than tax returns.

Micro-simulation models can simulate not only how taxpayers calculate tax liability given their incomes, but also how changes in taxpayer behavior in response to new tax rules affect revenue and the distribution of tax burdens. Although the behavioral responses themselves are estimated outside the micro-simulation model, a range of such behavioral responses can be incorporated into the model. For example, the Policy Economics Group models take into account the following five behavioral responses from the Tax Reform Act of 1986: 1) taxpayers will reduce the realization of capital gains in response to higher effective tax rates on such gains; 2) taxpayers will curtail their losses generated from "passive" activities due to the new passive loss restrictions; 3) fewer Individual Retirement Account deductions will be taken in response to the new IRA restrictions; 4) nonmortgage interest expenses and interest income will be reduced due to the phase-out of such interest deductions; and 5) charitable contributions will fall somewhat because their after-tax price has risen as a result of lower tax rates.

The general output of the tax simulation models is the calculation of tax liability for a given calendar year. However, the models also can be used to forecast revenue on a fiscal year basis. For this purpose, historical data are needed on estimated tax payments and withholding along with an understanding of how particular tax changes affect the timing of payments. Some tax proposals, such as changes in the rate schedule, will affect withholding as soon as the new withholding tables are put into place. Other changes, such as repeal of the investment tax credit, may affect primarily estimated payments. Still others, such as changes in the tax rate on capital gains, may not affect revenues until final payments are made when the return is filed. These various payment effects can be taken into account on a provision-by-provision basis for most tax reform proposals.

Further extensions include simulations of the combined effects of federal taxes and state taxes on individual taxpayers and even the interactions among tax systems. For example, it is possible to capture the effects of changes in property taxes on both state and federal liability resulting from the deductibility (or crediting) of one tax against another, the changes in federal liability resulting from changes in state income taxes, and for some states the changes in state income taxes resulting from changes in federal income taxes. It is also possible to model the credits that many states allow for taxes paid to other jurisdictions. As a result of such interactions, for example, a reduction in New York state taxes will increase taxes paid to New Jersey by New Jersey residents who work and pay taxes in New York.

Finally, the data bases themselves have an enormous research potential even without the associated tax models. They can be used by policy officials to obtain accurate profiles of the economic and social characteristics of state residents and to gain a better understanding of the amount of consumption and income that potentially can be made subject to tax.

IV. Evaluation of State Income Tax Systems

This section illustrates the general usefulness of micro-simulation models for policy analysis by using the tax models developed at the Policy Economics Group to evaluate some characteristics of the federal individual income tax and the income tax systems of a few selected states. Five states have been chosen for this analysis: California, Colorado, Nebraska, Oklahoma, and Virginia. These states have been selected to represent the various types of tax changes enacted at the state level in response to federal tax reform and to provide regional and economic diversity.

The five selected states vary in the amount of the windfall resulting from federal tax reform and also have responded quite differently to the federal tax changes.[2] California had a large windfall, over $1 billion, and returned it all to state taxpayers. Colorado had a moderate windfall and kept about half and returned about half. Colorado also greatly changed its tax structure, adopting a flat tax rate and a broader tax base. Nebraska received no windfall since its tax was calculated as a percentage of federal tax liability. However, the state adopted conformity with federal AGI in response to the federal tax changes. Oklahoma, facing serious fiscal difficulties, kept the entire windfall by maintaining its automatic link to federal AGI but otherwise did not change its tax system. Virginia returned all the windfall to state taxpayers and also restructured its own system. Table 1 presents a general description of the tax changes enacted in each state and in the federal tax law.

This chapter examines three characteristics of the federal and state income tax systems. The first is the progressivity of the tax system and is measured by an index of progressivity, developed by Professor Daniel Suits of the University of Michigan.[3] This index compares the distribution of family income with the distribution of taxes paid. For this purpose, as well as for all other tabulations in this chapter, tax liabilities are displayed by family and by a measure of comprehensive income (including all transfer payments and employer-provided fringe benefits) rather than by tax-filing unit and by AGI.

The index of progressivity measures whether a tax is proportional, progressive, or regressive. A proportional tax is one in which the share of the tax burden paid by each group of families is the same as its share of income. A progressive tax is one in which lower-income families have a lower share of the tax burden than they have of total income, and higher-income families have

Table 1.

Major Changes in the Federal Income Tax and the Tax Laws of Five Selected States

Federal Income Tax

- Changed the definition of AGI as a result of: repeal of dividend exclusion; taxation of all unemployment compensation; repeal of two-earner marriage deduction; cutback of IRA deductions; less generous depreciation deductions; disallowance of most passive losses; transfer of employee business expenses from an above-the-line deduction to an itemized deduction (above a floor of 2 percent of AGI); and repeal of capital gains exclusion.

- Changed itemized deductions as follows: phase-out of consumer interest deduction; repeal of state sales tax deduction; cutback of deduction for medical expenses.

- Changed other provisions of tax law: increase in exemption amounts; lower rates and flatter rate schedule; increase in standard deduction (formerly zero; bracket amount); tightening of minimum tax; increase in earned income credit; repeal of political contributions credit; repeal of investment tax credit.

California

- Lowered top rate from 11 percent to 9.3 percent;

- Lowered starting income level for top tax rate from $59,600 to $47,900 for married taxpayers filing jointly;

- Reduced number of brackets from 11 to 6;

- Raised personal exemption credit from $45 to $52 (in 1988, indexed for inflation);

- Strengthened the minimum tax;

- Allowed same IRA deduction as federal law (previously no deduction allowed);

- Provided higher child care credit;

- Increased conformity to federal AGI with respect to capital gains, business expense deductions, passive losses, interest and medical deductions, and depreciation.

Colorado

- Adopted flat tax rate of 5 percent (prior schedule had 11 brackets ranging from 3 percent to 8 percent with the top bracket starting at $14,150 and with 2 percent surcharge on high amounts of dividend and interest);

- Adopted federal definition of taxable income minus up to $20,000 in pensions (previously taxable income was equal to federal AGI plus the two-earner deduction minus federal tax liability minus up to $20,000 in pensions minus federal deductions except state and local income taxes);

- Increased standard deduction from the sum of $1,420 plus federal income tax to federal standard deduction;
- Increased personal exemptions from $850 to amount of federal exemption;
- Curtailed and phased out major credits except credit for taxes paid to other states.

Nebraska

- Adopted federal AGI conformity plus a percentage of federal alternative minimum tax (prior tax liability was 19 percent of federal liability);
- Increased standard deduction to approximate federal standard deduction prior to tax reform;
- Adopted federal itemized deductions except for state income taxes;
- Changed exemption amount to $1,130 in 1988;
- Adopted same tax brackets as under federal tax reform, but with rates ranging from 2 percent to 5.9 percent.

Oklahoma

- Did not change tax law;
- Continues to be tied automatically to federal AGI;
- Has a structure of tax rates that range up to 17 percent if federal taxes are deducted, 6 percent if not;
- Allows federal itemized deductions to be taken as state itemized deductions;
- Has a standard deduction that varies with AGI from minimum of $1,000 to maximum of $2,000;
- Provides personal exemptions of $1,000.

Virginia

- Raised the starting amount for top bracket from $12,000 to $17,000 by 1990 (top rate is 5.75 percent);
- Raised from $3,000 to $5,000 ($8,000 for joint returns) the AGI threshold for state tax liability;
- Raised standard deduction from maximum of $2,000 to $5,000 for joint returns, $3,000 for single returns, by 1989;
- Raised exemptions from $600 to $800 by 1988.

a higher share of the tax burden than of total income. In contrast, a regressive tax imposes a relatively higher tax burden on lower-income taxpayers. Under the Suits index, a proportional tax has a value of 0.0, a progressive tax has a positive value as high as 1.0, and a regressive tax has a negative value as low as -1.0.

The second characteristic of the federal and state tax systems we examine is the elasticity of the income tax. Generically, an elasticity measure is the percentage change in one variable in response to a 1 percent change in another variable. The elasticity of the income tax is the responsiveness of tax liabilities to changes in the underlying tax base. The aggregate tax base can change for various reasons, however, yielding an ambiguous definition of elasticity in some cases.

In general, changes in the base of the individual income tax over time can be separated into three components. First, the number of taxpayers can change; second, the real income of these taxpayers can change; and third, nominal values can increase because of inflation. Each source of increase in the tax base can have its own elasticity, and each measure of elasticity, in turn, will reflect various ways that each component can change. For example, if the number of taxpayers increases, and the new tax-payers are distributed among income classes in exactly the same way as the previous taxpayers, the elasticity of income tax liabilities with respect to a change in the number of taxpayers would have a value of 1.0. That is, a 10 percent increase in the number of taxpayers distributed in this way would increase tax liabilities by 10 percent. Although there is no necessity for the distribution of old and new taxpayers to match exactly, an elasticity of about 1.0 is a reasonable benchmark for changes in tax liabilities resulting from changes in the tax-paying population.

Similarly, if nominal values change as a result of inflation and not real growth, and if the tax system is fully indexed for inflation, the elasticity measure also should equal unity. In this case, nominal tax liabilities would increase proportionately with nominal income so that inflation imposes no higher level of real tax burdens. In an unindexed system, however, particularly one characterized by graduated tax rates, increases in nominal values can give rise to a greater than proportionate increase in tax liabilities, thereby causing real tax burdens to rise. That is, 5 percent inflation can cause tax liabilities to rise by more than 5 percent so that real after-tax income actually declines. In this situation, the elasticity of tax liabilities in response to an inflation-induced change in the tax base will be greater than unity. Finally, real income growth also can cause tax liabilities to increase. To the extent that liabilities increase more than proportionately, the elasticity in response to real growth is greater than one. If a tax system is not indexed, tax liabilities will increase by the same percentage whether the tax base increases as a result of real growth or inflation.

Any real-world change in the tax base is likely to be composed of some combination of real income growth per taxpayer, inflation, and an increase in the number of taxpayers. The elasticity measures presented in this chapter hold the number of taxpayers constant and reflect growth in aggregate real income.

The third dimension of state income tax systems we consider is tax relief at the low end of the income scale. Specifically, we examine two aspects of state tax systems from this perspective: 1) the number and percent of families no longer paying positive state income taxes as a result of state tax changes, and 2) the number of families for whom state income tax liabilities are greater than federal income tax liabilities (before the earned income credit).

V. Simulation Results

For the federal tax system and each state's tax system, micro-simulation models have been used to analyze the new tax laws. Before discussing the results, however, a few prefatory comments may be in order. First, we have attempted to capture only the main tax changes as sketched out in Table 1 and not every detail of the new tax laws. Second, we have estimated the state and federal tax changes as fully phased in, even though full phase-in will not occur for several years. Also, some simulations have been performed at 1986 levels of income and some at 1987 levels depending on the specific work we have done for the states in question. In general, the tax liability figures presented here should be regarded as representing the general change in each state's tax structure, not as a definitive calculation of the tax burden actually imposed by the state in a particular year. Tables 2 through 6 display a sample of information that can be obtained from the use of micro-simulation models. Each is discussed in turn.

Table 2 shows the distribution of income for the nation as a whole and for each selected state. It also shows the progressivity of the federal and state income taxes, both pre- and post-reform. As an important qualifier, however, these measures do not account for the full range of behavioral responses, such as portfolio shifts or labor supply responses, that might accompany tax reform, nor do they account for changes in corporate income taxation.

An examination of the four right-hand columns in the table shows that for the federal income tax before the Tax Reform Act

Table 2.

Distribution of Income and Tax by Income Class
Federal Income Tax (1986 Levels)

Income Class (000s)	No. of Families (000s)	Economic Income ($mil.)	Tax Pre- Reform ($mil.)	Tax Post- Reform ($mil.)	Percent Families	Percent Income	Percent Tax Pre- Reform	Percent Tax Post- Reform
Under $5	6,568.4	$ 14,927.0	$ 164.5	$ 131.4	6.88%	0.43%	0.05%	0.04%
5-10	9,035.9	69,111.0	228.4	−86.0	9.47	1.98	0.06	−0.03
10-15	9,178.7	115,020.0	2,688.9	1,588.3	9.62	3.29	0.74	0.49
15-20	9,078.3	158,646.0	6,767.5	5,163.6	9.51	4.54	1.87	1.59
20-30	15,715.6	389,565.0	25,725.2	22,490.2	16.47	11.14	7.10	6.94
30-50	25,006.7	965,732.0	83,219.0	75,334.5	26.20	27.62	22.98	23.23
50-100	17,574.1	1,161,733.0	123,077.7	115,294.0	18.41	33.23	33.99	35.56
100-200	2,453.7	328,787.0	52,156.7	47,373.6	2.57	9.40	14.40	14.61
Over 200	825.0	292,902.0	8,048.4	56,948.5	0.86	8.38	18.79	17.56
Total	95,436.4	$3,496,423.0	$362,076.8	$324,238.1	100.00%	100.00%	100.00%	100.00%

California Income Tax (1987 Levels)

Income Class (000s)	No. of Families (000s)	Economic Income ($mil.)	Tax Pre- Reform ($mil.)	Tax Post- Reform ($mil.)	Percent Families	Percent Income	Percent Tax Pre- Reform	Percent Tax Post- Reform
Under $5	554.9	$ 2,489.4	$ 23.1	$ 42.3	5.27%	−0.54%	0.18%	0.33%
5-10	718.7	5,462.1	−2.5	−2.9	6.83	1.19	−0.02	−0.02
10-15	745.7	9,431.6	−11.0	−18.0	7.09	2.06	−0.08	−0.14
15-20	992.4	17,490.2	46.9	25.7	9.43	3.81	0.36	0.20
20-30	1,789.5	44,937.0	406.8	330.8	17.00	9.79	3.11	2.58
30-50	2,665.3	104,608.9	2,047.0	1,825.1	25.32	22.80	15.67	14.21
50-100	2,469.9	171,195.8	4,743.6	4,758.2	23.47	37.31	36.32	37.05
100-200	486.1	62,246.2	2,689.9	2,718.6	4.62	13.57	20.60	21.17
Over 200	102.3	45,909.5	3,116.8	3,162.4	10.00	10.00	23.86	24.63
Total	10,524.8	$458,791.9	$13,060.5	$12,842.2	100.00%	100.00%	100.00%	100.00%

Colorado Income Tax (1986 Levels)

Income Class (000s)	No. of Families (000s)	Economic Income ($mil.)	Tax Pre- Reform ($mil.)	Tax Post- Reform ($mil.)	Percent Families	Percent Income	Percent Tax Pre- Reform	Percent Tax Post- Reform
Under $5	119.8	$ 254.2	$ 0.3	$ 0.1	8.84%	0.51%	0.03%	0.01%
5-10	117.6	852.3	1.3	1.7	8.68	1.70	0.12	0.14
10-15	117.6	1,474.0	10.4	10.2	8.68	2.95	0.93	0.83
15-20	115.5	2,024.4	31.1	32.1	8.52	4.05	2.77	2.61
20-30	229.7	5,746.7	105.2	112.5	16.94	11.49	9.38	9.13
30-50	362.7	14,324.8	320.0	338.9	26.76	28.64	28.53	27.51
50-100	243.9	16,200.1	389.2	418.8	17.99	32.39	34.69	33.99
100-200	38.9	5,504.0	151.2	174.5	2.87	11.00	13.48	14.16
Over 200	9.9	3,637.2	113.1	143.2	0.73	7.27	10.08	11.62
Total	1,355.6	$50,017.7	$1,121.8	$1,232.0	100.00%	100.00%	100.00%	100.00%

Nebraska Income Tax (1986 Levels)

Income Class (000s)	No. of Families (000s)	Economic Income ($mil.)	Tax Pre- Reform ($mil.)	Tax Post- Reform ($mil.)	Percent Families	Percent Income	Percent Tax Pre- Reform	Percent Tax Post- Reform
Under $5	44.7	$ 66.1	$ 1.6	$ 2.1	7.06%	0.30%	0.40%	0.45%
5-10	54.6	384.5	0.5	0.5	8.56	1.72	0.12	0.11
10-15	68.6	831.4	4.8	6.1	10.84	3.71	1.19	1.31
15-20	56.1	988.7	10.0	11.3	8.68	4.41	2.48	2.44
20-30	97.2	2,446.5	27.6	31.8	15.35	10.92	6.85	6.85
30-50	189.2	7,430.6	111.5	129.8	29.88	33.17	27.65	27.98
50-100	104.1	6,919.8	134.6	151.5	16.44	30.89	33.38	32.66
100-200	14.2	1,837.2	51.7	61.7	2.24	8.20	12.82	13.30
Over 200	4.8	1,496.1	60.9	69.1	0.76	6.68	15.10	14.90
Total	633.1	$22,400.9	$403.2	$463.9	100.00%	100.00%	100.00%	100.00%

Oklahoma Income Tax (1987 Levels)

Income Class (000s)	No. of Families (000s)	Economic Income ($mil.)	Tax Pre-Reform ($mil.)	Tax Post-Reform ($mil.)	Percent Families	Percent Income	Percent Tax Pre-Reform	Percent Tax Post-Reform
Under $5	135.2	$ 311.5	$ 1.3	$ 2.0	10.10%	0.82%	0.19%	0.22%
5-10	184.1	1,380.7	1.6	1.9	13.76	3.62	0.23	0.21
10-15	195.4	2,406.5	8.5	10.7	14.60	6.31	1.21	1.18
15-20	138.4	2,419.0	13.9	17.2	10.34	6.34	1.98	1.89
20-30	221.4	5,548.3	65.2	83.6	16.55	14.55	9.30	9.21
30-50	288.7	11,098.8	210.8	263.7	21.58	29.10	30.07	29.04
50-100	148.0	9,537.0	239.6	299.8	11.06	25.01	34.17	33.01
100-200	19.0	2,568.3	84.3	105.1	1.42	6.73	12.02	11.57
Over 200	7.8	2,867.7	75.9	124.2	0.58	7.52	10.83	13.68
Total	1,338.0	$38,137.8	$701.1	$908.2	100.00%	100.00%	100.00%	100.00%

Virginia Income Tax (1987 Levels)

Income Class (000s)	No. of Families (000s)	Economic Income ($mil.)	Tax Pre-Reform ($mil.)	Tax Post-Reform ($mil.)	Percent Families	Percent Income	Percent Tax Pre-Reform	Percent Tax Post-Reform
Under $5	162.6	$ 429.8	$ 7.2	$ 7.3	7.08%	0.51%	0.30%	0.30%
5-10	249.6	1,786.2	8.6	5.1	10.75	2.13	0.35	0.21
10-15	234.3	2,935.7	38.8	29.1	10.20	3.50	1.60	1.19
15-20	211.9	3,694.7	62.5	50.3	9.23	4.40	2.57	2.05
20-30	375.3	9,252.5	213.6	186.4	16.34	11.02	8.79	7.60
30-50	514.8	20,260.1	602.4	570.8	22.42	24.13	24.79	23.29
50-100	459.0	30,884.8	1,007.0	1,017.1	19.99	36.78	41.45	41.49
100-200	81.2	10,493.4	359.7	393.9	3.54	12.50	14.80	16.07
Over 200	10.6	4,224.4	129.9	191.3	0.46	5.03	5.35	7.80
Total	2,296.6	$83,961.6	$2,429.7	$2,451.3	100.00%	100.00%	100.00%	100.00%

of 1986 middle- and lower-income families (i.e., below $50,000) claimed a smaller share of income than their share of the population, but they paid an even smaller share of tax. Thus, the federal tax structure was progressive. After tax reform, the share of tax liabilities paid by this group declines and the share paid by upper-income taxpayers increases, reflecting a tilt toward even greater progressivity. For the states, California seems to have a particularly progressive tax system, and Colorado and Virginia much less progressive systems.

These results are confirmed in Table 3, which shows the Suits indexes of progressivity for the federal income tax and each state's income tax. Recall that a positive value of the Suits index indicates a progressive tax system and a negative value a regressive system.

Prior to tax reform, the five selected states and the federal income tax were all progressive, although to varying degrees. California had the most progressive system, followed by Oklahoma (tied to federal AGI), the federal income tax, and Nebraska. The Nebraska income tax was somewhat less progressive than the federal income tax even though state tax liabilities were calculated as a percentage of federal liabilities. The reason is that state liabilities were based on federal liabilities before the earned income credit. The tax systems of Colorado and Virginia were much less progressive because of lower personal exemptions and flatter rate schedules.

Table 3.

Suits Indexes of Progressivity

State	Pre-Reform	Post-Reform
Federal Income Tax[a]	.2443	.2487
California[b]	.3101	.3330
Colorado[a]	.1166	.1461
Nebraska[a]	.2204	.2213
Oklahoma[b]	.2545	.2687
Virginia[b]	.0988	.1545

Notes:
a. 1986 levels of income.
b. 1987 levels of income.

After tax reform, each of the six tax systems became more progressive. A major reason in all cases is the inclusion of all capital gains (rather than only 40 percent under previous law) and the elimination of tax shelters. As a result of these changes, taxable income increased by a much larger proportion at high income levels than at lower income levels. The income tax in Colorado became much more progressive even with a system having a single tax rate. This result occurs because under the prior law the top rate came into effect at a low income level ($14,150), and under the new law the personal exemption and the standard deduction have been increased to the higher federal levels. The Virginia income tax also became more progressive as a result of both a higher income threshold for the top tax rate (from $12,000 to $17,000) and a larger standard deduction and personal exemptions.

The California income tax became more progressive despite the flatter rate schedule because of more liberal credits, stricter conformity to federal AGI, and a stronger minimum tax. The Oklahoma tax system became more progressive because the tax base was broadened at higher income levels due to continued conformity to federal AGI. Also, the lower federal income taxes imply increased state taxes for those taxpayers claiming the deductibility option for the state (see Table 1). Progressivity of the Nebraska and federal tax systems did not change much because the higher personal exemptions and standard deductions were offset by a flatter rate schedule.

Table 4 shows the elasticity of tax liability with respect to changes in income. Somewhat paradoxically, the federal and state tax systems became less elastic after tax reform despite the increase in progressivity of each. Prior to tax reform, the real elasticity of the federal income tax and the income tax systems of

California, Nebraska, and Oklahoma were all in the vicinity of 2.0; that is, a 5 percent increase in real income across the board would increase tax liabilities by 10 percent. For Colorado and Virginia, the elasticity was on the order of 1.5; a 5 percent increase in real incomes would increase liabilities by 7.5 percent. The relative elasticities across states roughly matched the relative progressivity indexes prior to tax reform.

After tax reform, however, each income tax system examined here has lower elasticity. The reason for this outcome is that the elasticity measures are dominated by the flatter rate schedules and lower rates at the top of the income scale, whereas the progressivity measures are more affected by the reductions at the bottom. As incomes grow, the flatter tax rates generate less revenue than did the prior structure. Nonetheless, at the time they are introduced, the new systems are more progressive.

Oklahoma has the largest relative change in its elasticity. This is because many of its taxpayers were induced to switch from the highly progressive tax schedule, under which federal tax payments are deductible, to the flatter tax schedule with no deduction for federal taxes.

Policymakers should recognize the implications of the new flatter rate schedules; specifically, tax changes that are revenue neutral in the short run may not be revenue neutral over time. In a few states such as Nebraska and Oklahoma, the changes are fairly significant (a decline in elasticity of 12 percent and 14 percent, respectively).

Table 5 shows the change in the number and percentage of families with positive tax liability by state under the new federal

Table 4.

Elasticity of Tax Liability with Respect to Changes in Real Income

State	Pre-Reform	Post-Reform
Federal Income tax[a]	1.95	1.80
California[b]	2.19	2.04
Colorado[a]	1.57	1.49
Nebraska[a]	1.94	1.70
Oklahoma[b]	2.12	1.83
Virginia[b]	1.49	1.42

Notes:
a. 1986 levels of income.
b. 1987 levels of income.

and state tax laws. In each case, these new laws reduce the number of families with positive tax liability; i.e., they take families off the tax rolls. This is primarily due to higher personal exemptions and standard deductions.

Table 6 presents another dimension of the relationship between state and federal taxes; namely, the number of families with state income taxes greater than federal income taxes (before the earned income credit). In every state except Oklahoma, which did not

Table 5.

Change in Number and Percentage of Families
with Positive Federal and State Income Tax

	California				Colorado			
	Federal Income Tax		State Income Tax		Federal Income Tax		State Income Tax	
Income Class (000s)	Number of Families (000s)	Percent of Families	Number of Families (000s)	Percent of Families	Number of Families (000s)	Percent of Families	Number of Families (000s)	Percent of Families
Under $5	0.6	0.9%	−0.9	−0.4%	−1.1	−39.3%	−1.7	−85.0%
5-10	−7.8	−3.8	−6.0	−16.9	−8.2	−31.5	−6.0	−29.1
10-15	−32.2	−7.2	−31.8	−17.4	−9.8	−22.7	−6.3	−13.0
15-20	−20.2	−2.4	−16.6	−4.0	−7.0	−7.9	−3.0	−3.2
20-30	−165.2	−9.7	−218.5	−18.7	−5.6	−2.7	0.2	0.1
30-50	−78.6	−3.0	−139.4	−5.9	0.3	0.1	1.0	0.3
50-100	6.3	0.3	−9.9	−0.4	0.0	0.0	5.2	2.2
100-200	8.0	1.6	−0.2	0.0	0.0	0.0	0.0	0.0
Over 200	0.2	0.2	0.0	0.0	0.0	0.0	0.1	1.0
Total	−289.1	−3.2%	−423.3	−5.9%	−31.1	−3.1%	−10.6	−1.1%

	Nebraska				Oklahoma			
	Federal Income Tax		State Income Tax		Federal Income Tax		State Income Tax	
Income Class (000s)	Number of Families (000s)	Percent of Families	Number of Families (000s)	Percent of Families	Number of Families (000s)	Percent of Families	Number of Families (000s)	Percent of Families
Under $5	0.2	4.3%	0.3	+6.4%	0.6	9.7%	−0.3	−4.8%
5-10	−0.2	−3.1	−5.3	−46.1	−1.8	−7.2	−6.6	−22.2
10-15	−4.2	−11.3	−6.4	−16.2	−7.5	−9.1	−12.1	−13.5
15-20	−1.9	−4.4	−3.3	−7.4	−7.6	−8.2	−3.2	−3.6
20-30	−0.7	−0.9	−2.9	−3.3	2.8	1.4	4.1	2.1
30-50	+6.1	+3.3	+2.9	+1.6	2.8	1.2	3.2	1.1
50-100	0.2	0.2	0.0	0.0	0.9	0.6	1.7	1.2
100-200	0.1	0.7	0.1	0.7	0.2	1.1	0.6	3.3
Over 200	0.0	0.0	0.0	0.0	0.1	1.3	0.9	13.4
Total	−0.4	−0.1%	−14.7	−3.0%	−9.6	−1.1%	−11.7	−1.4%

	Virginia			
	Federal Income Tax		State Income Tax	
Income Class (000s)	Number of Families (000s)	Percent of Families	Number of Families (000s)	Percent of Families
Under $5	−1.7	−7.1%	−6.2	−25.1%
5-10	−7.8	−13.5	−26.5	−36.0
10-15	−18.7	−13.1	−13.4	−9.2
15-20	−23.4	−23.4	−13.1	−10.6
20-30	−8.8	−2.5	−1.6	−0.5
30-50	−2.4	−0.1	−2.3	−0.5
50-100	−0.7	−0.2	0.2	0.0
100-200	0.0	0.0	0.0	0.0
Over 200	0.0	0.0	0.1	1.0
Total	−63.7	−3.5%	−60.3	−3.4%

change its tax schedule, a smaller number of families after tax reform had higher state tax liabilities than federal tax liabilities. Thus, the states examined here did an even better job than the federal government in reducing taxes for lower-income taxpayers. After tax reform, there are fewer anomalous cases of taxpayers who pay higher taxes to their state governments than they pay to the federal government.

Table 6.

Number of Families with State Taxes Greater Than
Federal Taxes Before the Earned Income Credit

Income Class (000s)	California		Colorado		Nebraska		Oklahoma		Virginia	
	Pre-Reform (000s)	Post-Reform (000s)	Pre-Reform (000s)	Post-Reform (000s)	Pre-Reform (000s)	Post-Reform (000s)	Pre-Reform (000s)	Post-Reform (000s)	Pre-Reform (000s)	Post-Reform (000s)
Under $5	9.1	6.9	1.0	0.0	0.0	0.1	3.0	3.8	4.0	0.2
5-10	3.6	0.7	1.8	0.0	0.0	0.1	28.4	28.6	23.8	9.5
10-15	0.5	0.3	2.4	0.0	0.6	1.9	24.3	36.0	17.3	14.6
15-20	2.3	1.2	3.0	0.0	2.7	2.5	9.4	16.0	5.8	10.2
20-30	5.8	5.2	7.8	0.3	4.0	0.4	5.1	8.5	4.3	4.9
30-50	21.6	7.3	3.5	0.0	4.2	1.2	1.2	0.3	1.0	0.2
50-100	9.4	2.6	0.8	0.0	0.3	0.0	0.2	0.4	1.8	1.6
100-200	1.2	1.0	0.1	0.0	0.0	0.0	0.0	0.0	0.0	0.0
Over 200	0.3	0.2	0.0	0.0	0.0	0.0	0.0	0.0	0.0	0.0
Total	54.0	25.7	20.4	0.3	11.9	6.2	71.6	93.7	57.9	41.3

VI. Conclusion

This chapter's primary message is that computer-based micro-simulation tax models can be extremely useful tools in analyzing federal and state tax policies. We have used these tools to examine the federal and selected state individual income tax systems before and after tax reform. Three dimensions of each income tax system have been examined: the progressivity of each system, the revenue responsiveness to real economic growth, and the treatment of low-income taxpayers.

Our findings are that each of the tax systems examined became more progressive after tax reform but also less productive of revenue with respect to real economic growth. At the same time, thousands of federal and state taxpayers have been removed from the tax rolls and, with the exception of one state, fewer taxpayers pay higher income taxes to the state than to the federal government.

Notes

1. See U.S. Advisory Commission on Intergovernmental Relations, "The Tax Reform Act of 1986: Its Effect on Federal and State Personal

Income Tax Liabilities," Staff Information Report CSR-81, January 1988. The analysis and tabulations in this report were prepared by the Policy Economics Group of Peat Marwick Main & Co.

2. See Daniel B. Suits, "Measurement of Tax Progressivity," *American Economic Review* 67 (September 1977): 742-752.

3. For a detailed discussion of the response of states to the federal tax windfall, see Steven D. Gold, *The Budding Revolution in State Income Taxes* (Denver: National Conference of State Legislatures, 1987); and Steven D. Gold, Corina L. Eckl, and Brenda M. Erickson, *State Budget Actions in 1987* (Denver: National Conference of State Legislatures, 1987).

The Florida Sales Tax on Services: What Really Went Wrong?

by
James Francis

Taxation of service transactions by the states is widespread on a selective basis and inevitably will become more general.[1] As states and localities face mounting fiscal pressures, the inequity and economic distortion inherent in exempting the majority of service transactions while taxing most goods transactions will become increasingly unacceptable.[2]

Those interests that resist the taxation of service transactions have cited and likely will continue to cite Florida's experience in attempting to convince state legislatures to take minimal or naive approaches in expanding their sales tax bases. Only by mis-characterizing the events that shaped Florida's experience can such cases be made.

While reasonable people may differ as to the wisdom or efficacy of various technical provisions of Florida's legislation, the concept and execution of the tax were basically sound. Of the three key mistakes that led to the downfall of the tax, none had to do with the working of the tax itself. This chapter discusses the conceptual basis of the tax, refutes erroneous criticisms levied against it, and describes accurately the factors leading to its repeal.

Controversy #1: The Legislative Process

The initial enactment leading to the taxation of services was a prospective repeal of numerous sales tax exemptions, including the long-standing exemption for "professional, insurance, or personal service transactions." Passed in 1986 to take effect in 1987, it was characterized as a sunset bill in the same fashion as a host of earlier bills providing for prospective deregulation of various professions.[3] The legislation (Chapter 86-166, Laws of Florida) admittedly was bare bones as it related to services. It lacked conforming amendments to existing sections of law, it provided no resale exemption (that is, no tax-free "wholesale" sales of services among businesses), and it contained no exceptions—*all* service transactions occurring in Florida would have become taxable July 1, 1987, absent further legislation.

This legislation encountered surprisingly little political resistance, considering its scope, primarily for three reasons. First, the notion of closing sales tax loopholes had been popularized by the senate leadership for the preceding two years.[4] Second, evidence from a variety of sources indicated that the tremendous inflow of new residents was creating unprecedented levels of demand for governmental services and social infrastructure.[5] Third, the sunset approach had the effect of disarming opponents of the legislation. No lobbyists' client was affected, at least directly; prior sunset legislation rarely had resulted in consequential change;[6] and all previously untaxed special interests were in the tank together. As a result, each legislator with a special interest constituency was able to resist its pressure for exclusion from the sunset bill. After all, how could he make their case for exclusion to his peers, when they too were accountable to certain groups whose exempt status was subject to sunset?

Although not generally recognized at the time, the sunset mechanism was a procedural coup. Not only did it facilitate initial passage in 1986, but it also prevented wholesale reduction of the forthcoming tax base in 1987. Once the sunset legislation was enacted, those interests seeking continued exemption needed the concurrence of the house, the senate, and the governor, since any one of the three could fail to pass or threaten to veto legislation reinstating their exemption. Normally, an exempt group maintains its status by stopping a tax bill with the concurrence of only one house or the governor.

Because interest groups long accustomed to success in Tallahassee found their political leverage suddenly reduced, charges of railroading and excessive haste were levied against the 1987 legislature. In fact, the final implementing legislation was preceded by more study and critical evaluation than any other tax bill in Florida's history.[7] Two independent examinations were commissioned by the legislature in 1986. The first was a study of the legal, administrative, and revenue implications of the tax, spearheaded by the Department of Revenue. This effort included the drafting of model legislation for which the department used the services of Professor Walter Hellerstein, a nationally recognized scholar in tax law.[8] The second involved examination of the economic impact of service taxation by a special 21-person study commission with membership from the public and private sectors.[9] Of at least equal importance was the work of the House Finance and Taxation Committee chairman and his professional tax staff. Many hours were spent in meetings with the revenue department and representatives of each affected service industry group in an attempt to tailor the implementing legislation to each of their special problems and situations.

Moreover, opponents of the legislation had a full year to make their views or suggestions known. The failure of some affected parties to actively consider the consequences or mechanics of the tax until the eleventh hour hardly can be considered a legislative failure.

A number of parties, including the Department of Revenue, suggested that the 1987 legislature push the effective date of the broadened tax back to allow for more education and response time for rank-and-file taxpayers not privy to the legislative process. For budgetary reasons, the legislature held to the July 1, 1987, start-up date adopted a year earlier. But in recognition of the need for early taxpayer notification, registration, and agency rule promulgation, the legislature passed its detailed implementing legislation (Chapter 87-6, Laws of Florida) on April 23, 1987, an unprecedented early date for major legislation in a session running from early April to early June.[10] For the same reasons, the Department of Revenue began drafting its rules in December 1986.

Undoubtedly, more time between passage of the implementing bill and start up of the tax would have lessened apprehension among newly registered sales tax dealers, at least to a degree. As an element contributing to the demise of the tax, however, this shortcoming was only of marginal importance.

Controversy #2: Scope of the Tax

A second area of criticism relates to the scope of the tax. By flatly closing a single exemption for services, the sunset bill could have reached some $85 billion in previously untaxed transactions for a revenue yield of $4.2 billion in fiscal year 1988-89.[11] Despite posturing threats to let the sunset bill take effect unaltered, the legislature displayed a strong and active interest in paring down the list of impacted services. The final legislation resulted in only 33.4 percent of previously exempt service transactions being taxed.[12] And even if one assumes that money lending, insurance underwriting, and licensing of patented materials or processes are not services, an arguable proposition at best, the legislature still taxed less than half of the potential new service tax base (45 percent).[13] By comparison, taxed goods transactions represent 68.4 percent of the potential goods tax base, half again greater than the proportion of taxed services.

The real basis of complaint concerning the scope of the tax again rests on procedure. Antitax forces would have preferred an additive process requiring the legislature to vote to tax each activity on an individual basis. By casting a broad net and then discarding unwanted items, the legislature put itself in the advantageous role of primarily giving rather than taking away. As noted earlier, attacking each service industry separately via the build-up approach would have been far more difficult, particularly with respect to the professions.

Furthermore, broad imposition language followed by specific exemptions helps prevent unanticipated fiscal surprises from the judiciary, which, as a matter of interpretation, construes tax imposition narrowly. This approach also keeps the statute from becoming obsolete technologically or terminologically, as has been the case with many states' telecommunication taxes.

A necessary evil of this approach is that no matter how much research is done, certain transactions may be taxed that were never fully anticipated. In Florida, for example, private music teacher services were found to be taxable; the resulting political noise factor generally was considered to drown out the benefits from the revenue.

Nonetheless, music teachers and their brethren did not bring the tax down. Quick enactment of remedial exemptions is a certain cure for such problems. Far more difficulty would have been encountered if, for example, the law had specified that "data processing services" were taxable but the courts found "charges for time sharing of computers" to be beyond the scope of the tax. A court could reason that time sharing is different because it involves the payer renting property upon which he processes his own data. Remedial fixes to broaden the tax base generally are hard to enact and are particularly difficult after contentious initial enactments. And, most important, if a build-up approach is taken, what is the likelihood of a legislative body deciding separately to tax legal services, then to tax accounting services, and so forth? Failure to take a broad approach initially maximizes the difficulty a legislature will face in taxing professional services ultimately.

There is no legitimate economic reason for service transactions to be broadly excluded from a sales tax base.[14] To effectively build support of the tax, legislators must capitalize on the inherent unfairness of a tax system that discourages the consumption of manufactured goods and encourages consumption of services. Similarly, the most favorable change that inclusion of services can create in the overall incidence or economic burden of a sales tax will occur only with the inclusion of professional services in the tax base. Neither of these arguments can be advanced if only a handful of services are added to the tax base. Apart from political timidity, there is little to justify the taxation of barber and pest control services today while paying only lip service to the possibility of taxing legal and accounting services in some future year.

Nonetheless, if a stepwise approach appears most prudent, the above considerations suggest that the initial legislation define the tax base to include all services and at the same time provide exemptions with self-contained repeal dates for each block of services to be taxed in future years. When budgets for those upcoming years are prepared, they should anticipate revenues from the services scheduled for taxation in that year. This will serve to clarify costs and benefits for future legislatures.

Controversy #3: Pyramiding

A third criticism asserts that the resale or antipyramiding provisions of the Florida law were too narrow. What distinguishes a sales tax from a transactional gross receipts tax is that the former is limited to final sales whereas the latter applies to all sales. Exemptions for items purchased for resale effectuate the difference. Pyramiding occurs under the gross receipts approach to the extent that the object of taxation passes through various intermediate levels of commerce before final sale. Under a "pure" sales tax, the object of taxation is taxed only once at the final sale.

Conceptually, there are few disagreements on these points. Controversy arises, however, with respect to the desired level of purity in a sales tax and the definition of "final sale." The controversy is essentially no different whether goods or services are being taxed. From a strict economic perspective, a pure sales tax would never apply to a service or goods purchased by a business, since businesses are not final economic consumers. Only household purchases would be subject to tax.

Whatever the merits of such taxation, *no* state has chosen to levy a pure sales tax. All state sales taxes apply at least to some purchases by businesses. In testimony to the Sales Tax Exemption Study Commission, Professor Walter Hellerstein observed that conversion to pure sales taxation could so narrow tax bases as to result in intolerable rates.[15] It also should be noted that to the degree the incidence of the tax on business purchases falls on owners of capital, the regressivity of the tax generally is reduced. In Florida, approximately 25 percent of the old (pre-services) sales tax resulted from business purchases.

Rather than taxing selected business transactions arbitrarily as is done in some states, Florida's preservices resale policy was internally consistent and was based on a narrow definition of final sale. A business generally was considered to be a final consumer, so its purchase was taxable, if the item it purchased was not the object of consumption of some subsequent customer. Therefore, in contrast to a pure sales tax, the purchase of office furniture, computers and machines for business use, office supplies, productive machinery and equipment, electricity, business phone services, and office space rentals by businesses all were (and continue to be) subject to the sales tax in Florida.[16]

It is ironic that the considerable legislative attention devoted to the resale issue never centered on whether a "pure" sales tax would be applied to services or whether the prior-existing definition of final sale should be narrowed or broadened. Instead, the debate focused on which of two alternative sets of statutory criteria defining the resale of a service was most consistent with the *existing* resale policy for goods and which was most administrable.[17]

The narrower of the two ultimately was enacted into law.[18] The broader of the two was hailed by revisionists within the legislature and by most lobbyists as the remedy for complaints of excessive pyramiding.[19]

Policymakers in other states should be keenly aware that the pyramiding controversy in Florida was not over whether business purchases should ever be taxable. Generally, it was accepted throughout the deliberations that the tax would apply when the purchase of a service by a business was not made on behalf of a specific customer. The real dispute involved the mechanistic problem of defining those facts that distinguished services purchased for internal consumption by a business from those purchased primarily on behalf of the business' customers.[20]

Much of the appeal of extending sales taxes to service transactions lies in equalizing the burden of taxation between the goods and services sectors of the economy. To accomplish this, a state must address three fundamental concerns regarding sales for resale.

First, the philosophical basis or principle underlying a state's resale exemption for goods must be enunciated clearly and applied uniformly. Second, this principle must be adapted to service transactions. Third, a set of statutory or regulatory criteria must be formulated to allow sales tax dealers clearly to apply the resale principle in practice.

In Florida, tangible personal property (goods) can be purchased tax free for resale only if they themselves are resold or if they are incorporated physically into another item of tangible personal property to be resold.[21] Goods purchased by a business and necessary for its operation, irrespective of whether they are consumed in the process of producing other goods, are taxable, notwithstanding the "impurity" this adds to the economic notion of final consumption.

In attempting to draw as close a parallel to the goods criteria as possible, Florida's new tax legislation provided that services purchased on behalf of a business for a third party were exempt as purchases for resale, but those services consumed by a business, even though necessary in order to provide another service to its customers, were taxable.

As a result, court reporter services to a law firm were taxable, even though purchased by the firm in connection with the rendering of legal services to a client, just as the purchase of a published report or word processing equipment by the firm would be taxable. Conversely, a service station doing repair work on an automobile could farm out the recapping of a tire to a third party and purchase that service tax free for resale. This is because the garage did not consume the services of the recapper in the course of performing its own repairs; it parallels the tax-free purchase a repair shop could make of a new tire for resale to its customers.

What governed the applicability of the resale exemption was whether the item purportedly purchased for resale is the object of consumption by the final purchaser. In the garage example, this is clearly the case. However, a law firm client generally is seeking the best legal advice or representation the firm can render. He is unconcerned whether the firm needs court reporter transcripts, photocopies, law books, or dictating equipment in the course of its operations.[22]

The third concern is perhaps the most important because it controls how effectively the chosen policy is carried out in practice. Unlike an income tax where there is direct interaction between the tax administration agency and the taxpayer, sales tax administration relies on intermediaries to deal with taxpayers. These middlemen—sales tax dealers—are not tax experts and have little interest in subtle nuances or philosophical bases of tax law. Therefore, to be applied effectively and unambiguously, sales tax rules must be structured as a series of black and white litmus tests.

Because over 70 percent of the gross sales of services taxed in Florida were purchased by businesses, there was keen fiscal interest in proper application of the resale principle. Florida's solution was five straightforward statutory criteria that a service transaction must have met to qualify for the resale exemption.[23] The criteria keyed primarily upon specific facts of the transaction and provided a paper trail for audit purposes.

Due to the temporal nature of services, the lack of a parallel to the physical trail from manufacturer to final consumer that exists with goods, and the substantial revenue differences associated with various applications of the resale provisions, states should exercise considerable caution in this area with emphasis on the practical application of whatever resale philosophy is adopted.

Controversy #4: The Use Tax on Services

Beyond Florida's border, the most heavily criticized and most misrepresented provisions of the law involved its jurisdictional reach. Often repeated was the example of the Chicago office of a multistate business contracting for legal services from a New York law firm, with Florida having the audacity to tax the transaction. What often went unstated was the fact that a Florida tax would have applied *only if and to the degree* that the service was used or consumed in Florida. The underlying principle derives directly from the use tax on goods imposed by virtually all sales tax states.

If that same Chicago office of the same multistate business contracted for the purchase of a computer from a New York supplier, there would be a Florida tax on the transaction if the computer was delivered and used in Florida, and only the most ardent of antitax protesters would complain.

Use taxes, and exemptions or credits for out-of-state sales,[24] are long-standing features of most states' sales tax codes and are essential to the "level playing field" so often emphasized by economic development advocates. A level playing field exists only if the tax obligation faced by the purchaser in a given transaction is the same, irrespective of the location of the seller.

If a state imposes its sales tax only on those purchases its citizens make from in-state suppliers (that is, if it levies only a sales tax), those citizens have a financial incentive to buy from out-of-state suppliers or out-of-state offices of multistate suppliers. To avoid a tax-induced competitive disadvantage for local businesses and to close a tax avoidance opportunity involving multistate sellers, states impose use taxes to complement their sales taxes. A use tax applies when a sale occurs out of the levying state's jurisdiction, but use or consumption occurs within the state.[25]

Similar economic distortions occur if a state insists on taxing sales that occur within its jurisdiction when the purchaser is out of state (that is, when the item is used or consumed in another jurisdiction). A business located wholly within the taxing state will lose out-of-state sales since its foreign customers can avoid the tax by switching to a supplier in another state.[26] To the extent its out-of-state clientele is substantial, a business in this situation has an incentive to relocate. Multistate businesses serving out-of-state clients simply will begin serving those clients from one of their own out-of-state offices.

These economic realities are likely to be more prominent with respect to services than to goods. Service providers typically are more footloose than purveyors of goods since the former require less investment in physical plant space and inventory. Interstate service transactions are cost-effective because product delivery incurs minimal or no transportation costs. A telephone wire or an envelope can easily accommodate the tangible output of an accountant, stockbroker, lawyer, engineer, data processor, consultant, and so on. Many service businesses could migrate out of state yet continue effectively to service the same clientele.

As a result, one of the most durable tenets held by Florida policymakers was the necessity of effective provisions to tax all in-state consumption, irrespective of point of sale or performance, and exempt all out-of-state consumption, even if the service was performed and sold in Florida. Any other approach inevitably would harm the competitive position of in-state businesses.

The goods tax already worked in this fashion. The question was how to structure the service tax for the same result.

The situs rule that most states have for establishing the location of use or consumption with respect to interstate goods transactions is simple and long-standing: the point to which the seller or his agent delivers the product. While a purchaser could manipulate his tax obligation by taking delivery in one state but then actually using the product in another, at least three factors mitigate against this: increased handling and transportation costs that would offset the tax advantage; the existence of special tax rules relating to the duration of presence of the goods; and the likelihood of simply trading one state's tax for another's.

For services, physical delivery is an unworkable standard for several reasons. There may be no physical item to deliver, except for electrons traveling on a telephone wire. Where there is a physical item, such as a document, letter, blueprint, tax return, or legal brief, its size and intrinsic value are likely to be negligible relative to the value of the service. Transportation costs would not hinder efforts to manipulate delivery to avoid taxes. Rules as to duration of presence would be similarly ineffective thanks to copy machines and the lack of inventory records or purchase ledgers for services. And any of 49 other states likely would provide a tax-free haven for initial delivery, at least in the short run.

The unique nature of service transactions required that new rules be developed. In the final legislation, situs for use or consumption of services was established via two general and three special sets of rebuttable presumptions.[27] All were formulated to balance the competing goals of simplicity in application with accuracy of result.

The general rules for business purchasers defined consumption to occur in the state in which realty, tangible personal property, or a local market of the purchaser was located, if the service directly related thereto. As a result, consumption of landscaping, janitorial, or construction services was attributed to the site of the affected realty; equipment maintenance services were attributed to the site of the machinery;[28] and a consulting report on how to penetrate a specific existing market area better was attributed to the state in which the market existed.

If the service did not relate directly to a specific location, but instead related to the purchaser's business in general, consumption was defined to occur in the state in which the purchaser was doing business. For single-state businesses, the result is obvious.

For multistate businesses, the law borrowed a well-established income tax principle: formulary apportionment. Because of the inherent ambiguity and subjectiveness of dividing profits among the various individual activities of an integrated multistate business, taxpayers, tax administrators, and the courts all have come to accept the use of a relatively standardized, straightforward formula for the geographic assignment of profits. The formula is an average of three ratios: in-state sales to total sales, in-state property to total property, and in-state payroll to total payroll. These three factors have been found to reasonably represent the major business activities or sources that generate profits. Likewise, they reasonably represent business activity in general.

Thus, the presumption provided that nongeographic-specific services purchased by a multistate business were consumed in a state to the degree that its profits were attributed to the state. The tax was calculated by reducing the purchase price by the apportionment fraction and applying the tax rate.

In practice, any service of an overhead nature, such as preparation of federal tax returns, legal advice on corporate takeovers, and data processing of company payrolls, was deemed to be consumed by the business in general and therefore was apportioned across all states in which the business was present. Note that this approach applied in determining out-of-state consumption for exemption purposes as well.

For those taxpayers accustomed to the all-or-nothing delivery rules governing taxes on goods, this was a startling change. Although many reacted negatively to apportionment principles being incorporated into a sales tax, few offered realistic alternatives. Agreement was widespread that more presumptions should be enacted relating consumption to specific geographic sites. When pressed, however, no one was able to provide specific suggestions, other than for certain types of legal services.

Some corporations with headquarters out of state suggested that the apportionment rule be dropped and consumption of all overhead (nonsite-specific) services be attributed to the corporation's state of domicile. Needless to say, this suggestion was unpopular with businesses domiciled in Florida as well as with legislators interested in attracting corporate headquarters to the state. If a wider array of states taxed services, this suggestion may have been more popular. In the short run, however, it would have insured that all wholly Florida businesses paid tax on all of their service purchases, while most multistate businesses operating in Florida paid tax on very few of theirs, a politically unacceptable and economically questionable outcome.

For individual (nonbusiness) purchasers, the situs rules were different, recognizing the lessened likelihood of manipulation of point of delivery and the difficulty of use tax enforcement where no written records are kept. In this case, a service was presumed to be used or consumed in a state if it related directly to realty located there, or if it was represented by tangible personal property (e.g., accounting reports, legal documents, and so on) delivered into that state.

If no tangible personal property embodied the result of the service, then consumption was assigned to the location at which the greatest proportion of the cost of providing the service was incurred. A haircut, for example, would be ascribed to the state in which it was rendered, whether or not the recipient was a transient who "used" it mostly in another state.

Three sets of specialized rules governed selected situations: services provided to estates of decedents were presumed to be consumed in the last state where their residency was established; transportation services were presumed to be consumed 50 percent in the state of origin and 50 percent in the state of destination;

and advertising services were presumed to be consumed in a state in proportion to the audience in that state, measured by various readily available proxies.[29]

While some legitimate disputes occurred over the application of these provisions, most of the arguments surrounding them were really arguments against the tax itself. The reaction of the advertising industry, as discussed shortly, is a case in point.

The real bone of contention for multistate businesses was not the theory of the use tax but the cost of compliance.

To comply with the use tax requirements, a multistate business was required to identify those of its service purchases that were subject to apportionment and those subject to allocation (site specific to Florida). Use tax was self-accrued by the purchaser on those amounts. All argued that their accounting systems were not coded to extract total service purchases, much less categorize them as apportionable or allocable. Accounting system software would have to be changed and clerks trained to classify service purchase invoices properly.[30]

By rule, the Department of Revenue provided multistate businesses with the option of treating all service purchases as apportionable, substantially reducing the training needed for clerks. This option met with general disdain since the businesses then complained they would not be in a position to exclude service transactions eligible for various exemptions.

The cost of proper accounting, it was argued, would be substantial compared with the revenue generated, particularly if multistate purchasers were allowed to pay the tax directly to Florida vendors and self-accrue taxes only on purchases from out-of-state vendors. Their solution — at first implied and later expressed — was to require payment to Florida service vendors and essentially ignore purchases from out-of-state vendors.

If ignoring a problem constitutes a solution, this approach by all means qualifies. It begs the question of how to maintain a level playing field, because it presupposes that multistate purchasers will not shift to out-of-state suppliers of services, even though such a move would cut costs by 5 percent (or by whatever tax rate was in effect).

While it is reasonable to expect that businesses initially would maintain their existing sources of supply, observed behavior of multistate businesses with respect to other taxes strongly suggests that when cost-effective tax avoidance opportunities exist, they eventually will be taken.

The compliance cost argument has a short-term bias as well. As more states move to tax services, the ratio of costs to revenue will shift. In discussing the possibility of a sales tax on services in California, Gary Jugum, assistant chief counsel for the California State Board of Equalization, recently stated, "If you are interested in the technical aspects and applications of the 'new' California tax on service transactions, you should pay close attention to the events now occurring in Florida."[31]

Whether or not Florida's approach becomes the model for taxing services, someday, probably in the not-too-distant future, some state will tax services comprehensively. And sooner or later that state will come to grips with the use tax issue. The cost argument will be raised, but as other states follow the lead, such concerns will fade into history. How many legislators today are persuaded by arguments that the extra costs faced by multistate corporations in complying with state corporate income tax codes are prohibitive?

The use tax issue figured prominently in the national debate on Florida's service tax. In Florida, however, it was primarily the domain of technicians. Political leaders held firm to the level playing field notion and directed the technicians to minimize difficulties with the use tax without sacrificing its fundamental purpose.[32]

How, then, did this affect the mortality of the tax? Certainly, some multistate corporations took strong exception to what Florida did. Some went so far as to threaten to finance a citizen initiative drive to prohibit constitutionally the taxation of service transactions.[33] Others with large advertising budgets exerted pressure on the media to arouse public opinion against the tax. Many, however, expressed a willingness to work on various legislative or regulatory changes to overcome the difficulties they were experiencing with compliance.

In the final analysis, it appears unlikely that opposition to the tax by multistate corporations per se was a critical element in the downfall of the tax. The debate on the tax was not focused in the halls of the state house, where such firms are typically so effective. Instead, it raged in the popular consciousness and received inordinate media coverage. In such a form, politicians normally can overcome the resistance of outside special interests by appealing to the populist instincts of the electorate. When an issue is framed as pitting large out-of-state corporations against the interests of the average citizen and home state firms, it is not difficult to predict which way rank-and-file legislators will lean.

Unfortunately for proponents of the tax, events played out differently in Florida.

Controversy #5: Who Shot the Service Tax?

The tax on services, praised barely six months earlier by politicians of both parties as the key to Florida's future, was repealed in December 1987, in the third of three special tax sessions. The repeal bill, which only in the eleventh hour was amended to replace a portion of the revenues via a higher general sales tax rate, represented the culmination of a bizarre roller coaster of events (see chronology in the appendix following this chapter).

Certainly, the controversies discussed in this chapter did nothing to enhance the tax's chances. But these problems could have been redressed or ridden out, and all were of the nature one could have easily anticipated with an enactment of this type. Revision bills prepared in all three special sessions were aimed directly at solving or ameliorating these problems.[34]

Instead, the tax fell because of three logistical failures:

1) The governor's campaign rhetoric gave opponents an antitax message that was sellable to the electorate;
2) The media, aggravated by inclusion of advertising services within the tax base, were only too happy to bombard Florida's households with that message; and
3) Ill-conceived responses by leaders within both parties dissolved the coalition supporting the tax before an effective counterattack could be mounted.

During the course of the gubernatorial campaign in 1986, the mayor of the city of Tampa, now Florida's governor, characterized his opponent, a 12- year member of the Florida House, as "a man who never met a tax he didn't like."[35] The mayor's campaign theme was clearly against excessive government spending. He repeatedly vowed to "sweat $800 million of waste out of state government." Although he actually indicated support for the taxation of at least some services, it is clear that to the man on the street he was the antispend, antitax candidate. His postelection support of the service tax came as a surprise to many voters as well as to members of his own party.[36]

As with most service providers, the advertising media were not elated at the prospect of their sales becoming taxable. The industry commissioned an economic consulting firm to produce a report, heavily criticized by governmental economists,[37] which estimated a job loss of at least 46,000 and a drop in personal income of $2 billion two years after imposition of a tax on advertising.

(To reach this conclusion, one must assume that government will not spend the new revenue it collects.)

Whether it was a genuine fear of economic disaster, concern over governmental infringement on free speech,[38] pressure from big budget advertisers,[39] or fear of a domino effect across the states, the media were dead set against the "advertising tax." Repeated attempts by the Department of Revenue and the legislature to accommodate the technical problems faced by broadcasters and publishers did little to placate them. Unlike other service providers, the media were in a position to voice their objection easily and effectively.

In the same fashion that television viewers are convinced to want products they do not need and cannot afford, the advertisers effectively convinced Florida voters to oppose a tax they did need and could afford. The "public service" messages wasted little time upon the substance of the tax. Instead, they centered on the governor's support ("Billion-dollar Bob") of the "largest tax increase" in the state's history—"one which threatens to flatten Florida's economy."[40] Nowhere was there a discussion of public needs or tax alternatives. Nonetheless, the campaign was effective because it played directly upon the public's frustration with broken political promises. The governor unfairly was painted with a broad brush as one who immediately and completely broke faith with the voters. At one point, his approval rating fell below 30 percent.[41]

In the face of this pressure, either one or both of two courses of action would have been prudent: a public information campaign to counter that of the broadcasters, and/or exemption of advertising services, at least until the political situation stabilized. Neither was done because the coalition between the Republican governor and the Democratic legislative leadership disintegrated early on.

The service tax was a gift the 1986 legislature presented to the new governor (who was sworn in January 1987). He was in no way responsible for passage of the tax (sunset) legislation; he could argue for exemptions for favored industries; and he could produce a budget that realistically dealt with Florida's growth needs. He could have distanced himself from the tax by blaming it on his predecessor, taken credit for the newly enacted exemptions, and proceeded with his budget. Instead, in his first state-of-the-state address, delivered April 17, 1987, he bravely supported the tax. With respect to special interests opposing it, he said:

> For my part, every increase in pressure from those who would shirk their duty to Florida's future convinces me again that we are embarked on the right course. Under the leadership of Speaker Mills and Representative Patchett in the House and President Vogt and Senator

Jennings in the Senate [majority and minority leaders in each chamber] and the cooperation and support of all of you, I am confident we will stay the course and put this critical issue [taxation of services] behind us early in the session.

On August 22, after consulting with only two senators, and on the advice of his campaign strategist who was then serving as a co-chief of staff, the governor proposed letting the voters decide whether to retain the tax.[42] Proponents of the tax were somewhat surprised by this.

Because the hostile media campaign had led the voters to identify the tax as a symbol of political duplicity, few legislators were eager to pick up the torch. Whatever hopes the legislative leadership had of maintaining the coalition were dashed when the chairman of the state Democratic Party, with an apparent similar lack of consensus, publicly announced that Democrats would use the service tax issue against Republicans in the next election.[43]

With this, the fate of the service tax was sealed. While there were minor glimmers of hope, such as when the governor announced he might not continue to press for repeal after the second special tax session ended in deadlock, efforts to save the tax were too fragmented and ill planned.

The house speaker and senate president held public hearings around the state in an attempt to popularize the tax, but press coverage emphasized testimony of tax opponents. The chairman of the House Finance and Tax Committee worked hard on modified versions of the service tax, but his efforts seemed largely unilateral. When the legislature finally passed a referendum bill, the governor vetoed it, having moved on to demanding outright repeal. When it was proposed that advertising services be exempted, tax proponents seethed they would rather lose the tax than give in to media "blackmail." One special tax session ended after the House Finance and Tax Committee found it did not have a majority for any of three proposals: repeal, referendum, or revision.

Post Mortem

The Florida service tax was a classic case of snatching defeat from the jaws of victory.

Had the governor not campaigned so heartily against government spending, the media's antitax message would have been more obviously self-serving.

Had the governor not so boldly embraced the tax, proponents would have taken a more active role in selling it to the electorate and not been caught so off guard when he backed away.

Had advertising services been exempted, tax opponents would have been unable to saturate the airwaves.

Had initial political reaction to these problems been better thought out, the protax coalition might have mounted an effective salvage operation.

This chapter contains three fundamental messages for legislators in other states: 1) the piecemeal approach to service taxation is not the appropriate method because then the politically toughest but most important measures will likely never be taken; 2) a method must be found to make the self-serving, antitax posture of the media obvious for what it is. (One approach would be to tax advertising sales in a separate bill, after a general service tax has been implemented and accepted by the public;[44] another would be to tax advertising in a different—yet constitutional—manner, such as by denying the deductibility of advertising and promotional expenses for income tax purposes[45]); and 3) it must be recognized from the outset that the protax coalition must proceed on a consensus basis both before and after enactment.

Florida's legislation did not mark the end of service taxation, nor was it a nonproductive exercise. Given the valuable lessons it provided, Florida's experience may be characterized best as the end of the beginning of service taxation.

Notes

1. For example, in 1984, it was reported that 16 states taxed car washing, 33 taxed tire recapping, 27 taxed linen and towel supply services, 14 taxed dry cleaning, 17 taxed cable TV services, 33 taxed room rentals, 28 taxed telephone services, and 10 taxed house painting services. Source: *Survey of Sales and Use Taxation in the United States* (Pierre, S.Dak.: Business Research Bureau, The University of South Dakota, 1984). See also John Mikesell, "General Sales Tax," in Steven D. Gold, ed., *Reforming State Tax Systems* (Denver: National Conference of State Legislatures, 1986), pp. 217-221.

2. For an interesting account of the nature of the service sector in the United States and its domination of today's economy, see "Understanding a New Economy," *The Wall Street Journal*, December 23, 1986.

3. In 1976, the Florida Legislature created S.11.61, Florida Statutes, providing for periodic review via sunset of each "profession, occupation, business, industry, or other endeavor" subject to regulation. Since 1978, a once-every-10-year cycle has been in effect for such reviews.

4. These efforts occurred under the leadership of Senator Harry Johnston. Ironically, the house—generally known for creative work in this area—was at first reluctant to consider such legislation under the conservative leadership of Representative James Harold Thompson.

5. During this period, ongoing study by the State Comprehensive Plan Committee eventually concluded that the state had a $52.9 billion backlog of infrastructure needs directly attributable to population growth.

6. Since 1976, only two sunset bills (truck transportation and psychology) actually had eliminated statutory regulation. The psychology profession was reregulated a year later.

7. Only two tax bills in modern Florida history were comparable in scope with the service legislation: creation of the sales tax in 1949 and creation of the corporate income tax in 1971. There is nothing in the historical record for either to indicate research or evaluation approaching that given the service tax, although considerable care went into the drafting of the corporate tax bill.

In a letter dated September 9, 1987, to a member of the Department of Revenue, Professor Oliver Oldman, Learned Hand professor of law at Harvard University stated, "I have now gone through all of that material [from the Department of Revenue] to realize what an enormous effort you and your associates made in getting ready for this important new law....I will be showing the Blue Book [the department's report to the legislature—see note 8] to my students as an example of what a state ought to do whenever it produces important new tax legislation."

8. Florida Department of Revenue, *Report to the Legislature—Legal, Administrative and Revenue Implications of Chapter 86-166, Laws of Florida: Repeal of Sales Tax Exemptions for Services and Selected Transactions* (Tallahassee, Fla.: March 1987).

9. Sales Tax Exemption Study Commission, *Report and Recommendations of the Sales Tax Exemption Study Commission* (Tallahassee, Fla.: April 1987).

10. A second bill (Chapter 87-101, Laws of Florida), commonly known as the Glitch Bill, was passed on June 6, 1987. The bill originally was intended to provide minor technical corrections. As passed, it also contained a number of new exemptions and an industry-favored rewrite of the provisions applicable to construction services.

11. From the onset, controversy existed over the legal reach of the sunset legislation. The numbers in the text are based on inclusion of all services except pure labor, the interpretation given the bill by the Department of Revenue. If, however, the service tax also had functioned as a payroll tax (i.e., had reached labor services), its yield would have exceeded $7.6 billion in fiscal year 1988-89.

12. Considering labor services as a potentially taxable item, the taxed percentage would be 18.6 percent.

13. Two competing views existed as to the nature of transactions. The first held that all transactions fall into three categories: 1) purchase or use of property, 2) the purchase of services, and 3) the purchase of rights or intangibles. The second saw only two essential distinctions: 1) the purchase of property, either real, tangible personal, or intangible; and 2) the use of property, with the same three property types.

Under the second scheme, all uses of property are considered services since no permanent ownership rights are conveyed in the transaction. This latter system derives from the economic notion of capital—the embodied result of investment—and the benefits that accrue from ownership and/or control of capital. Capital can take the form of material capital (such as realty or tangible personal property), human capital (skills of persons, either intellectual or physical), or financial capital (money or stored purchasing power).

A transaction that gives the purchaser permanent control over capital and its attendant benefits is clearly different from one that vests only temporary control or benefit. The first classification scheme is flawed because use of property (e.g., rental of an automobile) is not distinguished from ownership and because no clear distinction exists between property use and services. The second classification more properly provides that temporarily purchasing the benefits of capital is a service, irrespective of the form of the capital. Therefore, renting an automobile, employing the skills of a lawyer, and borrowing money for a fee (interest) all are service purchases because they bequeath upon the buyer the benefits of capital for a limited time without providing permanent control.

The point for legislators is that when considering broadening sales tax bases to generally tax services, in parallel with the general taxation of goods, there is no a priori reason to exclude interest paid for the use of money. (Of course, social policy considerations may dictate certain exclusions, such as interest on home mortgages, student loans, and so forth.)

14. See, for example, Jerome R. Hellerstein, Significant Sales and Use Tax Developments During the Past Half Century," *Vanderbilt Law Review* 39 (1986): 962-972.

15. Remarks presented December 17, 1986. Tape recording on file with Florida Department of Revenue, Carlton Building, Tallahassee, Florida.

16. An exception exists whereby packaging materials used one time are exempt.

17. The enacted criteria provided that "a sale of a service shall be considered a sale for resale only if:

> 1) The purchaser of the service does not use or consume the service but acts as a broker or intermediary in procuring a service for his client or customer;
> 2) The purchaser of the service buys the service pursuant to a written contract with the seller and such contract identifies the client or customer for whom the purchaser is buying the service;
> 3) The purchaser of the service separately states the value of the service purchased at the purchase price in his charge for the service on its subsequent sale;
> 4) The service, with its value separately stated, will be taxed under this part in a subsequent sale, unless otherwise exempt pursuant to Section 212.0592(1); and
> 5) The service is purchased pursuant to a service resale permit by a dealer who is primarily engaged in the business of selling services. The department shall provide by rule for the issuance and periodic renewal every five years of such resale permits" (Section 212.02(19)(a), Florida Statutes, 1987).

The proposed revised criteria were "a sale of a service shall be considered a sale for resale only if:

> 1) The service provides a direct and identifiable benefit to a single client or customer of the purchaser;
> 2) The purchaser of the service buys the service pursuant to a written contract with the seller or other written documentation which identifies, by name or other evidence sufficient for audit purposes, the client or customer for whom the purchaser is buying the service;

3) The purchaser of the service separately states the value of the service purchased in his charge for the service on its subsequent sale; and

4) The service is purchased pursuant to a service resale permit by a dealer who is primarily engaged in the business of selling services" (Section 73, CS/CS/SB 5B, 1987 and Special Session).

18. The broader resale language if tightly enforced was estimated to reduce fiscal year 1988-89 revenues by about $135 million. If all business purchases were exempted, the reduction would have approached $900 million.

19. A related concern was whether expenses incurred by a service provider when passed on to his client and separately stated on the invoice to the client would be excluded in calculating the tax due on the transaction. Some members of the legal profession were particularly vexed that such charges were included in the taxable base, even though the tax on goods never provided such an exclusion, whether or not "pass through" charges were stated separately.

20. Discussions with tax administrators in Hawaii and New Mexico also heightened the Florida Department of Revenue's interest in an unambiguous statute that would be policed via readily ascertainable factual criteria, given the ephemeral nature of services and the lack of records comparable to those used to enforce resale provisions for goods transactions.

21. The physical incorporation criterion applies to component parts of a manufactured or fabricated good. It does not include tangible personal property that is merely "used up" in the production process, irrespective of how essential such inputs are to the final output.

22. If, however, the client expressly sought transcribed copies of depositions or testimony, the service resale exemption would apply to the court reporter's fee.

23. See note 17. Also, note that the fifth criterion dealt with the purported reseller's business activities. Legislative staff strongly argued that businesses whose primary source of receipts was not from sales of services were at best incidental resellers. Eliminating them from eligibility for the resale exemption would allow for more effective enforcement with respect to the remaining firms.

24. A credit for sales or use taxes paid to another state with respect to a given transaction has the same effect as an exemption for out-of-state sales, provided that the receiving state has a tax at the same or a higher rate. The lack of taxes on services in other states led to the exemption approach in Florida's law. Legislators should note the importance of requiring tangible evidence of use in another state, lest in-state dealers indiscriminately grant the exemption.

25. The statute provided that use or consumption occurred where the benefit of a service was enjoyed (Sections 212.059(2) and 212.0592(1)(b), Florida Statutes, 1987). The terms use, consumption, and benefit generally are used interchangeably in this chapter.

26. For example, an Atlanta resident purchasing goods from a Jacksonville business would owe a Florida sales tax and a Georgia use tax, absent a credit or an exemption from the Florida tax. Shifting the purchase to a Georgia dealer would give rise only to a Georgia sales tax obligation, since the complementary nature of a use tax precludes its imposition if the same state's sales tax applies.

27. All provisions as to localizing consumption were made rebuttable to avoid due process problems and in recognition of the lack of administrative experience under these provisions.

28.   This provision did not apply to services related to tangible personal property without situs, such as vehicles involved in interstate commerce.

29.   For example, noncable radio and television advertising was apportioned based on the ratio of in-state population to total population within the signal coverage area of those broadcasters carrying the message. Signal coverage area was based on engineering maps filed with the Federal Communications Commission. See Department of Revenue emergency rule 12AER87-44, Florida Administrative Code.

30.   A factor that aggravated compliance cost concerns arose because multistate firms convinced the legislature to exempt service transactions between commonly owned and controlled corporations. In arguing that such transactions involved internal activity within what was essentially a single business, the seeds were sown for treating integrated businesses composed of multiple corporations as single entities for other purposes as well. When applied to the allocation and apportionment provisions, this meant even more clerks would require training.

31.   Gary J. Jugum, "Taxing Services" (Paper delivered at the 1987 California Tax Policy Conference: Issues in State Taxation, San Francisco, November 13, 1987), p. 149.

32.   Legislative interest in use tax enforcement was so keen that two provisions were inserted, purely by legislative initiative. The first prohibited the issuance of state, county, or municipal licenses or permits unless the applicant attested that all applicable use taxes had been or would be paid (s. 212.059(6), Florida Statutes, 1987). The second required the use tax to be collected from a Florida purchaser by the out-of-state selling office of a multistate corporation with Florida nexus if the product of the service was represented by or embodied in tangible personal property delivered into the state, as well as under two other circumstances (Section 212.059(3), Florida Statutes, 1987).

33.   A south Florida attorney had begun a fledgling petition drive under the banner "STOP" (Sales Tax Oppressing People).

34.   The most comprehensive revision was contained in Part II of Committee Substitute for Senate Bill 5B, a bill passed by both houses during the second special tax session but vetoed by the governor.

35.   Widely quoted remark made during one of three televised debates between Bob Martinez and Steve Pajcic, candidates for governor in 1986.

36.   Vicki L. Weber, "Florida's Fleeting Sales Tax on Services," *Florida State University Law Review* 15, no. 14 (Winter 1987): 618-619. See, in particular, notes 37 and 38.

37.   See, for example, "Critique of the Wharton Econometrics Study of the Impact of the Sales Tax on Advertising," Division of Economic and Demographic Research, Joint Legislative Management Committee, September 28, 1987: interoffice memorandum.

38.   In an advisory opinion on the constitutionality of the tax on services, the Florida Supreme Court found the tax to be facially constitutional as to its application to advertising services, notwithstanding First Amendment arguments to the contrary. In Re: Advisory Opinion to the Governor, Request of May 12, 1987, Supreme Court of Florida, No. 70,533, July 14, 1987.

39.   It was common knowledge that considerable pressure was exerted by out-of-state advertisers on Florida broadcasters. Even after the national advertising boycott was terminated, Florida broadcasters complained that local "spot" advertising by such firms continued to be curtailed.

40.   Television advertisement developed by the Florida Association of Broadcasters.

41. "Martinez Still Maintains Bad Public Image," *St. Petersburg Times,* November 2, 1987.

42. "Signs Point to Trouble for Martinez," *The Orlando Sentinel,* August 30, 1987.

43. Martin Dyckman, "Cheap Shots on Sales Tax Won't Serve Democrats," *St. Petersburg Times,* September 20, 1987.

44. Outright exemption of advertising services appears questionable on equity grounds unless all business services are exempted—the "pure" sales tax approach.

45. Note that this approach automatically provides for apportionment of advertising services, although it would use the ordinary corporate formula rather than the special audience-based formula contained in the Florida law.

Appendix
Chronology:
Florida Sales Tax
on Services

Excerpted from the *St. Petersburg Times, The Orlando Sentinel,* and other news sources.

June 6, 1986—Legislature passes a bill repealing more than 100 exemptions from the 5 percent sales tax, including those for personal and professional services, effective July 1, 1987. Bill calls for a Sales Tax Exemption Study Commission of 21 persons to review exemptions and recommend which should be kept.

January 29, 1987—After a two-year study, a different group, the State Comprehensive Plan Committee, says public services are falling far behind population growth. The committee, chaired by Charles J. Zwick of Southeast Bank, recommends a sales tax on services to help meet $52.9 billion in state needs over the next 10 years.

February 10—New governor, Bob Martinez, in Tampa, announces his support for the tax.

February 18—Governor proposes a budget for 1987-88 that includes money from services and proposes cutting the sales tax rate from 5 to 4.5 percent.

March 2—Department of Revenue submits to the legislature the results of its year-long study of the legal, administrative, and revenue implications of taxing services.

April 6—The Sales Tax Exemption Study Commission issues its report after four months of study and public hearings. Its recommendations would provide service tax revenues of $934.8 million and $1,454.2 million in the first two years, respectively.

April 9—The service tax survives its first serious challenge and is approved by the Senate Finance and Taxation Committee.

April 15—The senate passes service tax package, 28-12.

April 16—The house passes its version of the tax, 84-35.

April 23—Following a flurry of activity, the full legislature approves a service tax package to generate an estimated $761 million the first year and more than $1.2 billion the second. The senate approves the tax 25-15 and the house 83-31. Governor quickly signs the bill.

April 29—NBC television network announces it will pull its 1988 affiliates' convention out of Orlando because of the service tax.

May 1—The Florida Bar sues the state, claiming the new law is unconstitutional.

May 5—The Florida Association of Broadcasters announces an advertising campaign calling for repeal of the tax.

May 6—A coalition of advertising and other groups called Sales Taxes Oppressing People announces a petition drive to prohibit the tax constitutionally. Meanwhile, the Association of National Broadcasters backs down from a possible advertising boycott.

May 12—Governor asks the Florida Supreme Court for an opinion on the constitutionality of the tax.

June 18—After four public workshop hearings, the Department of Revenue issues service tax rules.

July 1—The tax goes into effect.

July 2—Two major television networks ask their Florida affiliates to black out some nationally broadcast commercials to protest the tax.

July 14—The Florida Supreme Court, after briefs and oral arguments from affected parties, issues its advisory opinion saying most of the tax is constitutional.

July 23—Governor vows to veto any tax bill the legislature tries to substitute for the service tax.

July 29—Johnson and Johnson, the nation's 21st largest advertiser, ends its boycott of Florida advertising.

August 22—Facing falling approval ratings in polls, governor proposes a March 1988 referendum to let voters decide whether the tax should be banned in the state constitution.

September 3—Governor calls for a special session of the legislature to address the tax question.

September 14—Governor says he doesn't have the votes to force the referendum and says he'll work with lawmakers to study repealing or revising the tax.

September 18—After legislators reject his plan for a referendum, governor calls for legislators to repeal the tax and give him more control over the state budget.

September 21—Legislature convenes in first special tax session.

September 23—Standard and Poor's bond rating agency puts Florida on "credit watch" because of uncertainty of future state revenues. The watch could lead to lower bond ratings and higher costs for borrowing.

October 1—Governor announces that if the legislature will repeal the service tax and adopt some budget reform, he will support increasing the sales tax on goods from 5 percent to 5.5 percent. His plan would allow county commissions to impose an additional half cent for local use.

October 8—The house and senate approve a compromise measure giving voters the chance to choose between a revised service tax or an increase in the sales tax on merchandise. Governor vetoes it and calls the legislature into a second special session.

October 12—Lawmakers begin their second attempt to find an acceptable solution to the tax issue.

October 14—Hopelessly deadlocked, the legislature adjourns after nearly four weeks of special sessions. The service tax remains in effect. Governor hedges on whether he will try another session, but senate and house leaders set their own for December to wade into the issue once again.

November—House speaker and senate president hold public hearings around the state on the service tax and are met with orchestrated opposition to the tax.

December 8—Legislators begin third special session.

December 10—After about 37 hours of wrangling, the legislature repeals the service tax, effective January 1, and increases the five-cent sales tax by one cent as of February 1.

State Tax Relief for Low-Income People

by
Robert Greenstein
and
Frederick Hutchinson

Over the past several years, considerable attention has been paid at both the federal and state levels to increases in poverty in the United States. Much of the attention has centered on finding ways to reduce the incidence of poverty and promote self-sufficiency. A growing consensus has emerged that increasing opportunities to work should be a central component of any approach. This has led a number of states to institute programs designed to assist low-income families to move from public assistance to employment.

Complementing these efforts are reforms that reduce federal and state tax burdens on low-income working families. Such reductions permit these families to keep a greater portion of their earnings and thus enhance the advantages of work over welfare. After briefly reviewing how federal tax reform removed more than six million low-income families from the federal income tax rolls, this chapter focuses on ways the states can provide much needed tax relief for low-income people.

Federal Tax Reform: A Major Victory for Low-Income Working Families

The low-income provisions of the federal Tax Reform Act of 1986 were the product of a broad bipartisan consensus that working families with earnings below the poverty line should not have to pay income-related taxes. Politicians and policymakers recognized that rising federal tax burdens had pushed a substantial number of low-income working families into poverty and had thrust many who already were poor deeper into poverty. It also was believed to be unwise social policy (i.e., a work disincentive) to tax those, who in spite of their best efforts, could not seem to make economic ends meet. Such a policy diminished the financial advantages of work.

In fact, this consensus was sufficiently strong that low-income relief was expanded at each successive step in the federal tax reform process. The "Treasury I" plan, the Treasury Department's first comprehensive reform package that was altered before being proposed officially by the President, recommended removing working families with incomes up to the poverty line from the federal income tax rolls, while providing modest payroll tax relief for low-income families with children through expansion of the earned income tax credit. Treasury II, the proposal the President sent to Congress, followed suit, while expanding further the amount of payroll tax relief for low-income families. The bill passed by the House of Representatives provided more payroll tax relief for low-income families than the President's plan, while the Senate bill and the House-Senate conference agreement both improved on the low-income provisions of all previous proposals.

By the time the process had reached its conclusion, low-income families were relieved of $30 to $40 billion in federal income and payroll taxes over the following five years. This made the Tax Reform Act of 1986 the most significant piece of federal legislation in terms of low-income relief since the Social Security Act was amended in 1972 to establish the Supplemental Security Insurance (SSI) program for low-income elderly and disabled people. Under the federal Tax Reform Act, families of four with incomes at the projected 1988 poverty line received more than $1,000 in federal income and payroll tax relief. It should be noted, however, that this relief—as large as it is—merely returned the federal tax burden on these families to the levels of the late 1970s.

State Activity—The Next Frontier

Federal tax reform, which substantially broadened the federal tax base, provides both state policymakers and advocates for low-income people with an excellent opportunity to pursue tax relief for low-income people at the state level. Because most states tailor their definitions of taxable income to the federal tax code, many found themselves with a significant revenue "windfall" that could be either kept for needed expenditures or returned to individual taxpayers. Advocates for low-income people could make a strong case for tax relief for the working poor because state and local tax burdens on low-income households were heavier than federal tax burdens even *before* the federal Tax Reform Act. Specifically, Census data show that before federal Tax Reform, low-income families were paying more in combined state and local income, sales, and property taxes than in federal income and payroll taxes. The data also indicate that even prior to federal tax reform, the number of poor households paying state income tax was more than two-thirds greater than the number paying federal income tax.[1]

Income tax treatment of low-income working people at the state level had worsened in recent years, largely because of the erosion of state income tax thresholds (the income levels at which income tax is first owed). Prior to 1987, inflation had eroded the value of the threshold levels badly in many states. The Census Bureau reported that between 1980 and 1983 alone, the number of poor households paying state income tax rose by more than 30 percent. By failing to adjust their threshold levels to keep pace with inflation, more than half of the states with income taxes by 1986 had threshold levels at least $5,000 below the poverty line for a family of four.

Moreover, enactment of federal tax reform created a potential new problem at the state level. If states did nothing more than conform their definitions of income subject to taxation to the new federal definitions, then state income taxes on low-income people would go up further. An analysis by the Congress' Joint Committee on Taxation found that the federal Tax Reform Act increased the base of taxable income (before subtracting personal exemptions and the standard deduction) by 15.2 percent for households with incomes below $10,000 a year. This appears to have resulted from changes in the tax code such as full taxation of unemployment insurance benefits at all income levels (previously, unemployment insurance was tax free for single filers with incomes below $12,000 a year and for joint filers with incomes below $18,000 a year), the removal of a deduction for charitable contributions for non-itemizers, and the narrowing of the medical expense deduction.

The percentage increase in the base of taxable income for this low-income group was greater than that for any other category of taxpayers except for those with incomes exceeding $100,000.

In addition, in some states, the elimination of federal income taxes on low-income families paradoxically would cause the state income tax burdens of these families to rise. A number of states provide a deduction for federal income taxes paid for both itemizers and nonitemizers. The elimination of federal income taxes for low-income families would mean the loss of a state income tax deduction and a consequent increase in state taxes, unless other offsetting state tax reforms were instituted.

Moreover, some states also provide state income tax credits that "piggyback" on federal income tax credits—a family's state tax credit is simply a specified percentage of an equivalent federal credit claimed on the family's federal tax return. (The child care credit is an example.) If a low-income working family no longer owes federal income tax, it no longer may receive the federal tax credit (since there will be no federal tax liability for the credit to offset); if it no longer receives the federal credit, it could lose the state credit and see its state income taxes climb.

Thus, even with passage of federal tax reform, a large job remained to be done. Federal tax burdens on poor families had been returned to the level of the 1970s, while state tax burdens had risen—leaving total tax burdens on these families higher than they had been a decade earlier. Furthermore, in the absence of state tax relief for low-income families, passage of the federal Tax Reform Act would result in state tax burdens on these families increasing further.

State Income Tax Relief for Low-Income Families in 1987

The year 1987 proved to be a banner one for legislating state income tax relief for low-income families. Thirty-one states (or 76 percent of the 41 states with broad-based income taxes)[2] removed some or all low-income families from their income tax rolls by raising income tax thresholds. Twenty-seven of these 31 states raised tax thresholds for a two-parent family of four by $1,200 or more, including 24 states that raised the threshold for two-parent families of four by at least $2,200. An estimated two million low-income households were removed from state income tax rolls by state legislative action during 1987. Fifteen states do not impose any income taxes on families of four or fewer members with incomes below the poverty line, which is projected to be $12,234 in 1988.

Tables 1 and 2 illustrate the changes between 1986 and 1988 in state income tax thresholds and in state income tax liability for two-parent families of four with incomes of $10,000. In several states, the tables somewhat overstate the tax burden and understate the tax threshold because they do not take account of credits other than personal credits in those states that use them instead of personal exemptions. In Hawaii and New Mexico, those credits normally would raise the income tax threshold above the poverty line, bringing to 17 the number of states that do not tax poor families of four.

States have used a variety of measures to remove low-income families from state income tax rolls, from traditional methods such as increasing personal and dependent exemption and standard deduction levels to more targeted, innovative approaches such as establishing or raising "no-tax floors" and establishing a state earned income tax credit. These measures have varied in efficiency, as the next sections of this chapter explain.

Less Desirable Ways to Provide Income Tax Relief to Low-Income Households

Sixteen states reduced their income tax rates in 1987 and 1988. Generally speaking, rate cuts involve the loss of significant revenues for a state, provide little relief to low-income people, and do nothing to raise income tax thresholds. This was one of the lessons learned at the federal level with the 1981 tax cuts, which lowered tax rates in all tax brackets, yet failed to halt the erosion of tax thresholds due to inflation.[3] The result was that taxpayers at higher income levels received significant tax cuts, while taxpayers at low-income levels saw their tax burdens increase substantially over the next several years.[4]

Of the 16 states that lowered state income tax rates in 1987 and 1988, eight have continued to impose income taxes on a family of four with an income at the poverty line. The other eight states made other, more targeted adjustments that resulted in the raising of income tax thresholds above the poverty line.

A method of providing income tax relief that is more beneficial to low-income families than rate reductions is to increase the personal and/or dependent exemption(s). This approach raises the income tax threshold and is sensitive to family size. Twenty states and the District of Columbia raised their personal and/or dependent exemptions in 1987 or 1988.

Table 1.

State Income Tax Thresholds for Two-Parent Families of Four in 1986 and 1988

(Tax threshold is the level of income at which a family begins owing state income tax; the tax thresholds shown here have been rounded to the nearest $100. States are ranked according to the threshold in 1988.)

State	1986 Tax Threshold	1988 Tax Threshold	Change in Threshold from 1986 to 1988
1. Illinois	$ 4,000	$ 4,000	$ 0
1. Indiana	4,000	4,000	0
1. New Jersey	4,000	4,000	0
4. Kentucky	4,300	4,300	0
4. North Carolina[b]	4,300	4,300	0
6. Alabama	4,400	4,400	0
7. Arkansas[a]	5,000	5,600	+600
8. Hawaii[b]	5,300	5,900	+600
8. Virginia	3,700	5,900	+2,200
10. Montana	6,240	6,500	+260
11. Michigan[b]	6,000	7,200	+1,200
12. Iowa[a]	5,000	7,500	+2,500
13. Pennsylvania	5,700	8,000	+2,300
13. West Virginia	3,600	8,000	+4,400
15. Missouri[c]	6,900	8,200	+1,300
16. Arizona	8,400	8,400	0
17. Delaware	5,600	8,600	+3,000
18. Oklahoma[a]	5,830	8,900	+3,070
19. Georgia	6,100	9,000	+2,900
20. Oregon[b]	6,900	9,300	+2,400
21. Ohio	9,900	10,400	+500
22. Wisconsin[b]	9,200	10,800	+1,600
23. Utah	4,300	10,900	+6,600
24. Louisiana	11,000	11,000	0
25. Massachusetts[a]	6,400	12,000	+5,600
25. New Mexico[b]	12,000	12,000	0
27. Colorado[c]	6,200	12,800	+6,600
27. D.C.[d]	4,000	12,800	+8,800
27. Idaho[c]	8,000	12,800	+4,800
27. Kansas[b]	6,000	12,800	+6,800
27. Minnesota[b,c]	9,300	12,800	+3,500
27. Nebraska[f]	8,000	12,800	+4,800
27. North Dakota[c]	8,000	12,800	+4,800
27 South Carolina[c]	10,300	12,800	+2,500
35. Maryland[e]	5,830	12,900	+7,070
36. Maine	6,200	13,000	+6,800
37. New York	10,600	14,000	+3,400
38. Rhode Island[c]	9,600	15,100	+5,500
38. Vermont[b,c]	8,000	15,100	+7,100
40. Mississippi	15,900	15,900	0
41. California	14,300	18,100	+3,800

Notes:

Calculations are for a two-parent family with two children. The 1986 figures ignore all credits (except personal credits in those states that use them instead of personal exemptions) and assume that the taxpayer uses the standard deduction. The 1988 figures incorporate special credit provisions adopted by some states (e.g., Maryland, Pennsylvania, and Washington, D.C.) during the 1987 legislative sessions to reduce the income tax burdens on low-income wage earners.

    a. This level is based on a special no-tax floor, not on the personal exemption and standard deduction. Massachusetts' $12,000 no-tax floor (for married families) and Iowa's $7,500 no-tax floor (for married couples and heads of households) became effective in 1987.

    b. These levels do not take into account nonpersonal credits low-income households normally would receive that would raise their tax threshold and reduce their tax liability.

    c. This state adopts the federal personal exemption and standard deduction levels (except for Missouri, which adopts only the federal standard deduction, and Rhode Island, which adopts the federal Earned Income Tax Credit along with the personal exemption and standard deduction levels).

    d. Washington, D.C. exempts from the local income tax those families that have incomes up to the combined level of the federal standard deduction and the federal personal exemption. The exemption is achieved through the use of a special tax credit.

    e. Maryland established a state earned income tax credit that was designed to eliminate both state and local income taxes for low-income families of four or fewer persons that have dependent children and that have incomes at or below the poverty line.

    f. Although Nebraska's income tax is no longer a percentage of a taxpayer's federal income tax liability, the state did establish a no-tax floor for those families with incomes up to the combined level of the federal standard deduction and the federal personal exemptions.

Table 2.

State Income Tax for Two-Parent Families of Four
with Wage Income of $10,000 in 1986 and 1988

(States are ranked according to 1988 income tax.)

State	1986 State Income Tax at $10,000 of Income	1988 State Income Tax at $10,000 of Income	Change in Income Tax from 1986 to 1988
1. Kentucky	$281	$281	$ 0
2. North Carolina[b]	252	252	0
3. Pennsylvania[b]	216	211	−5
4. Indiana	180	204	+24
5. Alabama	156	156	0
6. Illinois	150	150	0
7. Iowa	245	144	−101
8. Arkansas[a]	165	130	−35
9. Michigan[b]	184	129	−55
10. New Jersey	120	120	0
11. Hawaii[b]	134	116	−18
12. Montana	112	109	−3
13. Virginia	185	93	−92
14. West Virginia	125	60	−65
15. Oregon[b]	233	50	−183
16. Delaware	106	45	−61
17. Oklahoma	33	33	0
18. Arizona	32	32	0
19. Missouri[c]	64	31	−33
20. Georgia	74	10	−64
21. California	0	0	0
21. Colorado[c]	130	0	−130
21. D.C.[d]	270	0	−270
21. Idaho[c]	40	0	−40
21. Kansas[b]	115	0	−115
21. Louisiana	0	0	0
21. Maine	39	0	−39
21. Maryland[e]	217	0	−217
21. Massachusetts	180	0	−180
21. Minnesota[b,c]	35	0	−35
21. Mississippi	0	0	0
21. Nebraska[f]	42	0	−42
21. New Mexico[b]	0	0	0
21. New York	0	0	0
21. North Dakota[c]	23	0	−23
21. Ohio	4	0	−4
21. Rhode Island[c]	22	0	−22
21. South Carolina[c]	0	0	0
21. Utah	212	0	−212
21. Vermont[c]	53	0	−53
21. Wisconsin[b]	40	0	−40

Notes: Same as Table 1.

Nevertheless, because all households in all income brackets benefit from the personal exemption, it is not well targeted and can be rather costly. And because of the costs involved, increases in the personal exemption usually must be sufficiently modest that they remove only a relatively small number of low-income households from the income tax rolls.

Raising the exemption level is most useful to low-income people in states in which the *dependent* exemption level has been lower than the *personal* exemption level for adults but in which action is taken to equalize the exemption levels. This exemption differential adversely affects families with children. Equalizing exemption levels—or at least moving them closer together—will improve the income tax status of low-income families with children and represents a desirable low-income reform as long as it does not pose too deep a drain on a state's treasury. In 1987, Georgia equalized its personal and dependent exemption levels, Arkansas and California equalized their personal and dependent tax credits, and New York increased its dependent exemption to $1,000, which is $100 above the state's personal exemption.

Targeted, Less Expensive Options

If costs become an issue, states can forego increases in the personal or dependent exemption for the opportunity to provide more meaningful tax relief to low-income people through other, more targeted and less costly options. Fortunately, a number of creative options can provide substantial income tax relief for low-income people at modest costs to states. One such option is to raise the standard deduction. Increasing the standard deduction is desirable; it reduces the amount of income subject to the income tax (just as raising the personal exemption would do) and thus raises the income tax threshold. Yet, unlike raising the personal exemption, raising the standard deduction does not reduce income taxes for *all* taxpayers and hence is a more efficient way to provide low-income relief. Twenty-two states and the District of Columbia increased the standard deduction in 1987 or 1988.

The standard deduction is used primarily by low- and moderate-income taxpayers whose deductible expenses are not large enough (if itemized) to exceed the value of the standard deduction. Higher-income taxpayers tend not to use the standard deduction, choosing to itemize their deductions instead. Because raising the standard deduction affects some but not all taxpayers (primarily those with low and moderate incomes), substantial tax relief can be provided at moderate costs through increasing this deduction. A state considering raising its personal exemption to provide tax relief generally would find that it could increase significantly the amount of relief going to low- and moderate-income taxpayers by raising the standard deduction instead.

Generally, the standard deduction amount varies according to filing status, and its structure varies from state to state. Many states have different standard deduction levels for married couples filing jointly, heads of households, and single taxpayers. As for structure, some states employ a flat standard amount, while in others, the standard deduction is a specified percentage of income up to a certain maximum dollar amount. In still other states where the standard deduction is a specified percentage of income, there are both minimum and maximum standard deduction amounts.

In those states whose standard deduction amounts are percentages of income, the value of the standard deduction for the working poor is compromised, since the deduction amounts tend to be quite low for families without much income. In 1987 or 1988, seven states that previously set their standard deduction levels at a specified percentage of the tax filer's income moved to adopt flat dollar amounts instead for their standard deductions. Such a reform is highly desirable for low-income working families and should be considered by states still maintaining the percentage-of-income approach.

Among those states that set their standard deduction as a percentage of income, the biggest problems occur in states that lack a minimum standard deduction amount. Without a minimum amount, the standard deduction is of the least value to the very families that need it most. If these states do not move to a flat standard deduction, they at least should consider establishing a minimum standard deduction at a reasonable level.

In 1987, Maryland, which formerly had a percentage-of-income standard deduction that lacked a minimum deduction amount, established such a minimum deduction level. Changing standard deductions to flat amounts, establishing minimum standard deductions, and raising standard deduction levels can provide significant relief to taxpayers with low incomes at a relatively modest cost.

An innovative (and progressive) standard deduction structure used by the state of Wisconsin may be of interest to states considering a change in this area. The deduction amount starts out high ($8,900 for low-income taxpayers filing jointly) and declines (or phases out) as income rises. The key here is to set the maximum amount of the deduction sufficiently high to provide the desired amount of tax relief for taxpayers with very low incomes.

A final standard deduction issue involves standard deduction levels for heads of households. At the federal level, there are three standard deduction levels—one for married couples filing jointly

($5,000), one for heads of households ($4,400), and one for single filers ($3,000). In a number of states, however, heads of households are required to use the same standard deduction as single filers.

Such an approach ignores the fact that the expenses of heads of households are much more likely to be similar to the expenses of married couples with families than to the expenses of single individuals. In states that have a lower standard deduction level for both heads of households and single individuals, a single-parent family can end up owing significantly more state income tax than a two-parent family with the same number of family members and the same income level.

Such an outcome violates the principle of horizontal equity that was a major impetus for federal tax reform—that taxpayers at the same income levels and with similar financial circumstances should shoulder a similar tax burden. In addition, such an outcome represents unwise social policy because it increases tax burdens for single-parent families and reduces the differential between work and welfare for them.

In 1987, several states that had two standard deduction levels—one for married couples and the other for singles and heads of households—made the heads-of-households' deduction level the same as that for married couples. Several other states followed the federal lead and established three standard deduction levels, with the level for heads of households set close to that for married couples.

It should be noted that while maintaining three standard deduction levels appears to be necessary at the federal level, this is not the case in many states. At the federal level, lawmakers contend that different standard deduction amounts for married couples and heads of households are needed because each filing category has its own separate tax rate schedule. These rate schedules must proceed from different standard deduction amounts for the different rate schedules to work. Many states, by contrast, do not have different rate structures for the various filing categories, and therefore, no technical problems are posed by having the same deduction level for heads of households as for married couples. Many states would not have to tamper with their tax rate structures to improve the equity of their tax codes and strengthen work incentives by equalizing the standard deductions for heads of households and married couples.

The No-Tax Floor

An even more targeted way to provide substantial low-income tax relief is to establish a no-tax floor, an income level below which no income tax is owed. Eight states currently have no-tax floors. One of them, Nebraska, established its no-tax floor for the first time in 1987. The other seven states with no-tax floors—Arkansas, Iowa, Maryland, Massachusetts, Oklahoma, New York, and Virginia—all raised their floor levels somewhat in 1987. Maine established a floor for 1987 only, but it replaced the floor in 1988 with increased standard deduction and personal exemption tax credits that eliminated income tax burdens for two-parent families of four or fewer persons and for single-parent families of three or fewer persons that do not owe federal income tax.

There are two major advantages to no-tax floors. First, a no-tax floor exempts significant numbers of low-income households from state income tax liability at little cost to the state. The cost is low because the floor benefits only those taxpayers with incomes at or below the floor level. Second, if a state ties its no-tax floor to the federal income tax thresholds, the state should find it much easier to monitor compliance with its own income tax system because it depends on Internal Revenue Service data to conduct its compliance programs. Trying to monitor low-income taxpayers who do not owe federal income tax and have not filed a federal tax return (and, consequently, are not in the federal data base) could prove to be difficult administratively and not worth the cost of the compliance effort.

It is worth noting that setting a state no-tax floor at a level equal to the federal threshold—which means setting the floor at a level equal to the combined value of the federal standard deduction and personal exemptions—is *not* the same thing as raising the state standard deduction and personal exemption levels themselves so that they are equal to the levels in the federal code.[5] The difference between these two approaches is of critical importance. Raising the state's standard deduction and personal exemption levels to the levels in the federal tax code would result in a state income tax cut for *all* taxpayers in *all* income brackets. This would likely result in a substantial revenue loss for the state. By contrast, setting a no-tax floor at a level equal to the combined value of the federal standard deduction and personal exemptions affects only low-income taxpayers. There is no impact on other taxpayers with incomes above the no-tax floor; they continue to use the state's regular deduction and exemption levels. As a result, raising the no-tax floor is a highly target-efficient way of providing low-income relief. It can remove poor families from state income tax rolls at a fraction of the cost of raising the state standard deduction and personal exemptions.

States employ a variety of approaches in establishing no-tax floors. Massachusetts and New York set different floor levels for single taxpayers and for married couples; for example, the floor thresholds in Massachusetts are $8,000 for singles and $12,000 for married couples. Arkansas sets different floor thresholds for single individuals, for those filing joint returns with no children, for joint returns with one dependent child, and for joint returns with two dependent children. Maryland and Oklahoma tie their no-tax floors to the federal filing thresholds for particular household types.[6]

In Nebraska, the no-tax floor is set at the income level equal to the combined value of the federal personal exemptions and standard deduction for which a household qualifies. For a two-parent family of four, this results in a no-tax floor of $12,800 in 1988, or slightly above the poverty line (projected at $12,234 for 1988).

A State Earned Income Tax Credit Targets Families with Children

Another well-targeted, although slightly less comprehensive, way of providing income tax relief to low-income taxpayers is to establish a state earned income tax credit (EITC) modeled on the federal earned income tax credit. The federal EITC is a tax credit designed to relieve the income and payroll tax burdens of low-income working families with dependent children. It is highly targeted because only families with dependent children and earned income are eligible for the credit. The EITC is less comprehensive than a no-tax floor because a floor eliminates income taxes for *all* households with incomes below it, including households without children.

The federal EITC is set at 14 percent of income for families with very low incomes (i.e., incomes below $6,250 in 1988). At an income of $6,250, an eligible family would qualify for the maximum credit amount, which will be $875 in 1988. Over a relatively small income range—between $6,250 and $9,840—the credit amount remains at $875. Between $9,840 and $18,590, the credit amount is reduced as income increases. The federal EITC is also refundable, meaning that to the extent that the eligible credit amount exceeds a family's income tax liability, the family receives a refund check from the federal government for the difference. The federal EITC is adjusted annually for inflation.

Establishing a state EITC has several advantages. First, as noted, the EITC is well targeted and cost-efficient. Second, the EITC is popular with both conservatives and liberals because it serves as a work incentive. Eligibility for the credit requires earned income, and for families with extremely low incomes, credit amounts increase as earnings grow. Moreover, the federal credit significantly raises the federal income tax threshold, while at the same time allowing families to ease into the federal income tax system.

The EITC is also quite attractive to advocates of "pro-family" policies since eligibility for the credit is limited to low- and moderate-income working families residing with their dependent children. Thus, a father who deserts his family becomes ineligible for the EITC regardless of how low his earnings may be.

One of the initial endorsements of the EITC concept came in 1972 from then-Governor Ronald Reagan of California in testimony before the U.S. Senate Committee on Finance. It became an integral part of the federal tax code in 1975, and it enjoys support from organizations ranging from low-income advocacy groups such as the Children's Defense Fund to conservative groups such as the Heritage Foundation.

At the state level, it is not feasible to design an EITC that perfectly mirrors the federal EITC. This is due to the cost involved in matching the dollar value of the maximum federal credit while at the same time making the credit refundable. Generally, states would use federal eligibility limits but set the amount of the credit at a specified percentage of the federal credit and make the credit nonrefundable.

Three states—Maryland, Rhode Island, and Vermont—have state earned income tax credits. The Maryland credit was established during the 1987 legislative session and is set at 50 percent of the federal EITC for which a family qualifies. It serves to raise income tax thresholds for low-income working families with children so that families of four or fewer members with incomes below the poverty line no longer owe state income tax. The Maryland EITC, which is nonrefundable, achieves this goal at a cost of only about $4 million per year.

The Rhode Island and Vermont credits exist because those states set their state income tax liability as a specified percentage of federal income tax liability after the federal EITC is computed. Vermont, which enacted its EITC in 1988, is the first state where it is refundable, like the federal EITC. In other words, if the amount of the credit is greater than tax liability, the taxpayer receives a refund.

Maximum Simplicity, Conformity, and Low-Income Relief

If state policymakers want to enhance simplicity while also ensuring conformity with federal changes, maintaining or improving progressivity, and providing substantial low-income relief, they may want to consider setting state income tax liabilities at a certain percentage of each taxpayer's federal income tax liability. Under this approach, a taxpayer need only transfer his or her federal income tax liability to the state income tax form, then multiply this liability by the state's designated percentage. Because federal tax reform removed all families living in poverty from the federal income tax rolls, adopting a tax structure that sets state income tax burdens as a specified percentage of the federal income tax burden ensures that the same families are removed from state income tax rolls as well. While this option substantially raises income tax thresholds, the specified percentage of federal tax liability can be set at a level high enough to avoid any revenue loss for the state. Three states currently follow this approach—Rhode Island, North Dakota, and Vermont. These states set their state tax liabilities at 22.96 percent, 14 percent, and 25 percent, respectively, of taxpayer's federal tax liabilities. No other states adopted this approach in 1987, while one state that previously had used it (Nebraska) dropped it.

A final option that can promote simplicity and conformity while providing extensive low-income relief is to adopt the federal definition of *taxable income.* Most states that conform to the federal code adopt the federal definition of *adjusted gross income,* which is income *before* personal exemptions and standard deductions are subtracted. *Taxable income* is income *after* subtracting personal exemptions and standard deductions. If a state conforms to the federal definition of taxable income, it effectively adopts the federal personal exemption and standard deduction levels. This approach, which was adopted by Minnesota and Colorado in 1987, has the effect of eliminating state income taxes on low-income households that owe no federal income tax. It can be costly, however, since it entails raising personal exemptions that affect all taxpayers. If such an approach is adopted, it may need to be accompanied by other provisions to reduce or offset its cost.

Many of the income tax relief options discussed in this section are quite inexpensive and can be tucked away into a larger tax package to minimize their fiscal impact. The key to reasonable revenue costs is targeting. If particular relief measures are targeted primarily to low-income or to low- and moderate-income people, their costs will be low. If more general measures are used, costs will increase.

Much Work Still Needed to Relieve Sales and Property Tax Burdens on the Poor

As previously mentioned, state and local sales and property taxes are generally more burdensome on low-income people than are state income taxes. While many states took steps in 1987 to relieve income tax burdens on low-income households, little progress was made in relieving sales and property tax burdens on them. Instead, these tax burdens rose in many areas.

That more progress was made in providing income tax relief may be due in part to the relatively low cost associated with removing low-income people from the state income tax rolls. In addition, the income tax "windfalls" due to be received by many states as a result of the changes in the federal income tax code led to measures to return some or all of the "windfall" to taxpayers, and income tax relief for the poor could be included as a part of such measures. That the federal government had just removed the poor from its income tax rolls, with broad bipartisan support, provided a powerful precedent.

Yet much of the progress made in providing state income tax relief for low-income families effectively was canceled out by state actions to raise sales and excise taxes. Some states offset much, and in some cases all, of the income tax relief they adopted for poor households in 1987 by raising regressive sales and excise taxes.

From the perspective of low-income people, a move away from reliance on the income tax as a source of state revenue is an unfavorable development. To the extent that states do not raise needed revenues through the income tax, which is generally the most progressive revenue source, and turn to sales and excise taxes instead, state tax codes become more regressive and tax burdens on low-income people increase.

A study published in January 1987 by Citizens for Tax Justice, a public interest and research organization, examined the regressivity of sales taxes. The study found that when measured as a percentage of income, the sales tax in the average state was 4.43 times more burdensome for families with incomes in the lowest income quintile (those families with annual incomes below $7,564 in 1986) than it was for the top 0.7 percent of families (those families with annual incomes above $527,241).[7] Moreover, for families in the lowest income quintile, the sales tax was 6.2 times more burdensome than the state income tax. By contrast, for the top 0.7 percent of families, state income taxes were 4.7 times more burdensome than the sales tax.[8]

In 1987, states enacted measures raising sales taxes by $2.4 billion, motor fuel taxes by $1.2 billion, and cigarette taxes by $0.3 billion.[9] These figures do not take into account approximately $0.5 billion in increases in miscellaneous taxes, most of which are also regressive. Not only do such regressive taxes disproportionately burden low-income people, but states relied much more heavily on increases in these taxes to raise additional revenues in 1987 and 1988 than on increases in progressive income taxes. As a result, much of the progress made by low-income people on the income tax front was offset by increases in other taxes that place a disproportionate burden on them. For example, Minnesota was one of the states that acted in 1987 to remove all poor families from state income tax rolls. Yet a study by Minnesota Citizens for Tax Justice found that this income tax relief for low-income households was offset fully by increases in a variety of state sales and excise taxes.[10]

The Sales Tax Credit Provides a Relief Option

As states raise sales taxes further and rely more heavily on them to raise needed revenues, there is a need for increased attention to measures that can provide sales tax relief for low-income families. Currently, seven states (Hawaii, Idaho, Kansas, New Mexico, South Dakota, Vermont, and Wyoming) have refundable sales tax credit programs that provide such tax relief for low-income people. These sales tax credits are available to low-income households regardless of whether they have earnings, since all low-income households pay sales taxes.[11]

Four of the seven states with sales tax credit programs (Hawaii, Idaho, New Mexico, and Vermont) administer their programs through the state income tax system. As such, the credit is used to offset state income taxes.[12] In addition, sales tax credits are refundable, meaning that eligible families can be sent a check for the amount of the credit, even if the credit amount exceeds the family's income tax liability.[13] Usually, the credit is adjusted for family size—for example, by basing the amount of the credit on the number of exemptions for which a family is eligible on an income tax return.

These state sales tax credits generally are targeted to benefit low- and moderate-income people. The targeting usually is accomplished by phasing out benefits at a certain moderate-income level. For example, in Hawaii, taxpayers receive a sales tax credit based on the number of exemptions they could claim for income tax purposes, with the amount of the credit reduced as family income rises. Taxpayers with incomes below $5,000 receive a credit equal to $48 per exemption. Taxpayers in the $9,000 to $11,000 income range receive a credit of $24 per exemption. The credit phases out at $20,000; taxpayers with incomes above this level do not qualify for it. During the 1987 session, Hawaii added an additional refundable sales tax credit to the one already in place. The new credit is designed to offset the sales tax on food and also is administered through the income tax system.

Sales tax credits do not tend to be very expensive. Costs are controlled because programs generally are targeted toward low- (or low- and moderate-) income people. Also contributing to the relatively small costs of sales tax credit programs is that participation rates generally fall well below 100 percent and tend to be low in the first years of a program.

Low participation rates point to the need for states with these sales tax credits to undertake vigorous publicity efforts so that low-income households may learn of their eligibility for the program and how to apply. Otherwise, households that do not owe state income tax are unlikely to learn of their eligibility for the sales tax credit. A promotional program should run at least for several years until policymakers are reasonably assured that knowledge of the program and its operation is widespread. Careful planning and promotional efforts, along with the careful collection of data, will indicate whether the intended beneficiaries are being reached.

Participation also can be enhanced by designing sales tax relief programs that are not complicated and thus do not discourage low-income households from applying. Eligibility requirements and instructions should be clear and straightforward. States also can process state income tax forms in such a way as to identify returns from low-income earners who may be eligible for the new relief program. Once identified, benefits can be provided automatically to these taxpayers if the taxpayers fail to fill out the proper lines for the credit on their returns. (This is how the IRS handles the federal earned income tax credit for working poor families. If a family eligible for the EITC files an income tax return but fails to fill in the lines for the EITC, the IRS will compute the EITC for the household and automatically provide it.)

Regardless of publicity efforts, however, program use still will not come close to 100 percent of those eligible for it. In every state with a sales tax credit, a significant proportion of the eligible low-income households do not apply for or receive the credit. Thus, the cost of a sales tax credit will be considerably less than would be the case with full participation. Policymakers should be sure to consider this factor when preparing cost estimates. Accurate cost estimates for a sales tax credit should assume a participation rate of well below 100 percent.

The Need for Low-Income Property Tax Relief

In most states, the heaviest tax burdens borne by low-income households are those that result from property taxes. In many areas, property tax relief is needed by low-income households as much or more than income tax relief.

The basic property tax relief program for low-income people is the circuitbreaker, which now operates in 31 states. The property tax circuitbreaker works in a fashion similar to its electrical namesake. Just as an electrical circuitbreaker shuts off the flow of electricity at a certain overflow point, so too does the property tax circuitbreaker shut off property tax payments when the tax consumes an excessive amount of income.

There are major differences among the circuitbreaker programs of the 31 states. Two of the most important are whether circuitbreaker programs are limited to the elderly and disabled and whether the programs are limited to homeowners. Of the 31 state circuitbreaker programs, 21 are limited either to the elderly (12 states) or to the elderly and disabled (nine states). The other 10 states cover nonelderly, nondisabled households as well.

Twenty-five of the 31 states cover renters as well as homeowners while six do not. In states covering renters, a specified percentage of a tenant's annual rental payments is assumed to represent a pass through of property taxes by the landlord. Typically, the percentage specified by the state falls in the 15 percent to 25 percent range.

In states with a circuitbreaker program that is restricted to the elderly and disabled, expanding the program to other low-income groups may constitute one of the most significant forms of tax relief for low-income people that the state can provide. Younger families that are poor are likely to need property tax relief even more than the low-income elderly do. The typical poor family with children tends to fall much deeper into poverty than the typical poor elderly person. Moreover, the elderly poor generally have lower housing costs than the nonelderly poor. Many low-income elderly homeowners have paid off their mortgages and incur no monthly rent or mortgage payments, unlike younger poor families.

As a result, an equitable and well-designed circuitbreaker program would cover all types of low-income households, regardless of age or disability. In 1987, Maine broadened coverage of its circuitbreaker from the elderly and disabled to all low-income households. If a circuitbreaker of this scope is considered too costly by a state, it at least might consider following the model established by Kansas, which covers three categories of low-income households under its circuitbreaker program: the elderly, the disabled, and families with children under 18.

The other area in which states can (and should) reexamine eligibility restrictions is with regard to renters. Low-income renters are often in acute need of property tax relief. Census data show that in 1983 (the latest year for which these data have been published), approximately half of all renter households with incomes below $7,000 a year paid at least 60 percent of their incomes for rent and utilities. Similarly, a General Accounting Office report found that the number of low-income households paying more than half of their incomes for rent and utilities rose 70 percent in just eight years—from 3.7 million such households in 1975 to 6.3 million households in 1983.

Moreover, while homeowners generally can deduct property taxes from their federal income tax liabilities, renters get no such deduction, although they too pay property tax (through their rent payments).

States initiating or broadening their circuitbreaker programs should make sure that any program expansion is publicized adequately. Experience shows that when eligibility for a tax relief program is expanded and encompasses poor households that do not have to file an income tax return, many in the enlarged pool of eligible households will not readily learn of the relief program or of their eligibility for it. For example, in Wisconsin, which has a circuitbreaker program available to all residents with incomes below $16,500 (regardless of homeowner status or age), the primary users of the program are elderly people. Data collected by the state's Legislative Fiscal Bureau show that 61 percent of those claiming program benefits receive Social Security or SSI benefits.[14] The reason generally given by legislators and Fiscal Bureau officials for the low participation by nonelderly residents is that the program was not originally available to the nonelderly and when the program was expanded to include them, the expansion was not well publicized.

The Wisconsin experience illustrates the importance of undertaking a public information effort if a circuitbreaker is instituted or eligibility for the circuitbreaker is expanded. Even then, participation will remain substantially below 100 percent of those who are eligible. These participation rate issues should be kept in mind when states estimate the costs involved in expanding a circuitbreaker. Cost estimates should not assume 100 percent participation in the program.

Publicize the Federal EITC

There is one other major area where states can contribute significantly to alleviating tax burdens on low-income people, and at little or no cost to the state. States can conduct public information campaigns designed to encourage low-income working families who have had no federal income tax withheld to file a *federal* tax return in order to receive a *federal earned income tax credit* benefit. Taxpayers must file a federal tax return in order to receive EITC benefits; because many low-income families have been removed from the federal income tax rolls by the federal Tax Reform Act, some of these families (those who receive a W-2 form indicating no federal income tax has been withheld) may feel that there is no need to file a return. This could be a costly omission, with some poor families foregoing as much as $875 (the maximum EITC amount in 1988).

It should be noted that if eligible families do file a federal tax return, they will receive the credit. If a return is filed, the IRS will itself compute a family's EITC benefit if the family is eligible but has failed to compute the EITC lines on its tax return.

There are several advantages to states of informing working poor families of the need to file a federal return. Such a state public information effort not only assists the family in question but also brings more federal funds into a state's economy. EITC benefits are 100 percent federally funded and tend to be infused into the economy rather quickly. In addition, by boosting the total compensation that results from working, the EITC can serve as a work incentive. As its benefits become more widely understood among low-income families, it may influence some families to rely more on work and less on public assistance.

Several cities and states are publicizing the expanded federal credit. Washington, D.C. has designed information bulletins and brochures for employers to distribute to their employees. Chicago publicizes the EITC through its Department of Human Resources, which uses direct service units as well as contracted agencies that have direct contact with clients who are likely to qualify for EITC benefits. Chicago also has encouraged public advocacy groups to assist in the publicity campaign. The city of Chicago also has publicized the EITC on radio and by distributing more than 100,000 fliers printed in English and Spanish.

Publicity efforts can include the following: 1) placing handouts at unemployment and welfare offices; 2) mailing notices to people who have received unemployment insurance during the previous calendar year; 3) mailing a notice to those who have left AFDC rolls due to increased earnings; 4) providing notices to public employees in the lowest grade levels; 5) placing public service announcements on radio and television (as done with tax amnesty programs in some states); 6) sending press releases to local newspapers, including minority and community papers in low- and moderate-income areas; 7) advertising through community service organizations and local churches; and 8) enlisting the cooperation of labor unions and large employers in notifying their members and employees in low-paying occupations.

Summary

The passage of the federal Tax Reform Act of 1986 led lawmakers in many states to make adjustments in state income tax codes in light of potential revenue windfalls that would have raised state income taxes. Overall, states chose to return more than $5 billion of the projected $6.1 billion windfall to taxpayers, and many states seized this opportunity in 1987 to provide income tax relief for low-income working people. Approximately two million low-income working families were removed from state income tax rolls in 1987.

This relief was badly needed. Census data show that even *before* federal tax reform, low-income families were paying more in combined state and local income, sales, and property taxes than in federal income and payroll taxes.

But despite the progress made in 1987, there is still much to be done at the state level to ease the overall tax burden of low-income people. Twenty-six states still impose an income tax on families of four with incomes below the poverty line (projected to be $12,234 for a family of four in 1988), and 20 states still tax families of four with incomes below $10,000. When states impose income taxes on poor families, the advantages of working over receiving public assistance are lessened.

For states interested in easing income tax burdens on low-income working people, several targeted, relatively low-cost options can be used. The no-tax floor that eliminates income taxes on taxpayers with incomes below the floor level and a state earned income tax credit (EITC) that can eliminate income tax burdens on most low-income families with dependent children are the most targeted ways to provide income tax relief for poor households.

The other relatively targeted and cost-efficient option for easing the income tax burdens on low-income people is to raise the standard deduction. The standard deduction covers a much larger number of taxpayers than would a no-tax floor or an EITC, but improvements in the standard deduction are better targeted than increases in the personal exemption that benefit taxpayers at all income levels.

Low-income people are also in need of sales and property tax relief. In most states, these taxes are far more burdensome on low-income households than are income taxes. In recent years, states have not made as extensive efforts to reduce low-income individuals' sales and property tax burdens as they have made with the income tax. In fact, the recent trend has been to cut income taxes and raise sales and excise taxes; in many cases, the net effect has been to increase the overall tax burden of the low-income population.

Nationally, in 1986, sales taxes were 4.43 times more burdensome on families with incomes in the lowest income quintile (those families with incomes below $7,564) than they were for the top 0.7 percent of families. Only seven states provide a refundable credit to relieve sales tax burdens on low-income people. These sales tax relief programs are generally inexpensive. It would be advisable for other states to explore instituting a sales tax credit for their low-income populations.

The property tax is the single most burdensome tax on low-income people, affecting low-income renters as well as homeowners. Property tax relief generally is provided through state circuitbreaker programs. Unfortunately, a majority of state programs are restricted to the elderly (or the elderly and disabled). Circuitbreakers would be more equitable and provide more relief to those in greatest need if they were expanded to cover the non-elderly, especially low-income families with dependent children. These families tend to have much higher shelter costs than the elderly since many elderly persons own their homes and have paid off their mortgages.

Finally, states can consider undertaking campaigns to inform low-income wage earners who have children of the advantages of filing a federal tax return so that they can receive the federal earned income tax credit to which they are entitled.

Notes

1. U.S. Department of Commerce, Bureau of the Census, unpublished data from 1984 Current Population Survey, prepared at the request of the Committee on Ways and Means, U.S. House of Representatives.

2. This chapter treats the District of Columbia as a state, which is why it refers to 41 states with a personal income tax.

3. This is not to suggest that the Economic Recovery and Tax Act of 1981 (ERTA) did not index federal income tax code provisions for inflation. On the contrary, all the provisions that combine to determine the income tax threshold and ultimately the income tax liability of low-income taxpayers were indexed with the exception of the earned income tax credit. But indexing for inflation did not begin until the 1985 tax year. Between 1979 and 1985, inflation took a heavy toll on the value of the personal exemption, the standard deduction, and the EITC. The rate cuts did not offset inflation's effects, and taxes for low-income people went up.

4. Robert S. McIntyre and Dean C. Tipps, *Inequity and Decline* (Washington, D.C.: Center on Budget and Policy Priorities, 1983), p. 23.

5. This is why Colorado, Idaho, North Dakota, South Carolina, and Vermont are not listed as having no-tax floors. These states tie their standard deductions and personal exemptions to the federal levels.

6. The federal *filing* threshold is a combination of the standard deduction and the minimum number of personal exemptions allowed a particular filing status. For example, the filing threshold for joint returns, regardless of the number of dependent exemptions claimed on the return, is $8,900 in 1988—the standard deduction ($5,000) plus two personal exemptions ($3,900). For heads of households, the federal filing threshold is $8,300 in 1988—a $4,400 standard deduction plus two personal exemptions ($3,900).

On the other hand, the federal *income* tax threshold is the income level above which the first dollar of federal income tax is owed. This threshold is a combination of the standard deduction, all personal exemptions the household would receive, and the earned income tax credit if the household qualifies.

The federal *filing* threshold for a two-parent family of four will be $8,900 in 1988, whereas the federal *income* tax threshold for this same family will be $15,116.

7. Robert S. McIntyre et al., *The Sorry State of State Taxes* (Washington, D.C.: Citizens for Tax Justice, January 1987), p. 3.

8. Ibid., p. 3.

9. Karen Benker, *Fiscal Survey of the States* (Washington, D.C.: National Association of State Budget Officers and the National Governors' Association, September 1987), Table A-14, p. 66.

10. Fritz Wiecking et al., *Two Steps Forward, One and a Half Steps Back: Tax Changes Made by the 1987 State Legislature* (St. Paul: Minnesota Citizens for Tax Justice, September 1987), p. 4. This point also is made in a recently issued study by the American Federation of State, County, and Municipal Employees (AFSCME). See Michael Mazerov and Iris J. Lav, *The Fairest of Them All: A Rating of State Personal Income Taxes for 1987 Returns* (Washington, D.C.: AFSCME), 1988.

11. Two of these seven states (South Dakota and Wyoming) restrict the credit to the elderly and disabled. Kansas restricts its credit to the elderly, the disabled, and families with children.

12. For illustrations of various sales tax credit programs, see Steven D. Gold, *State Tax Relief for the Poor* (Denver: National Conference of State Legislatures, 1987), pp. 74-78. Another useful discussion of sales tax relief options can be found in David Kahan with Robert Greenstein, *The Next Frontier: Relieving State Tax Burdens of the Poor* (Washington, D.C.: Center on Budget and Policy Priorities, April 1987), pp. 55-56.

13. Two of the other three states that have refundable sales tax credits have no income tax systems.

14. Therese Fitzsimmons, "Homestead Tax Credit" (Madison: Wisconsin Legislative Fiscal Bureau, 1987), p. 7.

State
Business Taxes:
The Policy and
Research Agendas

by
Michael Vlaisavljevich

Interstate competition and federal tax policy changes are dominant forces that have shaped state business tax policy in recent years and will help set the policy agenda for the next five years. This chapter has two objectives: 1) to identify and discuss business tax issues that are likely to confront state legislatures over the next five years, and 2) to indicate the research needed to evaluate policy alternatives and support sound fiscal management.

Political Tensions and Conflicting Goals Shaping State Business Tax Policy

Political tensions and conflicting objectives pull state business tax policies in very different directions.

The dominant political tension involves the goal of minimizing direct personal taxes versus the goal of competing successfully for capital investment and jobs. The populist political urge leads to taxation of corporations rather than individuals. While public finance theorists differ widely in their views of corporate tax incidence, it is agreed that some combination of individuals—shareholders, employees, or consumers—ultimately bear the burden of corporate taxation. Nonetheless, the political appeal of taxing businesses rather than resident individuals (voters) is often irresistible. This appeal is increased when business taxes are perceived to be exported to residents of other states.

The temptation to shift direct taxes from individuals to businesses, however, has been curbed by the increasingly intense competition among states for capital investment and jobs. States are now very sensitive to assertions that business taxes are excessive and present a barrier to attracting capital investment. Consequently, state policymakers are less likely to increase business taxes and run the risk of hampering state economic development.

On a theoretical level, a second conflict relates to the basic purposes and principles of state business taxation. Should state business taxes be based upon ability to pay or the benefits-received principle? The ability-to-pay principle is a familiar one and is embodied in the corporate income tax. A less familiar concept suggests that state business taxes are justified by the public service benefits that they receive from government and that the business tax structure should reflect this basic purpose. Business taxes based upon the benefits-received principle take the form of franchise taxes (based upon some measure of capital) or the value-added tax. The choice of a basic approach has significant implications in distributing the business tax burden among industries. It also affects the stability of state revenues since corporate profits are more volatile and uncertain than the broader franchise and value-added tax bases.

A third tension relates to alternative views of how tax policy should relate to state economic development. Conventional public finance theory emphasizes efficiency and economic neutrality. In this view, good business tax policy results in uniform effective tax rates across industries. An alternative view, however, asserts that tax policy can and should be tilted in favor of those industries that are targets for employment growth within the state.

Management Perspectives on State Business Taxes

An additional perspective on state business taxes concerns state fiscal and tax management. From the viewpoint of state revenue estimators and budget managers, the impact of federal tax reform on state revenues presents a major source of potential error and risk. The Tax Reform Act of 1986 included several provisions, described shortly, that federal tax analysts believe will have large revenue effects over the next several years. Because of their complex nature, these impacts are likely to unfold in unexpected ways as the new tax rules are clarified and implemented. Furthermore, future efforts at addressing the issue of the federal deficit as well as responding to the economic consequences of the Tax Reform Act suggest that additional changes in federal business taxes will have continuing impacts at the state level. The complexity of federal changes, past and future, will increase the uncertainty and risk associated with estimating state corporate revenues greatly—a difficult task under the best of circumstances.

From the viewpoint of state tax administration, federal tax reform creates both challenges and opportunities. The challenge concerns the burden placed upon state tax agencies in applying new and complex law correctly. The opportunity is exemplified by a number of states that have used the state response to federal tax reform as a vehicle to increase conformity with the federal code. Properly designed, these conformity efforts can result in reduced compliance costs for taxpayers as well as administrative efficiencies for state tax agencies.

Federal Impacts on State Business Taxes

The topic, federal impacts on state business taxes, is a broad one. Federal government actions affect state business taxes in many ways.

- Deregulation has made traditional state tax structures outmoded in the areas of telecommunications, financial institutions, and insurance. As a result, many states are faced with the need to modify their tax policies with respect to these industries.

- The efforts of the U.S. Treasury Department to discourage worldwide unitary taxation have contributed to a broad move to "water's-edge" taxation for those states that use combined reporting. Numerous unitary-related issues, however, remain to be resolved in many states, such as the treatment of foreign dividends and other foreign source income.
- Federal court cases continually redefine the bounds of permissible state tax policy, especially as it relates to discrimination against interstate commerce. Recent cases have invalidated state laws in the areas of insurance and trucking as well as a portion of the Washington business and occupation tax. These limiting federal cases should be kept in mind when states are designing tax incentives that favor in-state business activity.
- Federal legislation modifying taxable income affects the definition of the state corporate tax base since most states are coupled to federal law in this regard.

The comments in this section are focused primarily on the major impact that occurred in 1987—the state response to the Tax Reform Act of 1986 (TRA).

Estimating the Revenue Effect of Federal Tax Reform

The first challenge faced by states was to try to estimate the potential revenue gain or "windfall" from conforming to the corporate provisions of the federal TRA. The nature of the TRA provisions made it more difficult to estimate corporate compared with individual income tax provisions. Some states have built state personal income tax models that enable them to simulate tax changes directly using state-specific data. By contrast, however, states generally were not in a position to analyze several of the most important corporate changes using state-specific data.

Based upon federal estimates, the five federal changes (that have general application to state corporate taxes) with the largest positive revenue impacts are as follows:

1) Accounting changes relating to capitalization of inventory, construction, and development costs;
2) Accounting treatment of long-term contracts;
3) Modified depreciation and expensing provisions;
4) Repeal of reserve for bad debt for nonfinancial institutions; and
5) Accounting treatment of installment sales.

On the other hand, passive loss restrictions related to tax shelters could affect corporate revenue negatively. In essence, limitations upon tax shelter activity under the personal income tax could shift some losses to the corporate sector.

Given the complex nature of these provisions and the absence of usable state-specific corporate tax data, some analysts have turned to federal estimates as a basis for deriving state estimates. Three published studies attempted to address the question of the impact of federal tax reform on state corporate taxes.

The Committee on State Taxation (COST) of the Council of State Chambers of Commerce took a first cut at this question.[1] The authors of the COST study concluded that states would see double-digit increases in corporate taxes if no offsetting legislative actions were taken.

More recently, Robert Aten published an analysis of the impact of the federal tax reform on a national basis—not for individual states.[2] Aten's methodology carefully netted out those federal revenue-raising items that generally have no state counterparts. Such items include the investment tax credit, the alternative minimum tax, and provisions affecting insurance companies and financial institutions (industries usually subject to special rather than general state business taxes). The major corporate revenue-raiser at the federal level—the investment tax credit—had no direct impact on most states. Only a handful of states have general investment tax credits that are broadly available. (A number of states provide investment credits on a limited basis, for example, in enterprise zones.)

Aten estimated that the state corporate tax increase (after the state legislative response and taxpayer behavioral changes) would range from $1.0 billion to $1.4 billion. In percentage terms, the estimated increase is from 5 to 7 percent of total state corporate income tax receipts. These estimates rely on the Reagan administration's projections of profits that are higher than those developed by most other forecasters.

A third study by Robert Tannenwald of the Federal Reserve Bank of Boston analyzed federal impacts on six New England states (Connecticut, Maine, Massachusetts, New Hampshire, Rhode Island, Vermont).[3] This analysis carefully accounted for differences in state industry mix and prior differences in federal and state laws. Tannenwald's estimates of revenue gains range from between 12 percent in Massachusetts to 21 percent in Maine. These are estimates *before* any offsetting changes in state law.

Finally, most state governments were cautious in estimating corporate "windfalls." Based upon a survey of state agencies, the National Association of State Budget Officers reported corporate windfall estimates, before changes in state law, of under $1.0 billion.[4] This figure, however, was based upon incomplete data since some states had not yet completed corporate estimates.

In summary, estimates of state corporate tax windfalls from federal tax reform varied widely. Given the complexity of the major provisions affecting state corporate tax bases and the inability of states to validate estimates derived from federal data independently, most state governments used conservative estimates.

State Response to Federal Tax Reform Act of 1986

Most states conformed with federal base changes and either retained the potential corporate tax increase or used it for personal income tax reductions. Only nine states enacted reductions in corporate rates or other changes to offset (in whole or part) the windfall increase in corporate taxes: California, Colorado, Hawaii, Oregon, Maine, New York, Ohio, Pennsylvania, and South Carolina.[5]

Some states used federal tax reform to rationalize their corporate tax structure by increasing conformity with the federal definition of income or reshaping corporate tax policy. New York, for example, enacted a comprehensive package that followed the reform themes of base-broadening and rate reduction and that included the following provisions:

- Rates were reduced from 10 percent to 9 percent (8 percent under $200,000);
- The value of credits was reduced: The investment credit was reduced from 6 percent to 5 percent (4 percent for investments over $500 million). The employment credit rate also was scaled down;
- Other long-standing issues were addressed, such as amending the tax on capital to include a deduction for long-term debt.

At least in a few cases, states used federal tax reform to increase conformity with the federal code by eliminating pre-existing differences.

Wisconsin used federal tax reform to streamline the corporate tax by adopting federal taxable income as the starting point and eliminating over 70 federal-state tax base differences. The Wisconsin Department of Revenue initiated a legislative development process that involved consultation with major business and tax practitioner groups. This consensus effort proved critical late in the legislative process by building a broad coalition to resist amendments that would have unbalanced the corporate reform package.

California moved to address two areas of pre-existing differences that were significant concerns to the business community: the treatment of Subchapter S corporations and net operating loss carryovers. Previously, the state had no provisions for Subchapter S treatment for small business corporations. The new California law moves toward conformity with federal Subchapter S provisions. Net corporate income, however, will be subject to a 2.5 percent corporate surtax and out-of-state shareholders must agree to be taxed in California for the corporation to qualify for Subchapter S treatment. California also has moved toward increased conformity with federal net operating loss carry-forward provisions. Finally, the corporate tax rate was reduced from 9.6 to 9.3 percent.[6]

The move toward increased conformity is also notable in the area of depreciation. Because of the large potential revenue losses related to the adoption of the Accelerated Cost Recovery System (ACRS) enacted in 1981, many states deviated from federal depreciation treatment at that time. Subsequent modifications to ACRS, however, have led analysts in some states to conclude that little or no revenue loss was associated with conforming to the current federal depreciation provisions. Georgia, Virginia, and Wisconsin increased conformity with the new federal depreciation provisions in order to realize significant gains in terms of simplified compliance and administration.

State Business Tax Agenda for the Next Five Years

Two dominant themes can be expected to shape the state business tax agenda for the next five years: 1) interstate competition, and 2) the state response to federal tax policy change. The agenda will be defined further by the political tensions and conflicting objectives discussed earlier:

- The goal of minimizing direct personal taxes versus the goal of competing successfully for capital investment and jobs;
- Tax policy approaches based upon ability to pay versus benefits received; and
- The goal of economic neutrality versus the deliberate use of tax policy as a targeted economic development tool.

The management perspectives cited earlier also will influence the agenda. The two major concerns in this regard are:

- The risk of major revenue estimating errors due to federal tax reform; and
- The desire to ease compliance and administrative burdens through increased conformity with the federal code.

Interstate Competition

Interstate competition for capital investment and jobs is a predominant concern of governors and legislatures throughout the nation. Tax policy, relating to both businesses and individuals, generally is viewed as one of the tools in the economic development arsenal. From a policy perspective, some argue that this approach is a poor one, resulting in erosion of the tax base needed to finance a desirable level of public services, such as education and transportation. These public services are also important contributing factors to economic development. Nonetheless, a state cannot ignore a situation in which an above-average tax burden presents a barrier to economic development. States with relatively high business tax burdens compared with those of neighboring states will be under pressure to make changes.

The following issues are likely candidates for future state business tax agendas due to interstate competition concerns. It is essential to realize that all major taxes—not just the corporate income tax—are relevant to interstate competition and economic development. This point is developed in more detail later in the section on research needs.

- *Sales Tax on Business Equipment*—Sales taxes paid on business purchases often are overlooked in superficial comparisons of business taxes. The imposition of sales tax on machinery and equipment purchases is especially significant because it is a large up-front cost associated with capital investment, such as a new or expanded factory. As such, the sales tax on equipment is a "negative investment tax credit," which serves as a powerful disincentive to capital investment. Most states either exempt these transactions in whole or in part or tax these sales at a lower, preferential rate. Only 12 states fully tax manufacturer and contractor purchases of equipment or restrict exemptions to enterprise zone areas. (See Table 1.) It is noteworthy that Louisiana is considering sales tax relief for manufacturing equipment as an important economic development issue, even while faced with severe fiscal problems.[7]

- *Business Personal Property Taxes*—The property tax is generally the single largest state-local tax burden on a manufacturing business. The definition of the tax base and assessment policies—not just the rate of tax—are important determinants of property tax burdens. A clear trend has emerged to exempt inventories from the property tax. In addition to concerns about the difficulty of applying the property tax effectively and equitably to movable items, the inventory tax is a barrier to location decisions by wholesaling and distribution businesses. Thirty-three states plus the District of Columbia currently exempt inventories.[8] In 1987, North Carolina exempted inventories and coupled the change with an increase in the corporate income tax rate from 6 percent to 7 percent. Kansas also will exempt inventories beginning in 1989 as part of a comprehensive restructuring of its property tax.

- *Income and Franchise Tax Rates*—Corporate income tax rates are the most visible aspect of state business taxes. This feature is not likely to become a major economic development issue, however, unless the rates are far above the norm. Rates in a range of 5 percent to 8 percent are most common. Similarly, franchise taxes based upon some measure of capital (net worth or invested capital including debt) tend to become issues only when they are perceived to be excessive relative to those of neighboring states. The franchise tax has been a focus of the Texas Select Committee on Tax Equity not only because the rate is high but because it treats different businesses in an uneven manner. Corporations are subject to a substantial tax while firms organized as partnerships (including large master limited partnerships) escape tax in a state that does not have a personal income tax.

- *Taxation of Foreign Source Income*—The most controversial issue—the "unitary" issue—relating to foreign source income has been largely resolved. In 1987, Montana and North Dakota adopted "water's-edge" treatment of multinational corporations. Alaska is the only state that continues to use worldwide combined reporting on a mandatory basis. Important issues remain to be addressed in some states, however, such as the unitary treatment of "80-20" companies (U.S. corporations that have more than 80 percent of their activities

185

Table 1.

Sales Taxation of Equipment Purchases
by Manufacturers and Contractors (as of November 1987)

State	Taxable Status
Alabama	Taxable at lower rate
Alaska	No state sales tax
Arizona	Exempt for manufacturers
Arkansas	Exempt for new and expanding industries[1]
California	Fully taxable
Colorado	Fully exempt
Connecticut	Most are exempt
District of Columbia	Fully taxable
Delaware	No state sales tax
Florida	Exempt for new and expanding industries
Georgia	Exempt for new and expanding industries
Hawaii	Fully taxable
Idaho	Most are exempt
Illinois	Exempt for manufacturers
Indiana	Exempt for manufacturers
Iowa	Fully exempt
Kansas	Exempt[2]
Kentucky	Exempt for new and expanding industries
Louisiana	Exempt only in enterprise zones
Maine	Most are exempt
Maryland	Exempt for manufacturers
Massachusetts	Exempt for manufacturers
Michigan	Exempt for manufacturers[1]
Minnesota	Lower rate for new and expanding industries
Mississippi	Taxable at a lower rate[1]
Missouri	Most are exempt
Montana	No state sales tax
Nebraska	Exempt for new and expanding industries
Nevada	Fully taxable
New Hampshire	No state sales tax
New Jersey	Exempt for manufacturers
New Mexico	Most are exempt
New York	Exempt for manufacturers
North Carolina	Taxable at a lower rate
North Dakota	Fully taxable
Ohio	Exempt for manufacturers
Oklahoma	Exempt for manufacturers
Oregon	No state sales tax
Pennsylvania	Exempt for manufacturers
Rhode Island	Exempt for manufacturers
South Carolina	Exempt for manufacturers
South Dakota	Fully taxable
Tennessee	Exempt for manufacturers
Texas	Exempt only in enterprise zones
Utah	Exempt only for mining

State	Taxable Status
Vermont	Exempt for manufacturers
Virginia	Exempt for manufacturers[1]
Washington	Fully taxable
West Virginia	Fully exempt
Wisconsin	Exempt for manufacturers
Wyoming	Fully taxable

Notes:
1. Also exempt in enterprise zones.
2. Exempted by 1988 legislation.
   Source: *All States Tax Guide* (Englewood Cliffs, N.J.: Prentice Hall, 1987).

outside the United States) and state taxation of dividends from foreign subsidiaries.[9]

- *Corporate Apportionment Formula*—The method of attributing the income of multistate corporations to individual states is a major focal point of tax policy and litigation. Since most state corporate income taxes typically are paid by multistate firms, this is a critical step in the process of determining state corporate liability. The primary purpose of an apportionment formula is to allocate income in a manner reflecting the extent to which a firm is doing business in a state. The three-factor formula—which considers property, payroll, and sales—is the most common one that states use. Some states, however, also have evaluated apportionment formula alternatives from an economic development perspective. For example, Iowa uses a single-factor sales formula that tends to reduce the burden on firms that have a substantial investment in the state (as reflected by property and payroll) in comparison with the standard three-factor formula. Nebraska is also in the process of phasing in a single-factor sales formula. Thirteen other states give the sales factor a double weighting in the three-factor formula or allow some other method of giving sales an extra weighting.[10] States must be careful, however, in evaluating the revenue and distributional effects of apportionment formula options. Formula changes create considerable tax shifting in both directions that should be analyzed carefully.
- *Selective Tax Incentives*—States increasingly have turned to special tax credits, exemptions, and abate-

ments to compete with one another and attract major capital investment projects. These tax incentives take many forms—such as employment tax credits, investment tax credits, property tax abatements, and research and development credits. In most cases, these incentives are offered on a limited or selective basis. The provisions either are statutorily defined so that they are available only when certain conditions are met (e.g., well above- average employment growth or location in an enterprise zone) or are approved on a discretionary basis for specific projects. In 1987, Nebraska enacted a much-publicized package of employment and investment incentives. Many analysts, such as Ledebur and Hamilton, are critical of tax concessions and argue that they are not cost-effective and are inequitable.[11] Nonetheless, states often are expected to include tax benefits in packages designed to compete for major projects.

- *Comprehensive Business Tax Restructuring*—Business taxes can be structured in many different ways to raise a given amount of revenue. Different business tax structures will have differential impacts on the profitability of new investment, even while raising the same amount of total revenue. Consequently, it makes sense for states to analyze and evaluate business tax policy alternatives comprehensively in order to design an efficient general tax structure that encourages investment. Not surprisingly, states rarely undertake a comprehensive policymaking approach because of the incremental, crisis-oriented character of the political process. Recent business tax changes in Kansas are, however, a significant exception. The overall set of changes is a consequence of legislation enacted in 1988 and a property tax restructuring to implement an earlier constitutional amendment. Elements of the package included: 1) a property tax exemption for inventories; 2) strict rules for assessment of machinery and equipment that generally benefit long- lived equipment purchasers; 3) classification of real property resulting in some increase in taxes on commercial and industrial real estate; 4) sales tax exemption for machinery and equipment; and 5) favorable treatment of firms with high payroll to property/sales factor ratios under the corporate apportionment formula. While the author is not in a position to pass judgment on the net effects of this proposal, many of the elements of the package, such as favorable sales and property tax treatment of up-front business equipment purchases, are examples of general business tax policies with a meaningful investment orientation.

Response to Federal Tax Policy Changes

Federal corporate tax policy can be expected to have a major ongoing impact in setting the state business tax policy agenda during the next five years. Because most states use federal taxable income as a starting point in calculating state corporate tax liability, federal tax base changes generally affect state corporate tax receipts. As discussed earlier, states have found the corporate provisions of the federal Tax Reform Act of 1986 a major source of uncertainty. As the new President and Congress confront the issue of the budget deficit in 1989 and beyond, more federal business tax changes can be expected to ripple through to state treasuries. These impacts include:

- *Ongoing Revenue Impacts of the 1986 Tax Reform Act—* The precise impact of the 1986 TRA upon state corporate tax receipts is far from clear. A number of states reported corporate collections below estimates for the 1988 fiscal year. It is premature, however, to draw definitive conclusions regarding the extent of this problem or its causes. First, some state revenue analysts held out the hope that weakness in early receipts may be offset by stronger collections later when taxpayers who obtained extensions filed their returns. Second, further analysis is required to separate out economic and tax reform effects upon overall receipts. If actual corporate receipts are substantially different than estimates once the TRA impacts are reflected fully in collections, offsetting increases or decreases in corporate taxes may be proposed.
- *Future Federal Tax Changes—* The most dramatic federal tax policy option potentially affecting state business taxes is the value-added tax. The substance of the VAT is not discussed here since it is the subject of Chapters 14 and 15. Research tools needed to analyze the VAT are discussed, however, in the next section. Regardless of whether a VAT is enacted at the federal level, more corporate tax changes are almost certain

to come. Roughly half the revenue raised in the Omnibus Budget Reconciliation Act of 1987 comes from higher corporate income taxes. More tax increases in 1989 and beyond are, of course, possible as part of deficit reduction efforts. On the other hand, corporate income tax reductions are also possible in a VAT package, especially if a persuasive case can be made that certain TRA provisions have had an adverse economic impact. Although the content or even direction of future federal business tax changes is unpredictable, it is likely that states once again will be reacting to federal changes significantly affecting their tax policy and tax receipts.

- *Minimum Tax*—Most states have opted not to follow the federal lead in the area of the alternative minimum tax (AMT). The alternative minimum tax broadly redefines taxable income to include items that are not part of regular taxable income and are estimated to raise substantial revenue at the federal level. The AMT, however, is complex and controversial as to its economic effects. Ten states have some form of corporate AMT, although not all follow the federal approach in defining income. Most states have been cautious in proceeding in this direction because of great uncertainty regarding revenue and economic impacts. In addition, many states have franchise taxes that assure some tax will be paid by corporations doing business in the state, consistent with the benefits-received principle.

Research Needs

For many states, the experience of making policy in response to the Tax Reform Act of 1986 pointed out gaps in their ability to analyze the fiscal, distributional, and economic effects of policy alternatives. Some states were well equipped to analyze personal income tax impacts because they had invested in the development of personal income tax models that enabled staff to simulate policy alternatives. While these models could not capture behavioral effects, such as changes in the timing of capital gains realizations, with certainty, they could analyze the fiscal and distributional effects of policy alternatives. Many other states, however, were not able to analyze policy options using state-specific data.

Effective management of the policy research process requires anticipation of future issues and development of the necessary data bases and tools to analyze alternatives accurately.

The following types of research efforts are needed to provide reliable answers to the questions that legislators can be expected to ask if and when they address the business tax issues identified.

Multi-State Business Tax Comparisons

States considering development-related tax changes would benefit from a systematic approach to analyzing their business taxes. A comprehensive business tax analysis must:

- Consider all major taxes: property, sales, income, and franchise;
- Consider tax base as well as rate effects — e.g., sales tax treatment of business equipment, property tax treatment of inventories, corporate depreciation;
- Compare the impact of state taxes on profitability for relevant states and industries in a credible manner; and
- Analyze the effects of policy alternatives on profitability for key industries.

Table 2 is an example of the kind of information that is provided by such an analysis. Overall business tax burdens were calculated for six industries in nine states at both urban and rural locations. The model used for this analysis projects income and taxes over a multiyear period, taking into account timing differences, for representative firms in each industry. Tax impacts are portrayed as dollars of taxes per $100 of investment and as a percentage of pretax income.

Table 2 shows one of the tables produced by the model — dollars of tax per $100 of investment as an average for the six industries at the rural locations included in the study. Three important points can be observed:

- Property taxes are the single largest state-local business tax — three times greater than income taxes.
- The range of total taxes is significant across states, with taxes at the Kansas location more than double those at the New Mexico location.
- Although it is not a large item in most places, the sales tax on business purchases is significant when a high combined state-local rate is applied to equipment purchases, as is the case in Louisiana and Texas.

Table 2.

Annual Tax per $100 of Capital Investment
for Rural Locations, 1985

Metropolitan Area	Income Tax	Property Tax	Sales Tax	Franchise Tax	Unemployment Insurance	Workers' Compensation	Total
Dodge City, Kansas	$0.55	$1.88	$0.17	$0.03	$0.14	$0.19	$2.96
Kirksville, Missouri	0.26	2.17	0.07	0.03	0.09	0.15	2.77
Tupelo, Mississippi	0.43	1.49	0.05	0.10	0.13	0.18	2.37
Corsicana, Texas	0.00	1.45	0.22	0.21	0.09	0.26	2.23
Jonesboro, Arkansas	0.52	1.23	0.05	0.07	0.10	0.22	2.19
De Ridder, Louisiana	0.36	0.75	0.31	0.16	0.09	0.24	1.91
Ft. Collins, Colorado	0.41	0.96	0.06	0.00	0.10	0.32	1.86
Weatherford, Oklahoma	0.42	0.87	0.06	0.07	0.10	0.28	1.80
Durant, Oklahoma	0.42	0.80	0.07	0.07	0.10	0.28	1.74
Farmington, New Mexico	0.32	0.25	0.19	0.02	0.12	0.39	1.29
Average	**$0.37**	**$1.18**	**$0.13**	**$0.08**	**$0.10**	**$0.25**	**$2.11**

Note: Totals do not necessarily equal sum of lines due to rounding.
Source: *An Evaluation of the Oklahoma Business Climate* (Washington, D.C.: Price Waterhouse, 1985).

Similar results are provided for specific industries. In addition, the effects of tax policy alternatives can be simulated to assess their effect on business tax competitiveness.[12] It is important to note that Table 2 reflects laws in effect in 1985 and should not be interpreted as a current law comparison.

The advantage of this approach is that state decision makers would have an accurate way of determining the competitiveness of their current taxes and evaluating the relative merits of alternatives. As discussed previously, business tax policies can be structured to raise a given amount of total business tax revenue in a way that minimizes the impact on new investment in order to support the process of job creation. This view does not imply that taxes are the most important determinant of state economic development. Instead, a well-designed business tax policy should be viewed as one of many elements of an economic development program that includes investment in education and transportation, among other things.

Corporate Receipts Tracking and Analysis Systems

Although corporate income taxes comprised only 8 percent of total state general tax revenue in the United States in fiscal year 1985-86, the potential impact in terms of revenue shortfalls and budget problems is much greater. Because corporate profits fluctuate sharply over the business cycle, the corporate income tax is frequently a source of large revenue-estimating errors. At present, state corporate taxation is subject to even greater uncertainty due to the impact of federal tax reform and the likelihood of future changes in federal law that will continue to affect the definition of the state corporate tax base.

Currently, some state revenue research units have set up systems for tracking payments from large firms. These systems yield useful information on total collections and type of transaction (i.e., declarations, payments with return, refunds) by tax year. More detailed data, however, are needed to monitor and analyze federal tax reform impacts. As 1987 return data become available late in 1988, it will be possible for the first time to analyze the revenue impacts of key provisions using state-specific data. Continuing analysis of federal tax reform provisions is critical to doing accurate baseline revenue estimates because key provisions have important timing effects. Accounting provisions with large estimated revenue effects—such as uniform capitalization of inventories, completed contracts, installment sales, and bad debt reserves—have large initial impacts spread over the period of 1987 to 1990. In 1991, the revenue gains from these provisions fall sharply. On the other hand, depreciation and expensing changes are expected to lose revenue in 1987 and 1988 and then reverse and raise increasing amounts of revenue from 1989 to 1991.

It will be difficult for states to separate economic and TRA impacts on actual corporate collections. It should be possible, however, to test selected items on returns of major taxpayers by focusing on the 1 percent of filers who pay 50 percent or more of total corporate taxes in most states. A special effort is justified to provide timely information on federal impacts for revenue-estimating purposes.

Computerized Corporate Tax Model

Few states have invested in the development of corporate tax models enabling refined analysis of major business tax policy alternatives. Analyses are based upon actual state tax return data. A sample of corporate taxpayers is designed to produce valid estimates for the state corporate taxpaying population. Extensive information is keypunched from the sample returns. A corporate tax calculator is constructed so that tax policy alternatives can be analyzed with precision. The computer simulations show the amount and percent change in liability—by, for example, industry, size of firm, in-state versus out-of-state firm—that would result from alternative tax policies. This core data base can be expanded with financial data from other sources, such as Standard and

Poor's, in order to permit analysis of alternatives such as a state value-added tax. Public and private decision makers can be expected to demand good information on industry impacts in considering business tax policy alternatives.

Conclusion

Legislatures and governors will be confronted with important business tax policy and management decisions during the next five years. The priority assigned to job creation efforts translates into concern for the competitiveness of business taxes (as well as the quality of education and transportation systems). State budget and tax administrators will be challenged to monitor and analyze the complex impacts of federal tax reform in estimating revenue. Finally, future changes in federal tax policy related to deficit reduction efforts will place new business tax issues on the state tax policy agenda.

A somewhat limited tax policy agenda in 1988 may provide a breathing spell for states to organize their analytical efforts to improve their ability to make informed policy choices and to manage their fiscal affairs effectively. The sorting-out process in state economic development may well reflect the extent to which the leadership in the states responds to these challenges.

Notes

1. Committee on State Taxation, "State Income Tax Impact of Federal Tax Reform" (Washington, D.C.: Council of State Chambers of Commerce, 1987).

2. Robert H. Aten, "The Magnitude of Additional State Corporate Income Taxes Resulting from Federal Tax Reform," *Tax Notes,* August 3, 1987, pp. 529-534.

3. Robert Tannenwald, "The Effects of the Tax Reform Act of 1986 on New England's State Income Tax Revenues," *National Tax Journal* XL, no. 3 (September 1987): 456.

4. National Association of State Budget Officers, *Federal Tax Reform: The Impact on the States* (Washington, D.C.: National Association of State Budget Officers/National Governors' Association, 1987).

5. Steven D. Gold, Corina L. Eckl, and Brenda Erickson, *State Budget Actions in 1987* (Denver: National Conference of State Legislatures, 1987), updated to reflect subsequent legislation.

6. Thirty-seven of the 45 states with a corporate income tax recognize Subchapter S corporation status. Of the states that recognize Subchapter S status, California and Illinois are the only ones that impose a corporate franchise or income tax. Illinois exempts Subchapter S corporations from the general corporate income tax but imposes the personal property replacement income tax at a 1.5 percent rate.

7. See William Oakland, "Business Taxation in Louisiana: An Appraisal," in James Richardson, ed., *Louisiana's Fiscal Alternatives* (Baton Rouge: Louisiana State University Press, 1988).

8. As of November 1987, according to Prentice Hall's *All States Tax Guide,* the states that still imposed a tax on inventories were Alaska, Arkansas, Georgia (local option exemption effective in many counties and municipalities), Indiana, Kansas, Kentucky, Louisiana, Maryland, Massachusetts (except corporate inventories), Mississippi, Ohio, Oklahoma, Rhode Island (except manufacturers' inventories), Tennessee (except merchants' inventories unless held for lease), Texas, Vermont (local option), and West Virginia. Kansas exempted inventories in 1988.

9. The states are about evenly split on the issue of taxability of dividends received from foreign corporations. See William A. Raabe, ed., *Multistate Corporate Tax Almanac, 1988 Edition* (Greenvale, New York: Panel Publishers, 1988), pp. 99-104.

10. Ten states that place a double weight on the sales factor are Connecticut, Florida, Illinois, Kentucky, Massachusetts, New York, North Carolina (as of 1988), Ohio, West Virginia, and Wisconsin. In addition, Minnesota allows corporations to give sales a 70 percent weight, Missouri allows corporations to use either a one-factor or a three-factor formula, and Colorado permits the payroll factor to be excluded.

11. See Larry C. Ledebur and William W. Hamilton, "The Failure of Tax Concessions as Economic Development Incentives," in Steven D. Gold, ed., *Reforming State Tax Systems* (Denver: National Conference of State Legislatures, 1986), pp. 101-117.

12. These sample results are from Price Waterhouse, *An Evaluation of the Oklahoma Business Climate* (Washington, D.C.: Price Waterhouse, 1985). See James A. Papke and Leslie E. Papke, "Measuring Differential State-Local Tax Liabilities and Their Implications for Business Investment Location," *National Tax Journal* XXXIX, no. 3 (September 1986): 357-366, for a discussion of tax differentials as location factors.

Are States Overtaxing or Undertaxing Corporations?

by
Robert S. McIntyre

State corporate income taxes, although relatively low as a share of state revenues, are high in controversy. On the one hand, legislators worry that undertaxing corporations may cause public resentment and require higher taxes on ordinary citizens to pay for needed state programs. On the other hand, they are concerned that overtaxing companies may hurt their state's business climate, cost jobs, and lessen economic growth.

For the decade and a half preceding federal tax reform, most states followed the federal lead in undermining their corporate tax bases with various incentives. As a result, a situation in which many large profitable corporations were paying little or no federal income tax was duplicated too often at the state level. But faced with pressing revenue requirements, state legislators raised rates on those companies still on the tax rolls, thereby maintaining total corporate tax revenues at the state level even as federal corporate taxes plummeted.

As the eighties draw to a close, state governments are being called upon to lead the way in improving America's competitive position in world markets. Experts now point to better education and training, improved transportation systems, and the like as the keys to enhancing our standard of living and that of our children. To pay for these programs, many states will need additional revenues.

Fortunately, some help is at hand. The federal government has turned away from its previous policy of cluttering the tax code with loopholes and incentives, in favor of a fairer, economically more neutral system. Now, by conforming to the revitalized federal corporate income tax, states have the opportunity to improve the fairness and stability of their revenue systems and raise some of the revenues that they need to meet their added responsibilities.

Where Things Stand

All but a handful of states tax corporate profits earned within their borders. Only Michigan, Nevada, South Dakota, Texas, Washington, and Wyoming, homes to about 12 percent of the nation's population, have no general corporate income tax.[1] Indeed, except for Michigan, every state with a personal income tax supplements it with a corporate income tax.[2] Alaska and Florida are unusual in that their income taxes apply only to corporate profits,[3] as was briefly the federal practice in the early part of this century.

Top marginal corporate tax rates in states that have such taxes currently average 7.5 percent, and range from 11.5 percent in Connecticut to what amounts to 3.9 percent in Alabama and Missouri (5 percent minus federal deductibility).[4] Including states that have no corporate tax, the average top state corporate tax rate is currently 6.6 percent.[5] (See Table 1.) In fiscal 1986, states raised just under 7 percent of their tax revenues from corporate income taxes, with 30 states raising between 5 and 10 percent of their revenues from them. Six states raised more than 10 percent of their revenues from these taxes, while nine states with corporate income taxes raised less than 5 percent of their revenues from the tax. (See Table 2.)

As state legislators are well aware, state corporate income tax policy inevitably depends on what the federal government does. Most states generally follow the federal definition of corporate

Table 1.

State Statutory Corporate Tax Rates
Current Law, 1986, 1980, and 1970

State	1987	1986	1980	1970
Alabama*	3.9%	4.2%	3.7%	3.1%
Alaska	9.4	9.4	9.4	9.4
Arizona*	8.2	8.7	7.8	4.3
Arkansas	6.0	6.0	6.0	6.0
California	9.35	9.6	9.6	7.0
Colorado	6.0	6.0	5.0	5.0
Connecticut	11.5	11.5	10.0	7.4
Delaware	8.7	8.7	8.7	6.0
Florida	5.5	5.5	5.0	No Tax
Georgia	6.0	6.0	6.0	6.0
Hawaii	6.0	6.0	6.0	6.0
Idaho	8.0	7.7	6.5	6.0
Illinois	6.4	6.4	6.7	4.0
Indiana	7.7	6.9	5.9	2.0
Iowa*	10.7	11.0	8.7	6.5
Kansas	6.75	6.75	6.75	4.2
Kentucky	7.25	7.25	6.0	4.3
Louisiana*	6.2	6.6	5.9	4.0
Maine	8.93	8.93	6.93	4.0
Maryland	7.0	7.0	7.0	7.0
Massachusetts	9.5	9.5	9.5	6.9
Michigan	No Tax	No Tax	No Tax	5.6
Minnesota	9.5	12.0	12.0	7.0
Mississippi	5.0	5.0	4.0	4.0
Missouri*	3.9	4.2	3.7	1.2
Montana	7.02	6.75	6.75	6.25
Nebraska	6.21	6.21	4.46	2.5
Nevada	No Tax	No Tax	No Tax	No Tax
New Hampshire	8.0	8.25	8.0	6.0
New Jersey	9.0	9.0	9.0	4.25
New Mexico	7.0	7.0	4.8	4.8
New York	9.0	10.0	10.0	7.0
North Carolina	7.0	6.0	6.0	6.0
North Dakota*	8.2	8.7	7.0	4.3
Ohio	8.9	9.7	8.0	8.0
Oklahoma	4.8	4.8	3.8	1.8
Oregon	6.6	7.5	7.5	6.0
Pennsylvania	8.5	9.5	10.5	10.6
Rhode Island	8.0	8.0	8.0	8.0
South Carolina	5.5	6.0	6.0	6.0
South Dakota	No Tax	No Tax	No Tax	No Tax
Tennessee	6.0	6.0	6.0	4.8
Texas	No Tax	No Tax	No Tax	No Tax
Utah	5.0	5.2	4.0	3.7
Vermont	7.57	8.2	6.9	5.6

Table 1.
(continued)

State	1987	1986	1980	1970
Virginia	6.0	6.0	6.0	5.0
Washington	No Tax	No Tax	No Tax	No Tax
West Virginia	9.75	7.0	6.0	6.0
Wisconsin	7.9	7.9	7.9	5.9
Wyoming	No Tax	No Tax	No Tax	No Tax
U.S. Average	**6.6%**	**6.8%**	**6.5%**	**5.0%**
Average w/o No-Tax States	**7.5%**	**7.7%**	**7.5%**	**5.8%**

*Federal tax deductible under current law (rate adjusted by effective federal rate).

Notes:

Alabama:	5 percent statutory rate, with federal deductibility, in all years.
Alaska:	Top rate applies to taxable income over $90,000 in all years.
Arizona:	Statutory top rate of 10.5 percent, with federal deductibility in 1980 to current year. Eight percent top rate with federal and state taxes deductible in 1970. Top rate applies to taxable income over $6,000 in all years.
Arkansas:	Top rate applies to taxable income over $25,000 in all years.
Colorado:	Top rate currently applies to taxable income over $50,000; rate is scheduled to fall to 5 percent by 1993.
Connecticut:	State income taxes were deductible in 1970.
Hawaii:	State income taxes are deductible in all years. Top rate applies to taxable income over $100,000 currently, and to taxable income over $25,000 in earlier years.
Illinois:	Two tax rates: 4 percent and 2.5 percent currently and in 1986; 4 percent and 2.85 percent in earlier years.
Indiana:	Two tax rates: 3.4 percent and 4.5 percent currently; 3 percent and 4 percent in 1986; 3 percent and 3 percent in earlier years.
Iowa:	Half of federal income tax is deductible in all years. Statutory top rate of 12 percent over $250,000 currently and in 1986; 10 percent statutory top rate over $100,000 in 1980; 8 percent statutory top rate over $100,000 in 1970.
Kansas:	Top rate applies to taxable income over $25,000 in all years. Statutory top rate in 1970 was 6.75 percent, with federal deductibility.
Kentucky:	Top rate applies to taxable income over $250,000 currently and in 1986, and to taxable income over $100,000 in 1980. In 1970, top rate was 7 percent on taxable income over $25,000, with federal deductibility.
Louisiana:	Eight percent statutory top rate, with federal deductibility, on taxable income over $200,000 in 1980 and thereafter. No federal deductibility in 1970.
Maine:	Top rate applies to taxable income over $250,000 currently and in 1986, and to taxable income over $25,000 in earlier years.

Notes from Table 1 (continued)

Massachusetts:	Figures include a 14 percent surtax in 1980 and thereafter. State income taxes were deductible in 1970.
Michigan:	Repealed corporate income tax and replaced it with a 2.35 percent quasi-value-added tax in 1976.
Minnesota:	Top rate applies to taxable income above $25,000 in 1980 and thereafter. In 1970, top rate was 11.33 percent, with federal deductibility.
Mississippi:	Top rate applies to taxable income over $10,000 currently and in 1986; to taxable income above $5,000 in earlier years.
Missouri:	Five percent statutory top rate, with federal deductibility, in 1980 and thereafter. Two percent top rate with federal deductibility in 1970.
Montana:	Current rate reflects a new surtax.
Nebraska:	State income taxes deductible in all years. Top rate applies to taxable income over $50,000 currently and in 1986; over $25,000 in 1980.
New Mexico:	State income taxes deductible in all years. Statutory top rate of 7.6 percent, with state income taxes deductible; applies to taxable income over $1 million currently and in 1986.
North Dakota:	Top rate applies to income over $50,000 currently and in 1986; over $25,000 in earlier years. Current law provides for an alternative minimum tax of 5 percent of federal AMT income.
Ohio:	Top rate applies to taxable income over $25,000 in all years (over $50,000 in 1989); 1986 and 1987 figures include a 5.4 percent surcharge. The surtax expires after 1987.
Oklahoma:	State income taxes are deductible in all years. Federal income taxes were deductible in 1970. Statutory top rate is 5 percent currently and in 1986; 4 percent in earlier years.
Pennsylvania:	Statutory top rate of 12 percent, with state income taxes deductible, in 1970.
South Carolina:	Rate is scheduled to drop to 5 percent in 1989.
South Dakota:	No tax except on financial institutions in all years.
Tennessee:	Five percent statutory top rate, with state income taxes deductible in 1970.
Utah:	Four percent surtax for 1986. Statutory top rate was 6 percent, with federal deductibility, in 1970.
Vermont:	State income taxes are deductible in all years. Statutory top rate, 8.25 percent currently, 9 percent in 1986, and 7.5 percent in 1980; applies to taxable income over $250,000 in those years. Statutory top rate was 6 percent in 1970.
West Virginia:	Top rate applies to taxable income over $50,000 in 1980 and thereafter. Top rate is scheduled to drop to 9 percent by 1992.
Wisconsin:	Top rate applies to taxable income over $6,000 in 1980 and thereafter. Top rate was 7 percent in 1970, with state income taxes and federal income taxes up to 10 percent of income deductible.

Table 2.

Composition of State Tax Revenues in 1986
(as a Percent of Total Tax Revenues)

State	Corporate Income Tax	Personal Income Tax	Sales Taxes*	Property and Inheritance Taxes
New Hampshire	20.4%	5.1%	69.4%	5.0%
Connecticut	16.1	7.8	72.2	3.9
Massachusetts	13.9	47.2	36.2	2.7
California	12.4	36.8	45.6	5.2
New Jersey	11.4	24.6	61.4	2.7
Delaware	10.1	44.6	43.6	1.7
Alaska	9.6	—	84.2	6.2
Montana	9.5	27.9	53.9	8.7
North Carolina	9.2	39.5	48.5	2.8
North Dakota	9.1	11.9	78.3	0.7
Pennsylvania	9.0	24.9	61.8	4.4
Illinois	8.8	27.0	61.5	2.7
Georgia	8.5	39.6	51.1	0.8
Oregon	8.4	61.8	28.4	1.4
New York	8.4	50.9	39.3	1.4
Tennessee	8.2	2.1	88.8	0.9
Kansas	8.2	30.5	58.2	3.1
Rhode Island	7.6	32.4	57.3	2.7
Minnesota	7.5	39.8	52.3	0.4
Wisconsin	7.4	40.8	48.1	3.7
Louisiana	7.3	12.6	78.9	1.2
Kentucky	7.3	25.5	57.6	9.6
Arkansas	6.2	27.9	65.3	0.6
Vermont	6.1	32.1	60.8	1.0
Virginia	5.8	44.9	48.6	0.8
Idaho	5.7	34.4	59.5	0.4
Iowa	5.6	35.2	56.8	2.4
Maryland	5.4	41.3	50.0	3.3
Arizona	5.3	22.0	68.7	4.0
Florida	5.3	—	91.0	3.7
Ohio	5.3	30.6	63.5	0.6
Alabama	5.2	25.3	67.0	2.5
South Carolina	5.2	31.4	62.4	1.0
Mississippi	5.1	14.2	80.0	0.7
Colorado	5.0	40.8	53.3	1.0
New Mexico	4.9	7.0	87.3	0.7
Nebraska	4.9	31.4	63.0	0.7
Utah	4.9	33.1	61.7	0.4
Missouri	4.8	30.9	63.2	1.0
West Virginia	4.8	25.9	68.1	1.2
Maine	4.7	30.6	62.7	2.0
Indiana	4.1	29.8	64.4	1.7
Oklahoma	3.6	23.2	71.8	1.3
Hawaii	2.9	31.4	65.3	0.4
South Dakota	5.8	—	91.3	2.9

State	Corporate Income Tax	Personal Income Tax	Sales Taxes*	Property and Inheritance Taxes
Michigan	—	34.9	62.3	2.9
Nevada	—	—	96.8	3.2
Texas	—	—	98.9	1.1
Washington	—	—	83.9	16.1
Wyoming	—	—	86.2	13.8
U.S. Average	**7.4%**	**29.6%**	**60.0%**	**3.0%**
States w/CIT†	**8.4%**	**32.1%**	**56.7%**	**2.8%**
States w/o CIT	**—**	**11.6%**	**83.3%**	**4.9%**

*Sales tax figures include sales tax-type taxes, such as severance taxes and Michigan's Single Business Tax.
†CIT = Corporate income tax

taxable income (just as they usually do with regard to personal income) to avoid the large administrative difficulties in having significantly different tax forms and to obtain the federal government's help in tax enforcement.

Beginning in 1971 under President Nixon and continuing under various Presidents for the next decade and a half, the federal corporate income tax base grew narrower and narrower. One major federal change—the reinstatement and then expansion of the federal investment tax credit—did not affect the states directly. But constrictions in the definition of federal corporate taxable income, such as more generous depreciation write-offs, led to tough decisions at the state level. States had to either accept the federal changes, or, by refusing to conform, make state definitions of corporate taxable income more and more different from the federal definition.

In practice, state governments ended up on a corporate income tax treadmill. Faced with an increasingly loophole-ridden federal corporate tax code, reluctant (with a few notable exceptions) to deviate markedly from Uncle Sam's rules defining corporate taxable income but also confronted with growing revenue needs, states, in the aggregate, raced to increase statutory corporate tax rates to offset the revenue loss from conforming to the ever-narrowing federal corporate tax base.

In the 1970s, this process actually put state treasuries ahead of the game. Although state corporate taxable income as a share of corporate profits declined along with federal corporate taxable income (both fell by about 9 percent as a share of profits), and although some states followed the federal lead in adopting corporate tax credits, at the same time, 30 states increased their statutory corporate tax rates, while only two states cut them.[6] The average state statutory corporate tax rate (including states with no corporate tax) rose from 5 percent in 1970 to 6.5 percent by 1980.

These rate increases averted the state revenue losses that the narrower corporate tax base would have produced. In fact, from 1970 to 1980, state corporate taxes as a share of corporate profits rose by 16 percent—from 4.4 percent of profits in 1970 to 5.1 percent in 1980—while the federal effective corporate tax rate dropped almost a third.[7]

In the first half of the 1980s, however, states had a more difficult time preserving their corporate tax revenues. Due particularly to the sharp increase in federal accelerated depreciation write-offs enacted in 1981, federal taxable income as a share of corporate profits fell by 15 percent. Federal corporate tax credits grew as well, and federal corporate taxes dropped from 26 percent of profits in 1980 to only 17 percent by 1986, with dozens of well-known, highly profitable companies paying nothing at all.[8]

With some exceptions, states continued to conform to the federal base changes, and they too watched as profitable corporations dropped off their tax rolls.[9] Although 22 states increased their statutory corporate tax rates and only two cut them from 1980 to 1986, the average statutory rate went up only slightly (from 6.5 percent to 6.8 percent).[10] As a result, the average effective corporate tax rate in the states fell from 5.1 percent of corporate profits in 1980 to 4.6 percent in 1986—a 9 percent decline.

Thus, from 1970 to 1986, after a decade and a half of reacting to ever-expanding federal corporate tax loopholes, state governments had increased their average statutory corporate tax rate by almost 36 percent but had seen a mere 5 percent increase in their overall corporate tax collections as a share of corporate profits.[11] As a share of total state revenues, corporate taxes declined by 6 percent, from 7.9 percent in 1970 to 7.4 percent in 1986. A wide gap had developed between statutory rates and the effective rates companies actually paid. (See Figure 1.)

This corporate tax treadmill forced states to look to other taxpayers to bear the burdens of increased public demands for state spending and the decline in federal financial support to the states. From 1970 to 1986, total state revenues rose from 4.8 percent of the gross national product to 5.4 percent—an increase of 0.6 percentage points. Although state tax actions varied widely, in the aggregate, the entire change reflected higher state personal income taxes, which rose from 0.9 percent of the GNP in 1970 to 1.6 percent by 1986—an increase of 0.7 percent.[12]

Surely, states deserve congratulations for keeping their fiscal books in balance—a far cry from the federal government, which has seen every one of its major taxes except Social Security decline over the last two decades.[13] And surely, state legislators warrant a pat on the back both for maintaining corporate tax revenues in the face of the federal loophole onslaught and for generally relying on another progressive tax—the personal income tax—to pay for added state services.

But now, the federal government finally has provided some relief on the corporate income tax front. If they choose, state legislators finally can get some revenue benefit from all their efforts in raising statutory corporate rates over the past decade and a half.

The 1986 tax reform bill restored federal corporate taxable income to just over two-thirds of actual corporate profits (still less than 1980's 72 percent of profits, however, and far less than 1970's 80 percent). Repeal of the federal investment tax credit allowed a sharp cut in the federal statutory corporate tax rate—from 46 percent to 34 percent next year. Federal corporate taxes as a share of federal revenues and of the gross national product have been restored somewhat; the effective federal corporate tax rate has risen from 17 percent of profits to just over 20 percent; and the gap between the federal statutory and effective corporate rates has been narrowed substantially. (See Figure 2.)

By conforming to the most recent federal changes, states can restore their corporate income tax revenues and effective rates back to about their 1980 levels. And like the federal government, states can narrow the gap between statutory corporate tax rates and the effective rates that companies actually pay.

To be sure, the added revenues that potentially will flow into state coffers from federal tax reform will not spell revenue nirvana for the states. With corporate taxes providing less than 7 percent of total state revenues in fiscal 1986, the 11 to 18 percent expansion in the corporate tax base that federal conformity can offer (see Table 3) means only about a 1 percent increase in total state revenues. One percent or thereabouts, on the other hand, is nothing to sneeze at. A similar relative increase in federal revenues caused the President and Congress great consternation in 1987.

The Fairness Case for the Corporate Income Tax

Revenues, of course, are not the only issue with regard to corporate taxes. Equally important is tax fairness. From that point of view, the fact that all but a few states—and all except one of the states with a personal income tax—tax corporate profits is not surprising. Most taxpayers would view taxing the income of

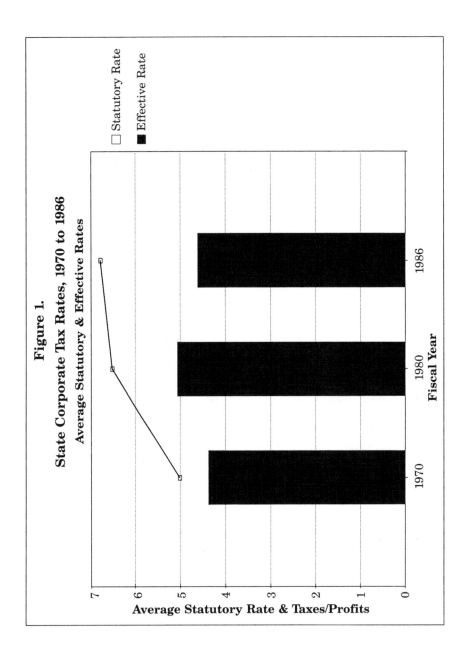

Figure 1.

State Corporate Tax Rates, 1970 to 1986

Average Statutory & Effective Rates

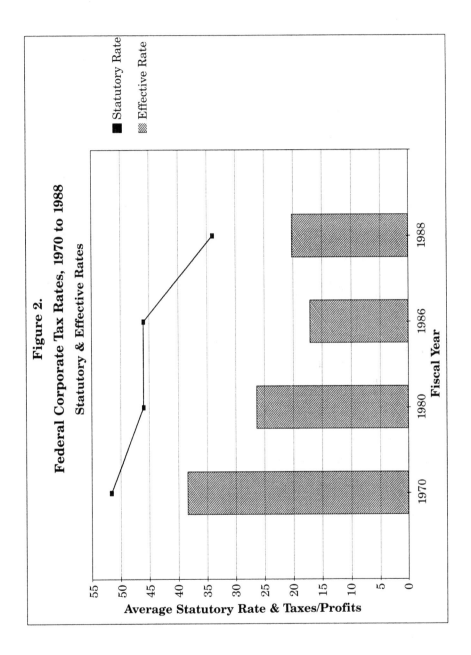

Figure 2.
Federal Corporate Tax Rates, 1970 to 1988
Statutory & Effective Rates

Table 3.

Revenue Effects of Corporate Changes in the 1986 Tax Reform Act (with federal fiscal year revenue impacts in billions of dollars)

Provisions	1989	1987-91
1. Items affecting corporate taxable income		
Inventory, etc., capitalization	$ 7.4	$ 32.2
Long-term contracts	2.2	9.6
Depreciation	0.2	7.7
P&C insurance companies	1.6	7.5
Bad-debt reserves (nonfinancial)	1.7	7.4
Installment pledges	1.4	7.3
Business meals & entertainment	1.3	6.2
Bad-debt reserves (financial)	1.2	5.0
Life insurance companies	0.9	4.0
Interest to carry tax-exempt bonds	0.7	3.4
Cash accounting	0.6	2.8
Public utilities	0.5	2.0
Liquidations & mergers	0.4	1.8
Sales tax deduction	0.3	1.3
Dividends received deduction	0.2	1.1
Agriculture, timber, oil, etc.	0.2	0.6
Troubled thrifts (reorg.)	0.0	0.3
Discharge of debt	0.1	0.3
Fringe benefits	0.0	0.2
All other	0.1	0.2
Regulated investment companies	0.0	0.2
Tax-exempt bonds	(0.0)	(0.1)
NOL carryovers (financial companies)	(0.1)	(0.3)
At-risk rules	(0.3)	(1.8)
LIFO, small business	(0.3)	(1.8)
Passive losses	(2.6)	(12.6)
Total, taxable income	**$ 17.7**	**$ 84.6**
2. Items affecting credits		
Investment tax credit	$ 25.1	$ 118.7
ESOPs	0.2	2.1
Finance leasing	0.3	1.4
Rehabilitation credit	0.2	0.9
Targeted jobs tax credit	(0.2)	(0.7)
R&D Credit	(0.8)	(3.9)
Total, tax credits	**$ 24.9**	**$ 118.5**
3. Other items		
Minimum tax	$ 5.1	$ 22.5
Foreign tax provisions	2.0	9.3
Compliance	0.3	2.1
Total, other	**$ 7.4**	**$ 33.9**
4. Corporate rate cut	$ (27.5)	$(116.7)
TOTAL, ALL	**$ 22.5**	**$ 120.3**

Provisions	1989	1987-91
Summary		
Taxable income	$ 17.7	$ 84.6
Tax credits	24.9	118.5
Other	7.4	33.9
Rate cut	(27.5)	(116.7)
Net Total	**$ 22.5**	**$ 120.3**
Estimated federal corporate tax collections		
Before reform	$ 103.5	$ 676.7
After reform	$ 126.0	$ 797.0
Effects on state corporate tax bases (% Increases)		
States using—		
Federal taxable income	14%	11%
Federal taxable income, including (if appropriate) alternative minimum tax income	18%	13%
Percentage of federal tax	22%	18%

Key: P&C = Property and Casualty
      NOL = Net Operating Loss
      LIFO = Last In, First Out (treatment of inventories)
      ESOPs = Employee Stock Ownership Plans
      R&D = Research and Development
Sources: Joint Committee on Taxation, *General Explanation of the Tax Reform Act of 1986* (May 4, 1987). Congressional Budget Office, *An Analysis of the President's Budgetary Proposals for Fiscal Year 1988,* February 1987.

wage earners and unincorporated small businesses while exempting the profits of major corporations as outrageously unfair.

The corporate income tax is an extremely progressive way to raise revenues. That's because ownership of corporate shares—or of capital in general—is heavily concentrated among the wealthy. Indeed, as recent papers by some quite conservative economists have illustrated, a central reason why the 1986 federal Tax Reform Act improved the progressivity of the overall federal tax system was that it strengthened the corporate income tax.[14]

The corporate income tax is different from many other kinds of business taxes in that it is not passed on to consumers in the form of higher prices. Since the income tax is a percentage of pretax profits, the pricing strategy that maximizes pretax profits also will maximize after-tax profits. If a company were to try to pass on its income taxes by charging more for its products, that would lead to reduced sales and reduced pretax earnings. And, therefore, it would lead to lower after-tax earnings as well. Thus, corporations would be foolish to try to pass on their income taxes.

Everyday experience confirms that companies don't pass on their income taxes. Prior to federal tax reform, wildly different effective tax rates existed among companies in the same industries. For example, from 1982 to 1985, Exxon paid more than one-quarter of its profits in federal corporate income taxes; Mobil paid less than 7 percent; and Texaco paid nothing (in fact, it got refunds). Yet a visit to any suburban street corner where these companies market their gasoline would show that all posted about the same price per gallon. So which company was passing on the tax? Similarly, banks had wildly different tax rates; yet all charged about the same interest rates on their loans. Again, which was passing on the tax?

To be sure, corporate lobbyists often do assert that the corporate tax is nothing but a hidden sales tax and therefore should be done away with. But the obvious question they must be asked is what should the corporate tax be replaced with? And their typical answer, ironically, is that it should be replaced with new or increased sales taxes, or, the equivalent, a value-added tax.

The lobbyists are right about one thing. States that don't have corporate income taxes do end up relying very heavily on sales taxes.

States with no general corporate income tax[15]	Percentage of revenues from sales, excise, and similar taxes[16]
Texas	99%
Nevada	97
South Dakota[17]	91
Wyoming	86
Washington	84
Michigan	62
Six-state average	83%
Compare all other states	57%

The regressivity that generally characterizes state tax systems buttresses the fairness case for the corporate income tax. On average, combined state sales, excise, personal income, and (mainly local) property taxes take far more of the income of the poor than of the rich.

State Sales, Excise, Property and Personal Income Taxes as Shares of Family Income, by Income Quintile[18]

(I = lowest, V = highest)

	I	II	III	IV	V, 15%	Top 5%	Top 0.7%
Sales, gas & tobacco	5.4%	3.9%	3.3%	2.9%	2.5%	1.6%	1.1%
Property	3.4	2.6	2.5	2.4	2.6	2.0	1.1
Personal Income Tax	0.5	1.8	2.4	2.8	3.2	3.4	3.3
Subtotal	9.3%	8.3%	8.2%	8.1%	8.3%	7.0%	5.5%

Taking account of corporate income taxes mitigates the regressivity of overall state systems considerably, although state taxes remain regressive.[19]

	I	II	III	IV	V, 15%	Top 5%	Top 0.7%
Corporate Income Tax	0.3%	0.3%	0.4%	0.5%	0.9%	1.8%	2.0%
Total	9.6%	8.6%	8.6%	8.6%	9.2%	8.8%	7.5%

By taking advantage of the increased corporate tax revenues available as a result of federal tax reform, states can mitigate the regressivity of their overall tax structures further. Each one percentage point increase in a state's effective corporate tax rate would take less than 0.1 percent of the income of low- and middle-income families but would take 0.4 percent of the income of the richest 5 percent.

The fact that corporate income taxes can be seen as ultimately a burden on shareholders also means that, in any given state, most of the corporate income tax is exported to citizens of other states—a happy result for legislators eager to deliver the most value for tax dollars to the voters within their particular jurisdictions.

If states don't take advantage of the increased corporate revenues available as a result of federal tax reform, they easily could end up making their tax systems more regressive by increasing sales or excise taxes. If this happens, state tax systems will become even less acceptable to voters, and states will be less able to meet their responsibilities.

Business Climate

Of course, when it's suggested that higher corporate taxes can help improve fairness and pay for needed programs, legislators often ask, "But what do corporate taxes mean for our state's 'business climate?'"

There is a school of thought, represented by the Grant Thornton annual "business climate" surveys, that says that the best place for business is where costs are lowest. This "least-cost" approach— antitaxes, antiunions, antiregulation—finds that places like North Dakota and South Dakota have the best business climates in America, while places like Massachusetts and California don't measure up.

But to suggest that states ought to emulate the economic policies of Taiwan, Korea, or Guatemala is wrong. It's wrong, first of all, because it forgets that the goal of economic development and a good business climate is to improve the well-being of a state's citizens, not drive their standard of living toward Third World levels. Just as fundamentally, it's wrong because it ignores the benefits that government spending, and therefore taxes, produce for businesses.

Recently, the Third World, least-cost paradigm for a "good business climate" has come under powerful attack. In a series of reports, the Washington-based Corporation for Enterprise Development has illustrated the common sense fact that businesses have an enormous stake in the quality of state services.[20]

Indeed, when business leaders are surveyed, what they usually say they care most about in deciding where to locate or expand are education, roads, labor force skills, and a state's quality of life. Likewise, most company managers understand that taxes are needed to pay for these things. Businesses, like all taxpayers, simply want value for their tax dollars. That's why Japanese corporations don't complain when they pay 30 percent of their country's tax load at both the national and the local level (far above U.S. figures). That's why several corporate executives in Texas recently testified in favor of a state corporate income tax—because they need the government's continued investment in improved education and other essential services to keep Texas on track in diversifying its economy.[21] That's why, in 1986, 20 local chambers of commerce in Colorado called on the state's General Assembly to increase taxes and emphasized that "the business community stands ready to pay its fair share of such an increase." "Colorado's future is at stake," said the business groups. "Without additional revenues, Colorado will be left little choice but to woefully underfund areas such as higher education, elementary and secondary education, our state highways, water resources and other vital capital construction and maintenance projects."[22]

Only through fair taxes, including corporate taxes, can states afford to pay for the services that benefit companies and people alike. Taxing the poor heavily, as many states do, simply doesn't raise much money, although it does impose much misery. Nor is it reasonable to expect middle-income taxpayers to shoulder the burden alone. If those with the greatest ability to pay don't carry their weight, then middle-income families rightfully will feel unfairly treated. And when middle-income people perceive that they are not getting full value for their tax dollars, they are likely to rebel.

States that fail to assess fair taxes on corporate profits must either: 1) forgo needed state programs, or 2) increase other taxes. If the absence of adequate revenues from corporate taxes leads to a poorer educational system, unrepaired or unbuilt roads, or similar problems, then businesses will have won a Pyrrhic victory.

Taking Advantage of Federal Tax Reform

The 1986 federal Tax Reform Act, enacted on a bipartisan basis with the support of one of the most probusiness presidents we've had in the last 60 years, shows that taxing corporations fairly is not antibusiness. The 1986 act granted states some relief from the federal loophole onslaught of the previous decade and a half and presents states with a rare opportunity to improve tax fairness while increasing revenues. As many business leaders now recognize, our country's economic future largely depends on states doing a better job in education and other services. Corporate taxes can play an important role in paying for those programs. Indeed, if states spend their added tax revenues wisely, increased corporate taxes will be good for people and companies alike.

To take full advantage of the opportunity of federal corporate tax reform, states should conform as fully as possible to the new federal corporate tax law. Besides adopting the expanded federal tax base for the regular corporate income tax, states also should piggyback on the federal alternative minimum tax, the new provision designed to assure that no profitable company gets away without paying taxes. Conformity to the minimum tax can be accomplished by requiring companies to use the larger of regular taxable income or alternative minimum taxable income as the starting point for computing profits to be apportioned to a state.

At the same time, state officials should keep the pressure on Congress to continue in the spirit of the 1986 Tax Reform Act to close the loopholes that remain in the federal code. Tax reform cut the cost of federal corporate "tax expenditures" from $120 billion a year to $62 billion, but much more remains to be accomplished. Since the states will share in the revenues from continued federal base-broadening, they have an important stake in lobbying Congress to keep up the good work.

States that heretofore have allowed companies to deduct their federal income tax payments in computing state taxable income should repeal this antiquated rule. Since the federal government already allows state corporate income taxes to be deducted, the problem of so-called double taxation is already abated. Moreover, states that retain federal deductibility could find their tax bases seriously eroded due to the increase in federal corporate tax payments as a result of the Tax Reform Act.

Conclusion

At a time when there is a renewed focus on the importance of education and a well-trained workforce in improving America's competitiveness, at a time when infrastructure is decaying and badly in need of repair, many states need added revenue to deliver the services that people and companies need. In those states, increased corporate taxes can pave the way to a better business climate and a more competitive America. Other states can use added corporate tax revenues to lighten the excessive burdens that sales taxes and property taxes impose on low- and moderate-income families. Some states may be able to accomplish both tax reform and improved services.

Corporations aren't overtaxed; on the contrary, until recently they were hugely undertaxed, with many getting away with paying little or nothing. In 1986, the federal government found the courage to restore some of its lost corporate tax base, thereby increasing federal corporate taxes by about one-fifth. The states should take advantage of the residual benefit—as much as an 11 to 18 percent expansion in their corporate tax bases on average—and put it to good use.

Notes

1. South Dakota's corporate income tax applies only to financial institutions. This limited tax nevertheless raises 5.8 percent of the state's limited revenues.

2. Michigan replaced its corporate income tax with a value-added tax in 1976.

3. In addition, Connecticut, New Hampshire, and Tennessee, which tax corporate profits, have only very limited personal income taxes.

4. The 7.5 percent average statutory corporate tax rate in 1987 (for states that have corporate income taxes) is down from 7.7 percent in 1986 (prefederal tax reform).

5. This 6.6 percent average statutory corporate tax in 1987 (for all states, including those without corporate income taxes) is down from 6.8 percent in 1986.

6. The most significant corporate income tax rate decrease between 1970 and 1980 was in Michigan, which repealed its corporate income tax in favor of a hybrid value-added tax, the Single Business Tax, which is roughly similar to a sales tax. The only other rate cut was in Pennsylvania, where the rate was reduced from 10.6 percent in 1970 to 10.5 percent in 1980.

7. The federal effective corporate tax rate fell from 38 percent in 1970 to only 26 percent by 1980. These and subsequent comparisons of corporate taxes and profits are based on comparing actual corporate tax payments with the sum of taxes paid and taxes avoided through special breaks, as reported by the congressional Joint Committee on Taxation in its annual compilations of "tax expenditures."

8. See, e.g., Joint Committee on Taxation, Study of 1983 *Effective Tax Rates of Selected Large U.S. Corporations* (November 28, 1984); Citizens for Tax Justice, *130 Reasons Why We Need Tax Reform* (July 1986).

9. States responding to a 1986 Citizens for Tax Justice survey reported that in fiscal 1985 about half the corporations filing state tax returns had paid no state corporate income tax. In several states, almost two-thirds of the companies filing returns paid no tax.

10. The 1980-86 statutory corporate tax rate hikes ranged from a 0.25 percentage point hike in New Hampshire to what amounted to a 2.3 percentage point increase in Iowa (the statutory rate was increased from 10 percent to 12 percent, and the deduction for half of federal taxes paid became less significant due to federal corporate tax reductions). Rates were cut from 1980 to 1986 only in Pennsylvania (minus 1 percentage point) and Illinois (minus 0.3 of a percentage point).

11. As a share of the gross national product, state corporate tax revenues were up by 7 percent from 1970 to 1986.

12.   In 1970, states got only 19 percent of their revenues from personal income taxes. Corporate income taxes supplied 8 percent; property, death, and gift taxes, 4 percent; and general and selective sales taxes and fees, 69 percent. By 1980, greater reliance on personal income taxes meant that states got 27 percent of their revenues from that source. Corporate income taxes had grown to 9 percent of revenues, and sales taxes had fallen to 60 percent (with the remaining 4 percent from property, death, and gift taxes). By 1986, corporate taxes had dropped to 7 percent of state revenues. Personal income taxes grew to 30 percent of state revenues. Sales taxes were constant as a revenue source at 60 percent. And property, death, and gift taxes were down to 3 percent of revenues.

13.   Since the 1960s, total federal taxes as a share of gross national product (excluding Social Security) have fallen dramatically: from 15.5 percent of GNP to 12.4 percent in 1986. Leading the way was the decline in corporate taxes, down from 3.8 percent of GNP in the sixties to 2.4 percent in 1980 and only 1.1 percent of GNP in 1983—but now back up to an expected 2.1 percent of GNP in 1988 after the 1986 Tax Reform Act. This decline occurred even as non-Social Security federal spending rose, from 16.4 percent of the GNP in the sixties to 18.2 percent in 1986 (entirely due to higher federal interest payments).

Federal interest payments (with the Social Security system's earnings excluded) grew from 1.4 percent of the GNP in the sixties to 3.4 percent in 1986. Not counting interest, the cost of federal non-Social Security programs fell as a share of the GNP, declining from 15 percent of the GNP in the sixties to 14.8 percent in 1986, and an expected 14.3 percent in fiscal 1988.

14.   See J. Gregory Ballentine, "The Short-Run Distributional Effect of Tax Reform," *Tax Notes,* June 9, 1986, p. 1035; Martin Feldstein, "Imputing Corporate Tax Liabilities to Individual Taxpayers," National Bureau of Economic Research, Working Paper No. 2349 (August 1987). See also Congressional Budget Office, *The Changing Distribution of Federal Taxes: 1975-90* (October 1987).

15.   Except for Michigan, these states also have no personal income tax either.

16.   Severance taxes, license fees, value-added tax, etc.

17.   Corporate income tax on banks only.

18.   Sales and excise tax figures reflect current law as of the end of 1987, and come from a Citizens for Tax Justice report *Nickels & Dimes: How Sales & Excise Taxes Add Up in the 50 States* (Washington, D.C., 1988). Property tax and income tax figures reflect 1985 law and are based on a 1987 CTJ report, *The Sorry State of State Taxes* (Washington, D.C.). The recent federal tax reforms have improved the progressivity of the personal income tax in many states since 1985.

19.   Corporate tax figures reflect state corporate tax revenues in 1986. Taxes are distributed according to each group's share of total dividends received.

20.   See Corporation for Enterprise Development, *Making the Grade: The Development Report Card for the States* (1987); and Corporation for Enterprise Development, *Taken for Granted: How Grant Thornton's Business Climate Index Leads States Astray* (1986).

21.   See Statement of Allen Holmes, Assistant Tax Officer for Atlantic Richfield Company, before the Texas Select Committee on Tax Equity (November 5, 1987), calling for "an income tax or a modified [corporate] franchise tax" based on income; statement of Bob Campbell, President of Texas Power and Light, on behalf of the Association of the Electric

Companies of Texas before the Texas Select Committee on Tax Equity (November 5, 1987), calling for "fair and equitable taxation of all entities," and arguing that the corporate franchise tax "should be significantly restructured or replaced with a fairer, more equitable tax that is reflective of the state's economy." But compare testimony of W. Humphrey Bogart, President of Fidelity Investments Southwest Company, before the Texas Select Committee on Tax Equity (November 5, 1987), arguing against imposition of a state corporate income tax but supporting enactment of a personal income tax.

22.　Letter from 20 Colorado chambers of commerce to all members of the Colorado General Assembly, April 2, 1986. The chambers' plea was answered. In May 1986, the Colorado legislature enacted several tax increases, including a one percentage point hike in the corporate income tax rate.

Constructive
State and Local
Tax Policy

by
David R. Burton

State and local tax policymakers must choose between two competing visions of what is constructive tax policy. One, represented ably by Robert McIntyre of Citizens for Tax Justice and his allies in Congress, is static and redistributionist. This view of desirable tax policy is cloaked in the rhetoric of fairness and equity and concentrates on the impact that any particular tax provision would have on income distribution.

The other view rests on the premise that the most desirable tax system is that which least impedes economic progress and has the least harmful impact on ordinary people's standard of living. The most important point to realize is that policymakers cannot have it both ways. If they pursue the redistributionist tax policies that Mr. McIntyre espouses, they are raising the stock of human misery in their jurisdictions.[1] Although redistributionist policies may satisfy some primitive need to tax business and the affluent, those policies will destroy jobs, reduce the standard of living, and ultimately force the very people they hope to tax out of the jurisdiction in question.

State and local policymakers do have an alternative to the destructive tax policies advocated by the Left. They can pursue carefully conceived policies designed to promote economic growth, job creation, and a higher standard of living.

Three basic sets of experiences can be used to demonstrate the relationship between tax policy and economic performance: the international record, the state record, and the federal tax policy record. The last of these three is the most compelling, rich, and familiar and will, therefore, constitute the bulk of this chapter. The impact of any state's tax policy on its economy probably will be less pronounced than that of federal policy simply because state taxes are lower than federal taxes and because all states' economies are interdependent. But in local economies where businesses can serve the same market from two or more different jurisdictions, the impact of taxes can be pronounced. Both people and businesses will vote with their feet and move to the lower tax jurisdiction.

A rigorous international comparison of the impact of tax policy on economic growth is difficult for lack of easily accessible data. Keith Marsden of the World Bank has demonstrated strong differential economic growth rates in developing countries that have differing tax burdens.[2] Countries that had low taxes, such as the Pacific rim countries, have prospered. Countries that pursued high-tax policies usually have remained poor.

Those that try to blame Third World poverty solely on lack of natural resources should reflect on the utter lack of resources at the disposal of Taiwan, South Korea, Hong Kong, or Singapore at the close of World War II. They adopted a low-tax, relatively free market development model and prospered accordingly. In fact, they no longer are considered part of the less developed world. They are called the newly industrialized countries.

Similar case histories of the successes of market policies and the tragedy of redistributionist economic policy abound. The best source of information on this subject is the two-year-old *Journal of Economic Growth* published under the auspices of the Center for International Private Enterprise, which in turn is funded by the National Endowment for Democracy.[3]

In Europe, income tax rates routinely reach 60 percent or more and are compounded with 20 percent or more value-added taxation and other taxes. Europeans have paid a dear price for these tax policies. The European Economic Community has increased employment only 1.3 percent in the last seven years, while the United States has created 13 million new jobs since 1980, an increase of 13.2 percent.[4] Europeans have learned to live with destructive economic policies (tax and otherwise) that have left over one-tenth of them out of work for almost a decade. Mr. McIntyre, in effect, is arguing for tax and other economic policies that would make the American economy like Europe's. Objective policymakers should cringe at the thought.

In 1983, Harris Bank of Chicago conducted a study systematically comparing the economic performance of states with their tax burdens. The bank found a strong inverse relationship between tax burden and economic performance.[5] Of course, this is not surprising to those that have seen their friends move from high-tax jurisdictions or talked to businesses trying to decide where to locate a plant. Nevertheless, the idea that people do not change their behavior in response to changes in taxation is one of those foolish ideas that is implicit in the redistributionists' view of the world. People are not nearly so stupid as the redistributionists would have us believe. People do respond to prices. And they do respond to taxes. Taxes are, economically speaking, nothing more than the price imposed by government for living or doing business in a jurisdiction.

The U.S. federal tax policy experience is a particularly rich area to examine the validity of that point because so many radical changes have occurred in federal tax policy over the years. State policymakers can analyze this record and glean a lot of useful information when deciding what tax policies they should pursue.

Let's travel back in time to 1980 and recollect some of the finer points of tax policy under the Carter administration. The top marginal tax rate was a modest 70 percent. A two-earner, middle-class family with about $50 thousand in income paid marginal rates of about 49 percent. More important, however, they could look forward to paying rates of 59 percent within eight years as their nominal income skyrocketed due to the effect of the 13 percent inflation rate in 1980. The same inflation that was driving the middle class into tax brackets once the exclusive province of the wealthy also was depriving the country of vital investment capital. High inflation and high interest rates made our capital cost recovery allowances increasingly anemic. Finally, the insidious estate and gift tax had become ubiquitous by 1980. In that year, everyone who died with an estate greater than $175,000 was liable for estate and gift tax. The idea that most middle-class Americans would have to retain legal counsel for estate planning was absurd.

The Carter administration seemed to have no comprehension that anything was wrong. It and its many supporters in government, academia, and the media were unable or unwilling to draw any connection between ever-increasing tax burdens and stagnant economic performance.

But President Reagan was elected and able to secure passage of the Economic Recovery Tax Act of 1981 (ERTA). This landmark piece of tax legislation was the centerpiece of the President's economic recovery program, and it has been an unqualified success. It had three major components. It cut marginal tax rates, enhanced capital cost recovery allowances, and dramatically reduced estate and gift taxes.

The act reduced individual tax rates to a maximum of 50 percent and cut them 25 percent across-the-board for the middle class. Perhaps most important, ERTA indexed tax brackets for inflation. No longer did the welfare state gain new revenues from the middle class by debasing the currency. Few states have indexed their tax brackets for inflation. But those legislators that want to avoid automatic inflation-caused tax increases at the expense of the middle class should reconsider indexing. ERTA also cut the individual capital gains rate from 28 to 20 percent. Perhaps a harbinger of compromises to follow, however, was the agreement by the administration to delay the effective dates of the tax cuts and tax indexing. The final 10 percent rate cut did not take place until 1983, and tax indexing did not take effect until 1985. Thus, some of the most constructive provisions in ERTA did not take effect until long after it was signed into law.

These rate reductions had a salutary impact on the economy. Lower rates reduced the relative price of work compared to leisure and thereby promoted work and employment. They reduced the tax bias against saving and toward consumption inherent in the income tax. Finally, they diminished economic distortion by reducing the value of tax shelters.

These reductions also dramatically increased the share of the overall tax burden borne by the wealthy. As Table 1 illustrates, those earning over $500,000 per year were paying 151 percent more taxes within three years of their tax rate being cut from 70 to 50 percent. Table 2 shows that these taxpayers' share of the overall tax burden grew from 3.1 to 7.2 percent over the same period. Only lower-income taxpayers paid fewer taxes.

These results are not difficult to understand if they are analyzed from a classical economic perspective and the focus of the analysis is on the effect of ERTA on after-tax incomes. The most affluent taxpayers saw their after-tax return for any extra dollar earned increase from 30 cents to 50 cents, or 67 percent. Lower-income taxpayers, in contrast, already paid comparatively few taxes and saw their after-tax income for any additional dollar earned go from 86 cents to 89 cents, only 3 percent higher. Thus, upper-income taxpayers responded to astounding increases in the after-tax reward to additional work or savings. The amount of additional income they chose to earn was sufficiently high that it

Table 1.

Federal Personal Income Tax Revenue by Income Class, 1981 to 1984

(Millions of Dollars)

Adjusted Gross Income (Thousands of Dollars)	1981	1982	1983	1984	Percentage Change, 1981-1984
$0-10	$ 7,945	$ 7,089	$ 6,273	$ 6,282	−20.9%
10-20	39,463	34,566	31,462	31,282	−20.7
20-30	55,617	51,966	46,320	44,778	−19.5
30-50	86,453	84,994	82,628	87,280	1.0
50-75	36,131	35,892	38,352	47,355	31.1
75-100	14,544	14,594	15,392	18,759	29.0
100-200	21,142	21,868	22,014	25,762	21.9
200-500	12,380	14,032	15,613	18,775	51.7
500+	8,623	12,591	16,122	21,647	151.0
Total	**$282,302**	**$277,597**	**$274,181**	**$301,923**	**7.0%**

Note: Totals do not equal sum of lines due to rounding.
Source: Internal Revenue Service, *Statistics of Income,* 1981-1984.

Table 2.

Distribution of Federal Personal Income Tax Burden by Income Class, 1981 to 1984

Adjusted Gross Income (Thousands of Dollars)	Percent of Total				Percentage Change (1981-1984)
	1981	1982	1983	1984	
$0-10	2.8%	2.6%	2.3%	2.1%	−26.1%
10-20	14.0	12.5	11.5	10.4	−25.9
20-30	19.7	18.7	16.9	14.8	−24.7
30-50	30.6	30.6	30.1	28.9	−5.6
50-75	12.8	12.9	14.0	15.7	22.5
75-100	5.2	5.3	5.6	6.2	20.6
100-200	7.5	7.9	8.0	8.5	13.9
200-500	4.4	5.1	5.7	6.2	41.8
500+	3.1	4.5	5.9	7.2	134.7
Total	**100.0%**	**100.0%**	**100.0%**	**100.0%**	**100.0%**

Source: Internal Revenue Service, *Statistics of Income,* 1981-1984.

more than compensated the government for the lower tax rates. Thus, ERTA's changes in the taxation of upper-income individuals promoted economic growth, enabled taxpayers to retain more of their own money,and increased federal and state revenues. Even Social Democrats who want, in effect, to exploit capitalism to fund a generous welfare state should support the rate cuts for upper-income taxpayers because these cuts raised federal revenues. Conservatives and libertarians support the rate cuts because of allegiance to ideas such as the sanctity of property. Pragmatists of all ideological stripes should be impressed with the positive macro-economic impact of the rate cuts. Only those who view economic success as sordid or immoral and deserving punitive taxation should remain opposed to ERTA's rate cuts.

Proponents of the Kemp-Roth tax cuts were not surprised by these unusual distributional effects of tax cuts for upper-income taxpayers. Precisely the same distributional and revenue effects were experienced when President Kennedy cut tax rates from 94 to 70 percent effective in 1964 and when tax rates were reduced steadily in the 1920s after the confiscatory rates imposed during World War I.[6]

ERTA reduced the tax bias against investment substantially. The new Accelerated Cost Recovery System (ACRS) combined with the Investment Tax Credit (ITC) approximated, in present value terms, the expensing of capital expenditures. Thus, the cost of capital declined, and during the recovery of the next several years, the size of the U.S. capital stock grew at robust rates. This new investment laid the foundation for the sustained economic growth we are enjoying now.

The specter of middle-class Americans being forced to retain legal counsel to conduct complex estate planning or otherwise forfeit most of their estate to the federal government no doubt helps the American Bar Association but most of us view that as a tremendous waste of society's resources. Yet, that was the situation in 1980, and there was no reason to believe it would have changed had President Reagan not been elected. Those most frustrated by the punitive estate taxes of the late 1970s were small business owners. More often than not, family farms, ranches, and businesses had to be sold out of the family, usually to large corporations able to pay cash quickly, simply to pay the estate taxes. Many states still maintain unduly high estate tax rates that have a disproportionately negative impact on small farms, ranches, and businesses.

In 1988, the maximum individual marginal tax rate is 33 percent, and the top corporate rate is 34 percent. These rates represent incredible progress compared with where they stood only eight years ago. Then, the individual rates were over twice as high at 70 percent, and the corporate rate was one-third higher at 46 percent. Rates as low as those in 1988 seemed like a pipe dream before Reagan came to Washington. Now they are a reality. These rate reductions represent powerful abatements to the tax disincentive to work, save, and invest and no doubt will lead to a healthier, more robust economy than in the late 1970s. All Americans will benefit from greater opportunities and an improved standard of living because of these dramatically lower tax rates.

Of course, the Tax Reform Act of 1986 is not all good news. The capital cost recovery allowances available to industries that invest in plant and equipment are inadequate. The higher cost of capital implicit in this new regime will reduce our capital stock, productivity, and competitiveness. But lower rates on corporations and their shareholders of the magnitude taking effect in 1988 go far to mitigate this effect.

Most forms of savings mechanisms that reduced the double taxation of savings implicit in an income tax were scaled back by the 1986 act. In particular, Individual Retirement Accounts and section 401(k) plans were made unavailable to millions of middle-class taxpayers trying to provide a sound basis for their retirement. It is the height of folly to cut back these plans dramatically when we need domestic savings to promote economic growth and when we know full well that within two decades tremendous pressures on the Social Security system will come to bear.

The 1986 act also substantially increased the capital gains tax rate—to 33 percent for individuals and 34 percent for corporations. This reversal of the successful 1978 effort to cut the individual capital gains rate from 49 to 28 percent and the further reduction in 1981 to a top rate of 20 percent are counterproductive. Higher capital gains tax rates are counterproductive economically and will cut federal revenues demonstrably. High rates reduce venture capital formation and hinder small businesses in raising capital. Perhaps most important, high capital gains tax rates reduce market liquidity by providing a powerful disincentive to realize gains. This "lock-in effect" of high capital gains rates actually costs the government revenue. Conversely, the capital gains rate reductions of 1978 and 1981 demonstrably increased federal revenues. Most economists that have analyzed the empirical data have concluded this. Substantial debate, however, exists over the magnitude of the gain. Of course, the government will secure that additional revenue while simultaneously promoting economic growth. Cutting the capital gains rate is about the only progrowth tax "increase" available to policymakers.

What is a state or local policymaker to make of all this? Simply that taxes matter. High taxes on business or individuals are destructive and, in the final analysis, will hurt those that can least afford to indulge in redistributionist fancies. Redistributionist tax policies quash opportunity, destroy jobs, and reduce the prosperity of all citizens. These considerations are all the more relevant this year as many states reconsider their tax systems in the wake of federal reform. Considered judgment may lead state policymakers to choose prosperity and growth over destructive, redistributionist practices.

Notes

1.   Of course, tax policy is only part of the answer. A host of other considerations matter as well.

2.   Keith Marsden, "Links Between Taxes and Economic Growth: Some Empirical Evidence," *World Bank Staff Working Papers,* Number 605, 1983.

3.   *Journal of Economic Growth,* Richard W. Rahn, Editor-in-Chief, National Chamber Foundation; 1615 H Street, N.W.; Washington, D.C. 20062.

4.   Telephone conversation with Joanne May, U.S. Department of Labor, Bureau of Labor Statistics, January 1988.

5.   Robert Genetski, "Taxes and Economic Growth," *Barometer of Business* (Chicago: Harris Bank, January 1983).

6.   For further information, see "Statement of U.S. Chamber of Commerce" on Tax Reform before the House Committee on Ways and Means, June 26, 1985.

XIV

Virtues
of a State
Value-Added Tax

by
Gerald H. Miller

The value-added tax (VAT) frequently has been discussed as a means of supplementing federal revenues or replacing current federal revenue sources. Most often, the VAT has been mentioned as a replacement for the Social Security payroll tax, the corporate income tax, or a portion of the personal income tax.

This chapter does not deal with the federal revenue issue but addresses the topic of whether states should rely on a state VAT as a replacement for other state business taxes. The VAT has been advocated as a revenue source for state governments—most often as a replacement for the corporate income tax—by prominent state-local finance experts such as Harvey Brazer, Richard Lindstrom, and James Papke. The author joins that chorus and encourages states to seriously consider replacing their existing business taxes with a statewide VAT.

This conclusion can be attributed to five important factors: 1) stability, 2) equity, 3) simplicity, 4) capital investment, and

5) progressivity. Let's keep in mind, however, that all states differ, and each factor should be considered in the context of the economic and political situation in each state.

Let's look at each point in more detail. For many, stability is not an issue on which to spend much time because the nation's economy has exhibited reasonably steady economic growth since 1982. A number of factors, however, may contribute to a greater interest and concern for this issue.

- Although the nation's economy has grown steadily, economic growth rates among the states have varied widely. In 1986, for example, the average annual change in personal income in the New England states was 7.7 percent, whereas in the Southwest the change was 0.8 percent.
- Because forty-nine states have a statutory or constitutional requirement for a balanced budget, revenue stability is important for effective fiscal and budgetary planning.
- From a program or service delivery standpoint, cutting budgets after they are enacted is probably the most disruptive policy action a state can take. Due to volatility in revenues and, in some cases, expenditures, states have been forced to act to balance their budgets after their fiscal year was already underway. For example, the number of states that had to take such action was 23 in 1982, 39 in 1983, and 24 in 1987.[1]
- Even though the U.S. economy has grown steadily in the last five years, most economists are forecasting a recession within the next two years. Such a downturn in the economy will do more to hurt state budgets than any other single event. A 1 percent increase in the national unemployment rate reduces state revenues by more than $3 billion. Therefore, any action that can reduce the impact of a recession on state budgets should be strongly considered.

When this recession comes, the most significant tax source that will show extreme volatility is the corporate income tax. This was true in the past, and it will be in the future. What has happened in the last few years? The figures below paint a clear picture.[2]

Year	Corporate Income Taxes	Total Taxes
	(percentage change)	
1983	−6.1	+5.3
1984	+17.9	+14.8
1985	+13.7	+9.1
1986	+4.1	+6.1

In fiscal year 1983, during the last recession, total state taxes increased 5.3 percent, but corporate income tax revenue was 6.1 percent below that of the previous year. Of the 15 largest states that imposed a corporate income tax, 10 had an absolute decline in the corporate income tax. Some states where corporate income tax revenue fell between fiscal years 1982 and 1983 are shown below.

Ohio	$133 million
Illinois	110 million
Minnesota	72 million
New Jersey	60 million
Pennsylvania	40 million
Colorado	35 million
Georgia	29 million

For all these states, this revenue fall-off produced difficult problems. During this same two-year period, the yield from the Michigan Single Business Tax, a form of value-added tax, with no change in rate or base, increased $52 million. State tax economists in Michigan estimate that if it had a corporate income tax instead of a VAT, the yield would have fallen more than $300 million.[3] The reason for this is obvious. The base of the corporate income tax (profits) is extremely volatile, whereas the base of the VAT is more diversified and, therefore, stable.

Fluctuations in corporate income tax collections may cause difficulty not only during weak economic times but also during periods of economic recovery because a large surplus is created and thus the extra revenue may be hastily spent. This raises the expenditure base, in turn creating problems during the next economic downturn. There is no question that replacing the corporate income tax with a VAT would increase stability. Therefore, depending on conditions in each individual state, a VAT should be looked at.

A second consideration of equal or more importance is the question of equity (fairness). The author is never comfortable talking about equity issues because one person's equity is another's tax burden. But in this case, the issues and evidence are so clear that more discussion and dialogue are essential.

One favorite statement about business taxation is that "we have a situation of comfortable inequity, and we need to move to a situation of uncomfortable equity, at least in the short run." Frequently heard is that "rough justice" is the best that can be expected. Replacing the corporate income tax with a VAT clearly meets this tax criterion.

The state corporate income tax can be criticized because it is not neutral as it applies to corporations versus partnerships, profit versus interest, and distributed versus undistributed income. By contrast, the VAT applies to all businesses and treats different kinds of income uniformly. Since the corporate income tax applies only to corporations, we need to examine further what this means with respect to equity (rough justice).

Florida's recent experience with expanding the tax base to services is relevant in this context. As Florida policymakers correctly assessed, a major segment of the state's economy—the service sector—basically was avoiding taxes. Examination of three key economic statistics clearly shows a tremendous transformation toward a more service-oriented economy.

> 1) Expenditures on services in 1982 accounted for 50 percent of all personal consumption. This figure was estimated to be 53 percent in 1987.[4]
> 2) Employment in service-producing industries shows even more growth. In 1982, 71 percent of employment was in service-producing industries. In 1987, the percentage was estimated to increase to 76 percent.[5]
> 3) From August 1986 to August 1987, over 90 percent of new jobs were in service-producing industries.[6]

The service sector is the fastest growing component of the economy, and policymakers must find a fair way, i.e., rough justice, to tax this sector. Success to date through using the sales tax to tax services has been limited.

Comparing the business receipts of corporations with those of unincorporated business by industry class is instructive. The percent of business receipts originating from unincorporated businesses rose steadily from 11.9 percent in 1980 to an estimated 20 percent in 1987. This is not surprising when the data by industry class are examined. Excluding agriculture, forestry, and mining, the service industry by far has the largest percentage increase. In all other industry classes, business receipts from unincorporated business are less than 10 percent; for services, they are greater than 40 percent.[7]

Thus, a growing percentage of business activity is escaping business taxation when states rely on a corporate income tax as the major source of business taxation. One final statistic from Florida's experience that further illustrates the importance of the service sector is that there were 125,000 new tax filers in Florida— a 25 percent increase—when the state imposed the sales tax on services for six months in 1987.

Three final points related to tax criteria deserve a brief discussion:

- *Simplicity or Convenience.* Michigan's repeal of eight business taxes and replacement of them with the Single Business Tax (VAT) leaves no doubt that the VAT is simpler and more convenient. All the information the taxpayer needs is present on other tax forms, so few, if any, administrative problems exist, assuming that the VAT is an addition-type consumption value-added tax with filing requirements identical to those of the corporate income tax.
- *Capital Formation.* A major claim made for the VAT is that it is more favorable for capital investment than a corporate income tax. Public policymakers should do all they can to encourage capital investment. Although the effect of state taxes in this area is small, it is clear that a VAT can have positive results with respect to capital investment compared with a corporate income tax.

This assumes a consumption-type value-added tax. The consumption-type VAT provides the most neutral treatment of capital assets. In the year of purchase, a firm may deduct the full value of the capital asset. Unlike the income-type VAT (where depreciation is deducted each year), the consumption VAT permits no adjustment for depreciation because to do so would be deducting the cost of the capital goods twice. In Michigan, depreciation is added back to federal taxable income.

The term *consumption VAT* is appropriate because the value added represented by capital equipment is not subject to tax until the equipment is consumed in the production process. In effect, the immediate tax rebate granted to users of capital equipment imposes the tax only once: on gross proceeds of the sales of the goods and services produced by the capital equipment. Funds are not tied up for tax purposes as under the income variant of the VAT.[8]

- *Regressivity.* One concern about a VAT is its regressivity, but there are ways to deal with income redistribution issues through the expenditure side of the budget or through other revenue sources such as the personal income tax. For example, services for low-income persons can be expanded, or a refundable tax credit can be provided.

One additional point worth mentioning comes out of Florida's experience. Since a VAT is similar to a retail sales tax, an analysis of Florida's experience is useful. A recent article by Karen Walby and David Williams[9] concludes that "taxing services should reduce the relative proportion of sales tax paid by low- and moderate-income individuals. As higher-income individuals tend to purchase more business and professional services, the sales tax should become less regressive." For fiscal 1989, they estimate that the average household in Florida would pay an additional $74 dollars in sales tax on services. In contrast, if an equal yield increase in the rate of sales tax on the existing base (excluding services) was imposed, this same household would pay $165 (more than twice as much). Therefore, it is reasonable to conclude that replacing existing business taxes with a VAT that covers services probably would reduce the relative proportion of state taxes paid by low- and moderate-income individuals.

In conclusion, the issue of rough justice or equity as it relates to business taxation will not go away. Pressure for needed services by state government will continue. It is imperative that state policymakers explore alternatives to improve their tax systems to make them as stable and responsive to economic and demographic changes as possible. State policymakers should place a value-added tax high on the tax reform agenda for the next five years.

Notes

1. National Association of State Budget Officers and National Governors' Association, *Fiscal Survey of the States* (Washington, D.C.: September 1987), p. 6.

2. Figures from *State Government Tax Collections* in 1986, 1985, 1984, 1983 (Washington, D.C.: Bureau of the Census, March 1987, February 1986, March 1985, January 1984).

3. Michigan adopted a modified VAT in 1976. The VAT replaced eight existing taxes, the largest being the corporate income tax.

4. Figures from *Economic Indicators* (Washington, D.C.: Prepared for the Joint Economic Committee by the Council of Economic Advisors, September 1987).

5. Ibid.

6. Ibid.

7. Internal Revenue Service, Department of the Treasury, *Individual Income Tax Returns—1982, Statistics of Income* (Washington, D.C.: October 1984).

8. Advisory Commission on Intergovernmental Relations, *Strengthening the Federal Revenue System: Implications for State and Local Taxing and Borrowing* (Washington, D.C.: U.S. Government Printing Office, October 1984).

9. Karen Walby and David Williams, "The Impact of Florida's Sales Tax on Services" (Tallahassee, Fla.: Office of Planning and Budgeting, 1987).

Should States
Adopt a
Value-Added Tax?

by
Robert J. Cline

The Changing State Fiscal Climate

 The dramatic changes in the structure of federal income taxation in the 1980s, combined with increased interstate and international competition for investment and jobs and a sharp reduction in the rate of growth of state revenues, have created a new fiscal environment in which to reevaluate the potential role of value-added taxation at the state level. The value-added tax may become an increasingly viable option as states look for new sources of revenue or substitutes for existing state taxes. The reduced value of state and local tax deductions to federal taxpayers, particularly the loss of the general sales tax deduction, is one example of the changing fiscal setting that may provide a new incentive for states to restructure tax systems to reduce the importance of retail sales taxes. Unfortunately for the states, the federal tax changes have occurred while a number of states are attempting to expand the retail sales tax base to include services. The tax policy challenge is clear: Can states find a politically and economically acceptable way to increase the importance of sales taxes in the state tax arsenal despite the loss of federal deductibility? A value-added tax offers one possible solution to this dilemma.

Interacting with the federal tax changes is the continued emphasis on developing effective state-local economic development incentives. The adoption of a state value-added tax could become a key element in future state economic policies. Many of the same forces that led Michigan to adopt the Single Business Tax (SBT) in 1975—slower revenue growth and increased vulnerability to interstate tax competition—once again are buffeting state economies in the late 1980s.[1] The following discussion examines these fiscal changes and looks at Michigan's unique experience with value-added taxation over the last 35 years as a possible guide for other states considering a VAT.

Tax Reform Act of 1986

The Tax Reform Act of 1986 should make a state value-added tax a more attractive alternative for several reasons. The structure of state tax systems may be affected most by the loss of deductibility of state and local sales taxes for federal taxpayers who itemize. State general sales and gross receipt taxes accounted for an estimated 33 percent of state tax revenue and 24 percent of state and local tax revenue in fiscal 1986. The loss of the sales tax deduction will increase the after-tax price of state and local spending for an average state taxpayer by an estimated 6 to 7 percent.[2]

This increase in the effective cost to state residents of using sales taxes to pay for state and local government will likely exert pressure on states to substitute deductible taxes for general sales taxes. Business taxes, which are still deductible under the federal personal income and corporate profits taxes, are possible candidates for increases, along with property and personal income taxes. However, greater interstate tax competition, which intensifies as the federal corporate tax rate drops from 46 to 34 percent, will make business tax increases less attractive to states concerned about maintaining a strongly positive business climate.

To the extent that the economic impact of value-added taxes is similar to that of a broad-based retail sales tax, businesses may not oppose the substitution of a value-added tax for retail sales taxation, especially if the taxation of intermediate products used by business can be reduced significantly. The VAT would be deductible by businesses on federal returns at a rate of 34 percent (compared with the top personal tax rate of 28 percent). If the VAT is viewed as a consumption tax, rather than a business levy, the existing balance between taxes on individuals and taxes on businesses could be maintained more or less with this substitution. As Courant and Rubinfeld have noted, "States that currently rely most heavily on sales taxes may encounter pressure to shift to a value-added tax, which would act much like a sales tax but also be deductible by businesses."[3]

In addition to those states that rely heavily on the sales tax, others attempting to reduce reliance on the property tax as part of educational finance reform efforts or as a continuing reaction to the property tax revolt also may want to look closely at a VAT. A switch to a value-added tax would maintain deductibility against federal tax liabilities while allowing a more diversified state-local tax structure with less dependence upon the property tax. As was the case in the early 1970s, increased reliance on sales or consumption taxes may become an important component of a new wave of school finance reform.

The 1986 Tax Reform Act also is affecting states by encouraging a change in the organizational form of doing business. With a top marginal tax rate for individuals below the highest corporate tax rate (28 percent versus 34 percent), businesses have a greater incentive to shift to partnerships and Subchapter S corporations from the corporate form of business organization. For many states, this structural change would reduce the number of firms paying a state corporate profits tax, and expanded individual income tax collections may fail to offset this reduction fully. A broad-based business tax that is relatively neutral in terms of the choice of business organization becomes increasingly more important in light of these structural changes. This neutrality is one of the real virtues of a value-added tax because it applies to all businesses, regardless of their legal form.

The Tax Reform Act of 1986 has affected state tax policy indirectly by rekindling the debate over the proper role of tax incentives in encouraging capital spending. A consumption-type value-added tax with immediate expensing of new capital investment provides many firms with approximately the same capital investment incentive created by the combination of the Investment Tax Credit and accelerated depreciation allowances repealed by the Tax Reform Act. A state consumption VAT could restore partially the capital investment incentives lost at the federal level. Although the relatively higher level of federal taxes on businesses may reduce the potential stimulative effect of such an incentive on investment spending significantly, individual states may view such an incentive as an important economic development tool.

A second major unresolved state tax policy issue is the question of whether consumption or income is a more equitable state tax base. With federal and state personal income taxes moving in the direction of effectively flat-rate taxes, states now may view a broad-based consumption tax as more acceptable on equity grounds, as well as on more generally acceptable efficiency grounds. As Richard Musgrave noted in an analysis of federal personal income tax rate changes under the Tax Reform Act of 1986:

> If the recent move toward reducing or abandoning effective rate progression over the middle to upper range were to continue, the trend might carry important implications for tax structure design....Indirect taxation of income at the source might take the place of a direct personal tax either via a schedular system with a uniform rate or an income type value added tax.[4]

As states reduce nominal (and in many cases, effective) personal income tax rate progression, the value-added tax could become a building block in a diversified, equitable state-local tax system. In addition to improving horizontal equity in state taxes, a VAT could reduce the regressivity of sales taxes by providing a practical means of effectively taxing the consumption of services, which represent an increasing share of spending as incomes increase. In effect, a flat-rate, consumption-based tax could be used as a new or substitute state revenue source with effective progression achieved by exempting certain products (such as food) or by increasing personal income tax exemptions or credits. One long-run implication of this structural change would be a greater reliance on indirect taxation at the state level.

State Efforts to Tax Services

Long-run structural changes in the patterns of consumption, production, and employment are interacting with recent federal tax changes to make value-added taxation more attractive. Since World War II, the service share of the gross national product (GNP) has risen from 58 to 68 percent, and the shift in the distribution of employment has been even greater. Of particular importance for state sales taxation is the fact that since 1948 the share of GNP in the "other service" category (personal, business, professional, and repair services) has increased from 11.5 to 15.0 percent, while its labor share increased by 10 percentage points. The share of GNP accounted for by professional services—including business, legal, and medical services—has more than doubled since 1948 and now stands at 10.1 percent.[5] It is this service component of GNP that is so difficult to tax under a retail sales tax. In Michigan, goods-producing jobs now account for less than one-third of wage and salary employment, while business, health, and personal services account for almost 22 percent of employment. A state retail sales tax that fails to tax consumer spending on services and incorrectly taxes these services when purchased as business inputs, will create increasingly large economic distortions over time.

It is also important to note that much of this shift of employment and output from commodities to services may be due to increased contracting out of business services that previously were performed within firms in the goods-producing sector. To the extent that the new service firms are noncorporate businesses, this shift would result in revenue losses under state corporate income taxes, which may not be offset by higher individual income taxes. These shifts exacerbate the existing problems of taxing business services under a retail sales tax. A value-added tax could be used to "recapture" some of this lost tax base and to tax these services in an economically efficient way that avoids pyramiding.

Florida's unsuccessful attempt to tax services is the most recent example of state efforts to extend the retail sales tax to a comprehensive list of services, including those provided by lawyers, accountants, advertisers, and personal service firms. The major problem with expanding the retail sales tax to include a comprehensive list of services is that a large percentage of services are purchased as business inputs. As already mentioned, if these purchases are included in the sales tax base, the tax becomes a gross sales tax with substantial pyramiding and undesirable economic distortions. In contrast, a consumption VAT would be equivalent to a comprehensive retail sales tax on goods and services without pyramiding.[6]

The Michigan Experience

The on-again, off-again Michigan experience with a value-added tax provides invaluable insights into the operational design of a state VAT and the likely political and economic pressures operating over time to modify a state's VAT. Michigan first experimented with an income-type value-added tax in the form of the Business Activities Tax (BAT) from 1953 to 1967. Following a fiscal roller coaster ride with a state corporate profits tax from 1967 to 1975, Michigan returned to the value-added tax with the adoption of the Single Business Tax (SBT) in 1975. The following discussion will focus on Michigan's recent experience with the SBT.[7]

Overview of the Single Business Tax

The Single Business Tax is Michigan's only broad-based state business tax. When adopted in 1975, it replaced or significantly modified eight other business taxes, including the personal property tax on business inventories, the corporate income tax, and the corporate franchise tax. The initial SBT tax rate (2.35 percent) was chosen to achieve a revenue-neutral substitution of tax sources, except for a one-time increase due to timing differences. At the time it was adopted in 1975, approximately two-thirds of the SBT revenue paid for reductions in state taxes on profits or net equity and one-third went to fund elimination of inventory property taxes.

The SBT is a tax on the additional value that business firms add to materials and inputs purchased from other businesses. As a value-added tax, the SBT can be viewed simply as a tax on the difference between a firm's sales and its cost of goods sold. Under Michigan's consumption-type VAT, a business firm's purchases of all goods and services, including capital purchases, are excluded from the tax base. Alternatively, the SBT tax base can be described as being equivalent to the firm's payments to labor (wages, salaries, fringe benefits, and other compensation) and to capital (profits, interest, dividends, rent, royalties, and depreciation on plant and equipment). In calculating the SBT tax base, firms follow this second approach by adding together payments to factors of production to determine value added.

Although the SBT is fairly easy to describe in theory, it is more difficult to understand the fundamental nature of the tax from its operational details. The confusion over the nature of the Michigan SBT can be seen in the U.S. Treasury Department's recent value-added tax study that stated: "Forty-five states have a retail sales tax, but none has a consumption-type value-added tax. (Michigan has an additive-type, income-based value-added tax which replaced its state corporate income tax, but has corporate profits in its base.)"[8] Although it does deviate from the pure form of a consumption-type VAT, the Michigan SBT is, in fact, a consumption-type value-added tax. Corporate profits are properly included as one of the payments to a firm's factors of production under the additive version of a VAT. The Treasury's inability to recognize the nature of Michigan's SBT should help other states appreciate the challenge Michigan faces in explaining this unique tax to business taxpayers.

As shown in Table 1, the value-added components of the SBT include labor compensation, business income (profits), dividends and interest paid, and depreciation. For tax returns filed in 1982-83, compensation accounted for 77 percent of the Michigan value-added tax base.[9] The remaining 23 percent of the base was payments to capital, including profits, interest, royalties, dividends paid, and depreciation.

The relative importance of compensation in value added varied significantly across industries in Michigan in 1982-83, ranging from a low of 47.6 percent in communications and utilities to a high of 95.6 percent in primary metals manufacturing. Industries with relatively high ratios of compensation to value added tended to be those with low or negative business income reflecting the severity of the 1979-82 recession in Michigan. Although firms in these industries reported low profits or even business losses, they were still subject to the SBT on compensation and the other components of value added.

The concentration of Michigan value added in manufacturing activities is clearly evident in the distribution of value added by industry. In 1982-83, almost 46 percent of the tax base was in the manufacturing sector with 21 percent of value added accounted for by the transportation equipment industry. Retail trade was the next largest sector with 19 percent of value added, followed by services with 16 percent. The combined Michigan value-added tax base in finance, insurance and real estate, and services was 19 percent, equivalent to the size of the retail tax base. Approximately two-thirds of the firms in the service industry, including hotels and lodging and personal, repair, business, and professional services, were noncorporate filers in 1982-83. While most of these firms would not be taxable under a state corporate profits tax, they were subject to the SBT.

The Michigan value-added tax base outlined in Table 1 can be viewed as a measure of "gross" value added because no deduction has been made for either depreciation or capital spending. Under the SBT, a firm doing business solely in Michigan is allowed to deduct annual capital expenditures for real and personal property from the value-added base. Multistate firms may deduct expenditures for real property located in Michigan and for personal property apportioned to Michigan using a two-factor (payroll and property) formula. The capital acquisition deduction, which is a fundamental component of the SBT structure, not an add-on investment incentive, makes the SBT a modified consumption-type value-added tax.[10]

Table 1.

Michigan Single Business Tax Base:
Components of Value Added, 1983

Components	Amount (millions)	Percent of Aggregate Tax Base
Compensation	$413,836.4	77.1%
Wages and salaries	336,612.3	62.7
Payroll taxes	25,840.0	4.8
Employee insurance contributions	26,754.3	5.0
Pensions and other payments	24,629.8	4.6
Business income[1]	38,957.1	7.3
Dividends and interest paid (net)[2]	4,269.8	0.8
Depreciation	76,469.7	14.2
Other additions and subtractions (net)	3,598.9	0.6
Aggregate tax base	$537,131.9	100.0%
Michigan tax base[3]	$ 61,179.0	

Notes:
1. Business income equals net business income reported on federal tax returns plus net operating losses, losses from partnerships, and taxes on income minus partnership income.
2. Interest and dividends paid ($49.6 billion) minus interest and dividends earned ($45.4 billion).
3. Aggregate tax base for firms doing business only in Michigan ($28.4 billion) plus apportioned tax base for multistate firms ($32.8 billion).

Source: Michigan Department of Treasury, *SBT Annual Return Analysis* (January 1986).

In 1982-83, capital acquisition deductions equaled almost $12.2 billion and reduced the SBT tax base by almost 20 percent. Approximately 80 percent of the deductions for new capital expenditures were for personal property located in or apportioned to Michigan. The largest percentage reductions in the tax base due to the capital acquisition deduction occurred in communications and utilities (57.8%), finance, insurance and real estate (55.8%), and mining (43.9%). The transportation equipment industry accounted for the largest dollar amount with over $3.5 billion of deductions. In the aggregate, manufacturing claimed 44 percent of total capital deductions in 1982-83, a little below manufacturing's share of value added.

The adjusted tax base (after deducting capital expenditures from gross value added) is the underlying net value-added tax base for the SBT. Data for 1982-83 show that this base is highly concentrated among large business firms in Michigan. Less than 5 percent of firms filing SBT returns had net value added greater than $1 million, but they accounted for over 75 percent of net value added attributable to Michigan. In contrast, 63.4 percent of the firms have net value added below $100,000.

There were clear winners and losers when the SBT was substituted for other Michigan business taxes in 1975. Tax burdens were increased substantially for many noncorporate firms and for businesses with a high ratio of value added or payroll to profits. To address the perceived inequities caused by the redistribution of tax burdens, a number of adjustments were made to the pure VAT foundation of the SBT, including the adoption of a statutory exemption and various base deductions and tax credits. The exemption was designed specifically to remove the majority of small businesses from the SBT. The exemption equals $40,000 but is phased out at the rate of $2 per $1 of total business income in excess of $40,000; therefore, the exemption is negatively related to profits. This is one of the SBT provisions introducing a profit-sensitive, ability-to-pay element into Michigan's VAT. The exemption is particularly important in reducing taxes in agriculture, construction, retail trade, services, and real estate, industries characterized by a large number of small firms. The statutory exemption reduced taxes by over $47.5 million for SBT filers in 1982-83.

A taxpayer's value-added base may be reduced further by either an excess compensation reduction or a gross receipts reduction. The excess compensation deduction reduces the adjusted tax base by the extent to which compensation exceeds 63 percent of value added. Almost 48 percent of the tax loss due to this deduction occurred in firms in durable manufacturing; retail trade accounted for 21 percent of the tax loss. This provision favors firms with high ratios of payroll to value added. In addition, it blunts the stimulative effect of the capital acquisition deduction because large capital investments may reduce the relative importance of compensation in value added and, as a result, the size of the excess compensation deduction. This deduction also creates greater instability in tax collections because it adds another ability-to-pay feature that is sensitive to profit swings over the business cycle.

The gross receipts deduction limits a taxpayer's taxable income to no more than 50 percent of gross receipts apportioned to Michigan. This calculation introduces a gross receipts tax alternative into the value-added tax structure with the undesirable effects of a pyramiding sales tax. However, only 15,000 firms, approximately 12 percent of SBT filers, used this alternative in 1982-83. Together, the excess compensation and gross receipts deductions reduced the Michigan tax base (before capital acquisition deductions) by 15 percent.

The SBT tax rate of 2.35 percent is applied to the net tax base remaining after all of the above adjustments. The resulting tax liability is reduced further by a number of allowable credits. The small business/low-profit credit added to the SBT in 1977 and significantly expanded in 1984 introduces yet another ability-to-pay element into the tax structure.[11] The credit is equal to one minus the ratio of business income to 45 percent of a firm's value-added base. The credit is available to firms with gross receipts less than $6 million, business income less than $475,000 ($95,000 for individuals), and business income less than 45 percent of the value-added tax base. The credit is phased out between $5 and $6 million of gross receipts and can reduce tax liabilities by up to 90 percent. For those firms qualifying for the small business credit, their after-credit tax liability changes roughly in proportion to the change in business income. If value added increases due to increases in other components of the base (compensation, for example), the marginal tax rate on the additional value added actually may be negative.[12]

Who Pays the SBT?

In 1982-83, 61 percent of Michigan businesses registered for the SBT either filed no SBT return or had no positive tax liability. This reflects the importance of the statutory exemption and various deductions and credits in reducing SBT tax liabilities. As a result, SBT tax liabilities are highly concentrated by industry and firm size. Approximately 8 percent of all Michigan firms had tax liabilities in 1982-83 in excess of $5,000, and they paid 90 percent of the SBT; the 66 firms with liabilities greater than $1 million paid 34.6 percent of the tax.

Table 2 indicates the distribution of SBT payments by industry. Manufacturing firms paid 47.7 percent of total quarterly payments in 1986, with 20.3 percent of payments concentrated in the transportation equipment industry. Wholesale and retail trade, finance, insurance and real estate, and services accounted for almost 38.8 percent of quarterly payments in 1986. Table 2 also shows the cyclical sensitivity of SBT quarterly payments by industry. Even with the profit-related components of the SBT, quarterly payments were relatively stable over the downturn from 1979 to 1982, with payments falling by less than 2 percent. A 15.1 percent decrease in payments in durable manufacturing was almost fully offset by significant increases in payments from services and communication and utilities. The data also show the longer-run diversification in the SBT base away from durable manufacturing toward service-producing activities.

For all firms, the overall effective tax rate (taxes divided by gross value added attributable to Michigan) was 1.44 percent in 1982-83. Rates were lower for smaller firms (tax base less than $100,000) because of the statutory exemption and the capital ac-

Table 2.

Distribution of Quarterly Single Business Tax Payments by Industry,
1979 to 1986

Industry	1986		1983		1982		1979	
	Amount (millions)	Percent of Total	Amount (millions)	Percent of Total	Amount (millions)	Percent of Total	Amount (millions)	Percent of Total
Agriculture and mining	$ 9.5	0.8%	$ 7.5	0.8%	$ 5.5	0.7%	$ 5.7	0.7%
Construction	38.8	3.1	24.7	2.6	26.5	3.2	29.7	3.5
Manufacturing	600.5	47.7	503.0	52.5	393.7	47.6	446.8	53.0
Nondurable	109.7	8.7	89.3	9.3	77.0	9.3	73.9	8.8
Durable	490.7	39.0	413.7	43.2	316.7	38.3	372.9	44.3
Metals	71.8	5.7	48.2	5.0	45.7	5.5	67.4	8.0
Nonelectrical mach.	53.9	4.3	40.7	4.3	42.0	5.1	47.8	5.7
Transportation equip.	255.7	20.3	256.0	26.7	166.1	20.1	196.9	23.4
Other durables	109.3	8.7	68.8	7.2	62.9	7.6	60.8	7.2
Transportation	21.6	1.7	16.4	1.7	13.1	1.6	10.6	1.3
Communications & utilities	99.4	7.9	64.9	6.8	49.4	6.0	33.4	4.0
Trade	252.4	20.1	188.5	19.7	187.4	22.7	189.9	22.6
Wholesale	52.2	4.2	33.6	3.5	33.0	4.0	32.6	3.9
Retail	200.2	15.9	154.9	16.2	154.4	18.7	157.3	18.7
Finance, insurance & real estate	70.3	5.6	30.4	3.2	34.6	4.2	37.6	4.5
Services and others	167.4	13.1	123.2	12.9	116.4	14.0	88.8	10.4
Total	$1,259.8	100.0%	$958.6	100.0%	$826.6	100.0%	$842.5	100.0%

Source: State of Michigan, Department of Management and Budget, *Executive Budget and Budget Message of the Governor,* various years.

quisition deduction. Tax burdens for middle-size firms were reduced primarily by the excess compensation and gross receipts deduction but were higher than for smaller firms. For the largest firms (value added in excess of $5 million), the effective rate falls slightly due to the excess compensation, gross receipts, and capital acquisition deductions.

The neutrality or horizontal equity of the SBT is seen in a comparison of effective tax rates across industries. The coefficient of variation in effective tax rates was .19 in 1982-83; in other words, the average difference in effective tax rates by industry was 19 percent of the statewide effective tax rate. The rates varied from 1.92 percent in mining to 1.06 percent in communications and utilities. Distribution of effective tax rates by size of firms shows coefficients of variation as low as .13 to .15 for a wide range of middle-size firms. As noted by the Michigan Department of Treasury: "In short, with the exception of the very smallest and largest firms, the SBT is remarkably neutral in treating equally firms of different types, but of similar size."[13] This is one of the real long-run strengths of the value-added approach to business taxation.

Revenue Dynamics

Michigan's SBT has proved to be both a productive and stable source of revenue. As shown in Table 3, SBT collections in fiscal 1987 were 15.6 percent of total state taxes, not significantly below the 16.7 percent share at the peak of the last state economic expansion. Compared with other state taxes in Michigan, SBT collections in fiscal 1987 were 55 percent of total sales and use tax collections (at a rate of 4 percent) and 45 percent as large as net personal income taxes (at a flat rate of 4.6 percent).

The last column in Table 3 also shows that SBT collections are relatively stable over the business cycle, especially in comparison with state corporate profits taxes.[14] In fiscal 1979, SBT collections were 1.13 percent of Michigan personal income. This ratio dropped only to 0.93 percent in 1982, the trough of the last recession. By 1987, SBT collections had rebounded to 1.13 percent, which matched the 1979 ratio. The relatively moderate cyclical swing in SBT collections compared with personal income occurred without a tax rate change over the entire cycle and with only minor adjustments in the definition of the tax base.

Michigan's experience with the SBT suggests that the capital acquisition deduction serves as a built-in stabilizer for business tax collections. Because capital spending is procyclical, the deduction moderates both the rise and fall in SBT revenues over the business cycle. Between 1977 and 1979, the SBT tax base (gross value added) grew 9.5 percent, while capital acquisition deductions jumped 36.7 percent. In the downturn of the cycle, the tax base fell 6.3 percent from 1979 to 1981, and capital deductions dropped by 3.5 percent. In addition, the fact that depreciation subtracted in determining federal taxable income is added back in determining Michigan value added further insulates the SBT

Table 3.

**Michigan Single Business Tax Revenues,
Fiscal Years 1978 to 1987**

Fiscal Year	Amount (millions)	Percent of State Taxes	Percent of Michigan Personal Income
1978	$ 899.4	16.7%	1.12%
1979	1,001.3	16.7	1.13
1980	917.0	15.5	.97
1981	942.2	15.1	.94
1982	943.1	14.5	.93
1983	1,041.7	14.2	.97
1984	1,280.5	15.1	1.09
1985	1,378.4	15.5	1.11
1986	1,495.8	16.2	1.16
1987	1,497.6	15.6	1.13

Source: State of Michigan, Department of Management and Budget, *Executive Budget,* various years, and Department of Treasury.

base from the instability created by the frequent and substantial changes in federal depreciation rules since 1980. This automatic decoupling feature of a state consumption VAT should appeal to state legislatures facing the uncertain future caused by structural federal deficits.

The fact that the ratio of SBT collections to personal income in 1987 equaled that in 1979 suggests that the long-run personal income elasticity of SBT revenues is approximately 1.0. Many analysts consider a unitary elasticity to be a reasonable target for automatic revenue growth in today's go-slow environment of increased public sector accountability. Michigan's version of a value-added tax appears to meet the twin policy objectives of adequate long-run tax base growth and moderate short-run swings in revenues.

The political advantages of the short-run revenue stability and long-run growth potential in the SBT can be appreciated by noting that the SBT tax rate has not changed since the tax was adopted in 1975 in spite of the steepest recession since the Depression. The fact that the SBT applies to both corporate and noncorporate firms also contributes to the stability of the rate. Douglas Drake has summarized this aspect of the SBT as follows:

> The Single Business Tax is a basically neutral approach to business taxation that is well-suited to Michigan's volatile and highly cyclic economy. A similar tax might be well-suited for other states with cyclical economies. The SBT is very pro-investment and pro-profit, and perhaps its greatest benefit to the business community—the broad political base that provides resistance to rate increases—grows out of the major criticism of the tax: that it affects too many businesses. In other words, what some businesspeople feel is a bad tax for them as individuals is very good for the business community as a whole.[15]

Michigan's Experience: Implications for the Design of a State VAT

Benefit Versus Ability-to-Pay Taxation

After 35 years of experimentation with value-added taxation, the basic question of how to tax businesses fairly still is being debated in Michigan. The theory of value-added taxation is quite consistent with the view that business taxes should be imposed on firms in line with the government goods and services that they consume. A firm's value added is viewed as a reasonable proxy for the level of use of these services. This line of reasoning leads to the conclusion that a firm with zero or negative profits still should pay taxes, just as it still must pay labor, energy, material, and other production costs. In contrast, ability-to-pay proponents—including business people in general—view the income tax as a more equitable tax. If a firm does not make a profit, it should not pay a tax according to this view. Michigan business firms with low profits or losses strongly object to the SBT on these grounds.

Michigan's experience with the BAT and the SBT suggests that it is extremely difficult for a state to adopt a "pure" version of a consumption-type VAT. And once adopted, it is even more difficult to protect the VAT from relentless political pressure to introduce profit-sensitive components into the value-added structure on ability-to-pay grounds. Only one year after the adoption of the SBT, major adjustments were made to reduce the tax liabilities of unprofitable (often small) businesses, including the adoption of the small business credit. Agriculture production also was excluded from the SBT in 1977 more to relieve the tax burden on unprofitable farmers than to reduce the potential regressivity of the tax on consumer purchases of food.

The excess compensation deduction, the small business credit, and the vanishing statutory exemption all increase the variability in the SBT compared with a pure value-added tax. The interaction of all these ability-to-pay elements, particularly the excess labor compensation and small business credits, adds complexity to the system, increases the variation in effective tax rates across firms and industries, creates a less stable tax base, and results in a less effective incentive for capital investment. Ironically, these are the characteristics of the corporate profits tax that were viewed as undesirable when the SBT originally was adopted as a substitute for the corporate profits tax in 1975.

States adopting a value-added tax should guard against the continual pressure to convert a VAT into a complicated, indirect business profits tax. The prognosis for the outcome of this struggle in Michigan is uncertain. The authors of one of the most comprehensive studies of the SBT reached a rather pessimistic conclusion: "Like the BAT before it, the SBT has come to represent a compromise between the rival concepts of value-added taxation and profits taxation, and through successive amendments is likely to resemble a corporate profits tax more and more in the future."[16]

Taxation of Multistate Firms

The treatment of interstate sales and multistate businesses under a value-added tax is a critical issue in the design of the tax. In theory, if the VAT is viewed as a benefit tax levied to pay for government goods and services provided to businesses, it follows that the tax should be based on production within a state. It also suggests that sales to out-of-state customers should be subject to VAT, but sales to state consumers and businesses by out-of-state firms should not be taxed. Under this production or origin version of the VAT, a state would tax a greater portion of the value of sales being sold out of state (and possibly a smaller portion of imports) than under current retail sales and use taxes, which follow the destination principle of taxation.

Theory suggests that an origin-based VAT should apportion the value-added base to the state of production using payroll and property located within the state. However, the SBT continues to use the three-factor formula (payroll, property, and sales) to apportion the tax base for multistate firms. As a result, a portion of the value added attributed to Michigan for multistate firms reflects production outside Michigan and a portion of the value added within Michigan is not subject to the SBT. In a state like Michigan, with a large manufacturing sector that exports to out-of-state consumers, the three-factor formula is attractive from the viewpoint of such firms.

Michigan's three-factor formula was challenged recently in a 1985 state court of appeals ruling.[17] The court ruled that the SBT taxpayer could use a two-step procedure for allocating the value-added tax base to Michigan. The taxpayer apportioned the non-compensation base using the three-factor formula but used separate accounting to identify actual compensation in Michigan, not apportioned compensation. This ruling provided out-of-state firms with an opportunity to reduce substantially SBT liabilities when the payroll factor was significantly lower than the overall apportionment factor. Public Act 39 of 1987 was passed to reaffirm the legislative intent of using the three-factor formula to "fairly represent" a taxpayer's business activity in Michigan.

The three-factor formula, borrowed from the corporate profits and individual income tax structures, and first used in Michigan under the BAT, creates a mixture of origin (payroll and property) and destination (sales) elements in the SBT. The rationale for using the three-factor formula to apportion profits is the difficulty in identifying the geographic location of "profitable" activities. While the profit component of the value-added tax base creates similar apportionment problems, labor compensation (almost 77 percent of the SBT value added in 1982-83) is easier to allocate to a specific state. For this reason, the alternatives of an origin-based apportionment formula or a destination-based formula deserve closer attention in the design of a state VAT. The choice of the apportionment structure is perhaps the most important decision to be made in designing an operational version of the value-added tax.[18]

Structuring a Value-Added Tax

As the discussion of Michigan's experience illustrates, a state seriously considering the adoption of a VAT first must decide how to structure the tax. This decision will be guided by the rationale for adopting a VAT. If the tax is viewed as a substitute for the corporate profits tax (or other taxes on capital), the additive approach to calculating value added (Michigan's SBT) may be preferred. Most of the information needed to identify value added already would be available in the federal tax return, and taxpayers would be familiar with this approach to determining the base. The additive approach, however, tends to focus attention continually on the ability-to-pay arguments against the VAT. It is also difficult to explain clearly the unique nature of a VAT when it is presented in the form of an income tax.

If a VAT is viewed as a substitute for a sales tax, the subtraction method (Michigan's BAT) probably would be a better approach in designing a VAT. Tax calculations would focus on sales data and the cost of goods sold and other business expense information from the federal tax return. While a firm's tax liability should be the same under either approach, the consumption tax nature of the VAT appears to be more evident under the subtraction approach. If the VAT is a substitute for a sales tax, a destination VAT would mirror the typical state sales/use tax structure.

The structure of a state VAT also will be heavily influenced by administrative considerations and the technical difficulties of applying a VAT to some industries. In Michigan, as in most countries using a VAT, agriculture is excluded from the value-added tax.[19] This exclusion often is defended on equity grounds (exempting food from the tax) and on administrative grounds (excludes a large number of small and low-profit businesses). Government activities also are universally excluded from value-added taxes.

Banks and insurance companies are particularly difficult to tax under a VAT. The fundamental problem is defining and accurately measuring the value added by financial institutions. Unfortunately, from the viewpoint of VAT administration, financial services often are provided at prices significantly below the actual cost of the services. The difference is covered by the spread between the bank's interest earned on loans and investments and interest paid for funds. In the absence of direct, comprehensive measures of the dollar value of services of financial institutions, a bank's value added is measured most accurately by the sum of factor payments, including labor costs and net profits.

This additive approach to defining a bank's value added is the approach used under Michigan's SBT. In recognition of the unique nature of this industry, banks include interest earned and exclude interest paid from the SBT base, the reverse of the SBT treatment for other firms. Although financial institutions are subject to the SBT in Michigan, the complexities involved suggest that states seriously should consider taxing financial institutions under alternative taxes (such as a net income or insurance premiums tax) if a VAT is adopted.[20]

Equity Issues

Regardless of how a state VAT is structured, it is useful to think of the tax as similar in economic impact to a comprehensive retail sales tax. The question of who pays the tax—consumers or factors of production—depends upon market conditions. It has been argued that a destination-based VAT is most likely to be borne by consumers in an open economy, such as an individual state. The reasoning is that all sellers in a regional market, whether local or from outside the region, would have to charge higher prices to recoup the tax. As a result, prices would reflect the tax and consumers would bear the tax burden. This would be particularly true for services provided locally. This result assumes, however, that the VAT would be imposed on all imports into a state that compete with in-state production. In contrast, if the VAT is levied as an origin-based tax (exports are taxed but imports are not), it is more likely that competition from businesses (particularly manufacturing) outside the state—firms not subject to the VAT—will prevent state producers from fully passing the VAT along in higher prices to consumers. Local goods and services that are sheltered geographically from competition, however, would have more flexibility in raising prices.

To the extent that a state VAT is borne by in-state consumers through higher prices for goods and services, it raises vertical equity concerns. Unfortunately, the ultimate incidence of tax burdens under a state VAT will be determined by a number of complex factors, including the degree of competition in economic markets for inputs and outputs, the pattern of consumer spending by income level, and the extent to which services are included in the VAT base. Given the resulting uncertainty concerning the actual distribution of tax burdens under a state VAT, the vertical equity issue is unlikely to be a significant factor in the political decision to adopt a state VAT.[21]

Michigan's experience in substituting a VAT for other state business taxes, including the corporate profits tax, indicates that the short-run redistribution of tax burdens across industries and individual firms within industries will be debated much more intensively than longer-run changes in the ultimate distribution of tax burdens by individuals. Compared with a corporate profits tax, a broad-based VAT is almost certain to increase tax burdens on unincorporated, labor-intensive, and low-profit businesses. Firms in the service sector will experience relatively large increases in effective tax rates and, therefore, will be vocal opponents of a VAT. State legislatures must be prepared to deal with the political pressures generated by such a redistribution of tax burdens if a VAT is adopted.

Conclusion

According to Henry Aaron in a recent discussion of a national VAT, "The value added tax belongs to a class of issues sufficiently interesting and attractive never quite to die, but not sufficiently appealing ever to be adopted."[22] In contrast, Michigan's experience has demonstrated that a state VAT is a practical and viable option. Compared with a state corporate profits tax, a value-added tax is relatively attractive if judged on the basis of economic efficiency, revenue stability, long-run growth potential, and horizontal equity across firms and industries. A consumption-type VAT offers states an opportunity to replace a business tax system that discriminates against capital investment with one that favors capital spending.

Compared with a retail sales tax, the value-added tax has two attractive advantages: It does not tax intermediate goods purchased by firms, and it can be extended effectively to cover a significant portion of consumer spending on services. This second advantage will grow in importance as the structural shift from goods to service industries continues.

Whether viewed as a consumption tax or a general business tax, the adoption of a VAT offers states an opportunity to implement the basic principles underlying the Tax Reform Act of 1986 at the state level. The VAT is a broad-based, low-rate general business tax that achieves a remarkable degree of horizontal equity in the distribution of tax burdens across industries and firms. For this reason, the VAT is ideally suited to a state business tax policy aimed at reducing overall tax rates and removing specific, targeted subsidies from the tax code. While it probably will take a significant fiscal crisis to prod states into taking a serious look at the value-added tax, the longer-run advantages of this low-rate, broad-based, procapital approach to business taxation eventually may lead additional states to join Michigan in the value-added tax arena.

Notes

1. For a detailed discussion of the economic and fiscal conditions contributing to Michigan's adoption of the modified VAT in 1975, see U.S. Advisory Commission on Intergovernmental Relations, *The Michigan Single Business Tax: A Different Approach to State Business Taxation,* Report M-114 (Washington, D.C., March 1978).

2. Estimated percentage presented in Paul N. Courant and Daniel L. Rubinfeld, "Tax Reform: Implications for the State-Local Public Sector," *Economic Perspectives* 1, no. 1 (Summer 1987): 91.

3. Courant and Rubinfeld, "Tax Reform," p. 96.

4. Richard A. Musgrave, "Short of Euphoria," *Economic Perspectives* 1, no. 1 (Summer 1987): 67.

5. An excellent overview of the shift in GNP and employment shares between goods- and service-producing sectors is found in Mack Ott, "The Growing Share of Services in the U.S. Economy—Desperation or Evolution?," *Federal Reserve Bank of St. Louis Review* 69, no. 6 (June/July 1987): 5-22.

6. The fact that a state VAT would avoid the serious pyramiding problem of sales taxes on business purchases of goods and services was noted in George Mundstock, "Florida Services: You Only Tax Twice?," *Tax Notes,* June 15, 1987, pp. 1137-1138.

7. The BAT was a modified, income-type VAT using the subtraction method: value added equaled gross receipts minus purchases from other firms and depreciation on real property. The following references provide a detailed analysis of the design and operation of the BAT: Robert D. Ebel, *The Michigan Business Activities Act* (East Lansing: Michigan State University, 1972); Peter A. Firmin, "The Michigan Business Receipts Tax," *Michigan Business Report,* No. 24 (Ann Arbor: University of Michigan, 1953); Clarence W. Lock, Donovan J. Rau, and Howard D. Hamilton, "The Michigan Value-Added Tax," *National Tax Journal* VIII, no. 4 (December 1955): 357-371; James A. Papke, "Michigan's Value-Added Tax After Seven Years," *National Tax Journal* XIII, no. 4 (December 1960): 350-363.

8. U.S. Department of the Treasury, *Tax Reform for Fairness, Simplicity, and Economic Growth,* Volume 3, *Value-Added Tax.*

9. The SBT data reported here is from the Taxation and Economic Policy Office, Michigan Department of Treasury and is based on tax returns for firms with tax years ending between December 1982 and November 1983. Detailed data for 1980-81 is presented in "Analysis of the Michigan Single Business Tax," Taxation and Economic Policy Office, Michigan Department of Treasury, Lansing, Michigan, January 1985.

10. Under the consumption VAT, the full deduction of capital expenditures provides an immediate tax savings for the purchasing firm that offsets the VAT tax liability on the value of the plant and equipment. As a result, the tax is imposed only on consumption spending with investment spending (saving) excluded from the base. The capital costs will appear in the value-added base in the future when depreciation is added back as capital is used up in the production of goods and services for consumption. For this reason, Michigan's SBT can be viewed as a broad-based tax on consumption. It should be noted that the immediate expensing of capital investment means that the SBT is not "neutral" in its treatment of capital and labor as inputs. In fact, this provision favors capital because immediate expensing effectively exempts capital income (but not the cost of capital) from taxation.

11. For detailed information on the small business credit, see "Impact of the SBT Small Business Credit," Taxation and Economic Policy Office,

Michigan Department of Treasury, Lansing, Michigan, March 1987.

12. The impact of the interaction between the small business credit and other components of the SBT on effective tax rates is discussed in Michigan Department of Treasury, *Analysis of the Michigan Single Business Tax*.

13. Michigan Department of Treasury, *Analysis of the Michigan Single Business Tax*, p. 7.

14. SBT collections dropped 5.9 percent from fiscal 1979 to 1981. In sharp contrast, Michigan's corporate profits tax receipts fell by almost 44 percent in the 1970-71 recession.

15. Douglas C. Drake, "Michigan's Single Business Tax: A Review and Analysis," paper prepared for the House Taxation Committee, Lansing, Michigan, January 1984, p. 13.

16. Robin Barlow and Jack S. Connell, Jr., "The Single Business Tax," in Harvey E. Brazer, ed., *Michigan's Fiscal and Economic Structure* (Ann Arbor: University of Michigan Press, 1982), p. 679.

17. See Jones & Laughlin Steel Corporation v. Department of Treasury, 145 Mich. App. 405 (1985).

18. This issue is discussed in detail in Richard W. Lindholm, *Value-Added Tax and Other Tax Reforms* (Chicago: Nelson-Hall, 1976), pp. 92-93. It is interesting to note that the BAT contained a sales-factor-only apportionment formula when adopted in 1953. Because of its questionable constitutionality and undesirable burden distribution by industry, it was replaced by the three-factor formula in 1955. While in effect, the sales factor included all sales in Michigan plus 50 percent of sales in interstate transactions. Under the SBT, the additive approach to determining value added seems most consistent with an origin-based view of the tax: The tax should be paid where production occurs or incomes are produced.

19. See Charles E. McLure, Jr., *The Value-Added Tax: Key to Deficit Reduction?* (Washington, D.C.: American Enterprise Institute, 1987), Chapter 8, for a detailed discussion of the problems in applying a VAT to particular business activities.

20. U.S. Department of Treasury, *Value-Added Tax,* Chapter 6, discusses the formidable problems of taxing financial institutions under a VAT. As noted in the study, "The practical problems of taxing financial services have led all European Economic Community (EEC) countries to exempt the basic lending activities of banking, insurance, and related financial establishments from the value-added tax" (p. 49).

21. The U.S. Advisory Commission on Intergovernmental Relations, *The Michigan Single Business Tax,* p. 26, reached this conclusion in summarizing the 1975 legislative debate over the SBT. As pointed out by Harvey E. Brazer, "Michigan's Single Business Tax—Theory and Background," *Proceedings of the Sixty-Ninth Annual Conference on Taxation, National Tax Association—Tax Institute of America,* 1977, pp. 62-69, it is very likely that the SBT will be borne in the long run by the same immobile factors of production that would have paid the repealed Michigan business taxes.

22. Henry Aaron, "Consumption Taxes: Revenue, Structural and Equity Effects," *Tax Notes,* May 17, 1982, p. 527.

About the Authors

David R. Burton is the manager of the Tax Policy Center of the U.S. Chamber of Commerce, which he joined in 1984. He holds a B.A. in economics from the University of Chicago and a J.D. from the University of Maryland School of Law.

Robert J. Cline is professor of economics at Hope College. He has served as the director of tax research for the Michigan Department of Management and Budget and conducted studies for the U.S. Advisory Commission on Intergovernmental Relations, the U.S. Treasury Department, and several states. He has a Ph.D. in economics from the University of Michigan.

Harley T. Duncan is executive director of the Federation of Tax Administrators, a position he assumed in 1988. Previously, he was the director of the Kansas Department of Revenue for five years and served on the staffs of the National Governors' Association and the U.S. Advisory Commission on Intergovernmental Relations.

Corina L. Eckl is a senior staff associate for the National Conference of State Legislatures. Among her many publications are annual reports on state budget actions, which she has co-authored for four years. She is a graduate of the University of Colorado with a degree in political science.

James Francis is director of tax research for the Florida Department of Revenue. He was responsible for the agency's investigation of the legal, administrative, and revenue implications of taxing services and served as the legislative liaison on that issue. Previously, he served on the Florida House of Representatives staff for eight years.

Harvey Galper is the National Director for Tax Analysis at Peat Marwick Main Co.'s Policy Economics Group. He was formerly the director of the Office of Tax Analysis of the U.S. Treasury Department and a senior fellow at the Brookings Institution.

Steven D. Gold is director of fiscal studies for the National Conference of State Legislatures. This is the 10th book on state and local finances that he has written or edited. He also has authored dozens of articles and serves on the editorial boards of three scholarly journals on public finance issues. Prior to joining NCSL in 1981, he was professor of economics at Drake University.

Robert Greenstein is the executive director of the Center on Budget and Policy Priorities, a Washington, D.C.-based organization that he founded in 1981. Previously, he was the administrator of the Food and Nutrition Service of the U.S. Department of Agriculture, which is responsible for federal food assistance programs.

Frederick Hutchinson is the director of the State Tax Project of the Center on Budget and Policy Priorities. Previously, he was a tax analyst for Bread for the World, a Christian antihunger movement. He has testified before numerous congressional and state tax committees.

Helen F. Ladd is a professor at Duke University's Institute for Policy Analysis and Public Affairs. She was previously on the faculty of the Kennedy School of Government at Harvard University and is one of the leading researchers in the field of state and local public finance.

Robert S. McIntyre is director of Citizens for Tax Justice, a coalition of labor, public interest, and citizens' groups that lobbies for more progressive taxes. His research that showed the low taxes paid by many large corporations is widely credited with contributing to the impetus for passage of the 1986 Tax Reform Act. Prior to joining CTJ, he was the director of the Public Citizen's Tax Reform Research Group.

Gerald H. Miller is executive director of the National Association of State Budget Officers, which he joined in 1983. He served as the Michigan budget director longer than any other person and played a leading role in enactment of Michigan's Single Business Tax.

Stephen H. Pollock is a senior consultant at Peat Marwick Main Co.'s Policy Economics Group and has participated in estimating the effects of federal tax reform in a large number of states. Previously, he was on the staff of the Kansas City Federal Reserve Bank. He received a Ph.D. from the University of Maryland.

Richard D. Pomp is professor of law at the University of Connecticut Law School and chairman of the Institute on Taxation and Economic Policy. From 1981 to 1987, he directed the New York Tax Study Commission. He has served as a consultant to many cities and states, the U.S. Congress, and foreign countries, including the People's Republic of China. He is a magna cum laude graduate of Harvard Law School.

Michael Vlaisavljevich is the senior manager for state and local tax analysis for the Washington, D.C. office of Price Waterhouse. He previously directed the Research and Analysis Division of the Wisconsin Department of Revenue and managed tax policy development and revenue estimating under three governors. He also served as tax policy supervisor for the Wisconsin Legislative Fiscal Bureau.

Robert C. Witzel is the senior director for state and local tax for RJR Nabisco, Inc. He worked for the Ohio Department of Taxation from 1972 to 1977, when he joined the tax department of R.J.-Reynolds Industries. He received a J.D. from Ohio State University.

Index

Ability to pay, 38, 178, 183, 247-48
Accountability, 8, 53-54
Adequacy of revenue, 8, 32-37, 50, 58
Administration of taxes, 8, 59-60, 83-106, 184; and federal tax reform, 14, 54, 179; and sales tax on services, 131-41
Alcoholic beverage taxes, 12, 51, 56, 60, 70
Alternative minimum tax (corporate), 24, 181, 190, 214
Apportionment: of income, 187; of value added, 248-49
Audits, 75, 85-97, 102-06
Balance as a goal of tax policy, 2, 31-46, 51-52
Banking taxes, 6, 53, 59, 70, 179, 250-51
Behavioral distortions, 39-40. *See also* Efficiency
Benefit taxation, 8, 38, 51, 178, 183, 247-49
Brassieres, taxation of, 91
Broadening of tax bases, 14, 26-27, 51, 58
Business climate, 75, 178, 212-13, 219-26
Business taxes, 2, 4, 6, 51, 54-55, 57, 60, 88-98, 101-06, 177-254. *See also* Corporation income tax, Sales tax on services, Value-added tax
Capital formation, 224, 231. *See also* Venture capital
Capital gains, 21, 115, 124, 225
Certainty of a tax system, 50, 58
Cigarette taxes. *See* tobacco taxes
Circuitbreakers (for property tax relief), 20, 171-73
Complexity of tax provisions, 88-98. *See also* Simplicity
Compliance: costs, 52-53, 60, 90-98, 184; and federal tax reform, 14; and sales tax on services, 136-41. *See also* Administration of taxes
Conformity to federal income tax, 14-24, 26, 117, 167, 182, 205, 214
Corporation income tax, 177-95, 197-217, 227-32; administration of, 101-06; compared to value-added tax, 252; rates, 18-19, 23-24; reform of, 4, 6, 21-24, 88-90; reporting beneficiaries of tax preferences, 73-76; revenue, 12, 16, 58, 69-70
Deduction of federal income tax payments, 17, 214
Deduction of state-local taxes on federal income tax returns, 235-37
Depreciation, 183, 208, 224, 237, 241-42
Deregulation as motivator of tax reform, 7, 179
Distortion of resource allocation. *See* Efficiency
Distribution of tax burdens, 57, 115-26, 219-26, 238, 251. *See also* Incidence, Progressivity
Diversification of revenue, 31-46, 51-52, 58, 238
Earned income tax credit, 20-21, 165-66, 170, 173-75
Economic change as motivator of tax reform, 7, 15-16

Economic development, 2, 8, 84-98, 136, 178, 183, 236-38. *See also* Business taxes
Efficiency of resource allocation, 7, 32, 39-40, 58, 108-10, 221, 245; under Florida's sales tax on services, 133-41
Elasticity, 3, 8, 37-38; of personal income tax, 120-27; of sales tax, 15-16, 26-27, 50, 58
Enterprise zones, 88-89
Erosion of tax bases, 26. *See also* Service sector, growth of
Excise taxes, 12-14, 51. *See also* Alcoholic beverage taxes, Insurance taxes, Tobacco taxes
Fairness, 8, 32, 38-39, 51-52, 58, 101, 108-10, 213, 229-30
Federal tax reform: 115-27, 221-26, 235-38; and corporations, 4, 74, 177-83, 189-90, 197-215; in the future, 7-8, 10, 189; and the poor, 4, 153-76; and simplicity, 84; and state tax reform, 5, 7, 11, 14-24, 47
Fees and charges, 48, 51
Fiscal condition of the states, 7, 12
Flat tax, 15, 238
Franchise tax, 185
Goals of tax policy, 31-63, 87-97, 108-12
Heads of household, income tax treatment of, 162-63
Horizontal equity, 8, 38, 52, 59, 109, 163, 238, 245
Incentives: created by taxes, 57, 220-26, 238; for business, 73-76, 183-89
Incidence, 38-39, 52, 210-12, 251
Indexation, 20, 120-21, 222
Information needed to design tax reforms, 8-9
Insurance taxes, 6, 53, 179-80, 250-51
Interest on late tax payments, 102
Interstate tax competition, 2, 26, 40-41, 54-55, 177, 184-88, 236
Investment tax credit, 66, 73-74, 88-89, 181-84, 203-05, 208, 224, 237
Itemized deductions, 15-20, 118-19, 155
Job creation, 8, 88-89, 96, 220, 235. *See also* Economic development
Limitations on taxes, 31
Lincoln Institute of Land Policy, 47
Local government aid, 54, 60
Local taxes, 6, 12, 41-42, 48-50, 59-60. *See also* Property tax
Low-income persons. *See* Poor, tax relief for
Mandates on local governments, 54, 59
Marginal tax rates, 14-23, 26-27, 125
Micro-simulation models, 3, 112-28
Motor fuel tax, 12, 51
No-tax floor, 164-65
Outlook for state tax reform, 5-8
Passive income and losses, 115-16, 181, 208
Penalties, 104
Personal exemption (or credit), 14-20, 115, 124, 157, 161
Personal income tax: incidence of, 121-27, 211, 222-24; reform, 5, 6, 14-21, 92-93, 107-28; revenue, 12, 31

257

Piggyback on federal income tax, 20, 167; of tax credits, 156

Political obstacles to tax reform, 6-7, 48, 178; at federal level, 14; in Florida, 130, 142-45

Poor, tax relief for: 4, 14-21, 52, 58, 92, 121-27, 153-76, 214

Principles of good tax policy, 2, 14, 31-63, 67-70

Progressivity, 3, 8, 20, 25-26, 38-39, 52, 59, 109-10, 117-27, 210-12

Property tax: and assessment reform, 53, 59; burden on the poor, 168-73; on business, 185, 188, 191; reform of, 6; revenue, 32-46

Rainy Day Funds, 50, 58

Recession, 12, 84. See also Fiscal condition of the states

Redistribution of tax burdens, 15, 52

Regressivity, of local taxes, 50, 52; of property and sales taxes, 39, 211; of value-added tax, 232, 238. See also Progressivity

Reports about how the tax system operates, 54, 57, 60, 72, 116-27, 191-94

Research capacity for developing tax reforms, 70-71, 107-28, 190-94

Resource allocation, 8, 55-56

Revenue estimates, 86, 184

Sales tax: burden on the poor, 168-71, 211; on business equipment, 184-88, 191; compared to value-added tax, 239, 250, 252; exemptions, 90-92; income tax deduction for, 235-36; rates, 18-19, 25; reform of, 6, 24-25, 58; revenue, 12-13, 16, 32-46, 211, 239; on services, 3, 6, 15-16, 24-27, 129-52

Service sector, growth of, 15-16, 230-31, 238-41. See also Sales tax on services

Severance taxes, 12-13

Simplicity as a goal of tax policy, 8, 52-53, 59, 84-98, 108-12, 167, 231

Social policy, taxes as an instrument of, 55, 60

Stability as a goal of tax policy, 8, 27, 37-38, 50, 57, 228-29, 246-47

Standard deduction, 14-20, 124, 161-63

Statute of limitations, 103

Subchapter S corporations, 24, 183, 237

Tax brackets, number of, 17

Tax credits, 92, 169-74. See also Circuitbreaker, Earned income tax credit, Investment tax credit

Tax expenditure budgets, 53-54, 59, 65-81

Tax expenditures, 3, 55-56, 65-81, 88-92, 214

Tax rates, 17-24, 40-41, 95, 157, 182, 185, 197-98, 220-25, 244

Tax reform, definitions of, 8; studies, 15

Tax Reform Act of 1986. See Federal tax reform

Tax relief, 8, 121

Tax revenue, amount of, 12

Tax structure, 12-14, 31-46

Taxable income, federal, 16-17, 118, 167

Technological change, 7

Telecommunications, taxation of, 6, 16, 53, 59, 70, 132, 179

Tobacco taxes, 12, 51, 56, 60, 70

Transportation, taxation of, 6, 180

Truth in taxation (for property tax), 53, 59

Understandability of tax system, 8, 52

Uniformity. See Horizontal equity

Unitary taxation, 180

U.S. Advisory Commission on Intergovernmental Relations (ACIR), 2, 31-46, 48, 67

Use taxes, 136-41

Utilities taxes, 59, 70

Value-added tax, 4, 189, 227-54; federal, 7-8

Venture capital, 89-90, 225

Vertical equity, 38-39, 52, 109. See also Progressivity

Windfall from federal tax reform, 14-24, 115-17, 174, 181-82, 211-15